Paula Nicolson
and
Rowan Bayne

# Psychology for Social Work Theory and Practice

Fourth Edition

palgrave
macmillan

THE BRITISH ASSOCIATION OF SOCIAL WORKERS

First published as *Applied Psychology for Social Workers* 1984
Second edition 1990
Third edition 2006
Fourth edition published as *Psychology for Social Work Theory and Practice* 2014

Published by
PALGRAVE MACMILLAN

Palgrave Macmillan in the UK is an imprint of Macmillan Publishers Limited, registered in England, company number 785998, of Houndmills, Basingstoke, Hampshire RG21 6XS.

Palgrave Macmillan in the US is a division of St Martin's Press LLC, 175 Fifth Avenue, New York, NY 10010.

Palgrave Macmillan is the global academic imprint of the above companies and has companies and representatives throughout the world.

Palgrave® and Macmillan® are registered trademarks in the United States, the United Kingdom, Europe and other countries

ISBN 978–0–230–30316–4

This book is printed on paper suitable for recycling and made from fully managed and sustained forest sources. Logging, pulping and manufacturing processes are expected to conform to the environmental regulations of the country of origin.

A catalogue record for this book is available from the British Library.

A catalog record for this book is available from the Library of Congress.

Typeset by Cambrian Typesetters, Camberley, Surrey, England, UK

Printed in China

# Brief contents

# Contents

# List of figures, boxes and tables

## Figures

## Boxes

## Tables

# Acknowledgements

Paula would like to thank Catherine Gray of Palgrave Macmillan for encouraging both of us to write this book. Writing this also brings back memories of the late Jo Campling, whose support sustained both of our interests in psychology applied to social work theory and practice over nearly thirty years. My colleagues, at Royal Holloway, University of London and on the MA in Consulting to Organizations at the Tavistock and Portman NHS Foundation Trust helped, in different ways, to shape my ideas. Of course I also want to thank Derry Nicolson, Kate Nicolson, Malachi and Azriel for support and happy distractions.

Rowan would like to thank Katherine Bayne and literally hundreds of my colleagues and students very warmly for helping me increase my understanding and appreciation of applied personality theory in particular and communication skills (interviewing, assertiveness, counselling) generally. I am especially grateful to Paula for asking me to teach interviewing to her social work students, suggesting we write the first edition of this book and taking the lead with it and subsequent editions.

PAULA NICOLSON
ROWAN BAYNE

# Introduction: why study psychology?

This book takes over from our *Applied Psychology for Social Workers*, first published in 1984, since when there have been many changes in social work organization, training and delivery, as well as in psychology as an academic and applied discipline. However, the challenges remain the same even if the context, organization, process and management structures are different. Social workers work with people. That means that a working knowledge of psychology is vital because each one of us individually, in our families, friendship and work groups expresses ourselves psychologically through our thinking, behaviour and emotions.

Social workers and psychologists also have shared value systems which are articulated through their professional ethical and anti-oppressive codes of conduct. Both social workers and psychologists recognize that many people who seek their help are underprivileged or excluded in some way and seek to support service users both practically and emotionally. Throughout the book we will be providing examples to demonstrate how this works.

Our book, which achieved its third edition in 2006, proved to be one of the top twenty best-selling books of the *Practical Social Work* list commissioned by the late Jo Campling. While the social work curriculum and general landscape have changed, the ongoing brief from the Department of Health (DoH) still situates 'psychology' at the core of many areas of social work practice (Parton, 1996; Nicolson, 2014).

Psychology is the science (as well as the art) of working with people in one-to-one, family, community and political relationships. Without an appreciation and grasp of psychology it would be difficult to practise effectively as a social worker or to care for oneself as a professional in such a tough, emotionally taxing, but ultimately rewarding profession. Psychology, therefore, continues to be a popular and essential component in the training of social workers and even a cursory examination of the social work curriculum and the outline of social work courses, across the

English-speaking world in particular, reinforces this observation. Psychology 'happens' immediately, in that when humans face each other for the first time a number of activities – conscious and unconscious, above and beneath the surface – take place as we assess the other person and reflect on ourselves in social encounters. As you will read later, an understanding of human motivation, empathy, personality, asking open questions, listening and checking carefully that you have understood, underlie all professional interaction. The immediate situation you face when you meet any service user for the first time is to find out all the relevant details from the practical through to the emotional ones.

Each social worker is also faced with having to make the right decision on each occasion, taking care to ensure that they are making the correct impression on the other person. The better the skills and insights applied to the initial interview, the lower the risk.

Every human exchange in professional social work draws upon implicit and explicit psychological knowledge, as you will see as you read on and illustrated in Figure I.1. This includes the ability to communicate with other people using techniques that improve with practice; the ability to understand ourselves through reflection on our behaviour; and the ability to draw on a variety of theory making sense of personality and emotion, all of which contribute to meaningful communication and effective practice. Social workers need to know what takes place between people and within themselves and what happens for their service users living in their wider networks. Social workers and psychologists also need to ensure that their practice is both ethical and anti-oppressive taking account of social inequalities and social exclusion which may come about through differences in gender, ethnicity, abilities and opportunities constrained through poverty and unemployment. Competence in cognitive, emotional and practical skills lead the social worker to understand more of what is happening in interpersonal encounters both above and beneath the surface.

All social work courses continue to include, in some form, development through the life-span, the theory and practice of human communication, understanding other people, personality, emotions and behaviour and the psychological elements of human systems such as work and care organizations and the family. The social work curriculum in the UK gives greater than ever priority to the study and understanding of human growth and development. Psychology and social work theory and practice therefore remain intrinsically linked (Beckett and Taylor, 2010; Nicolson,

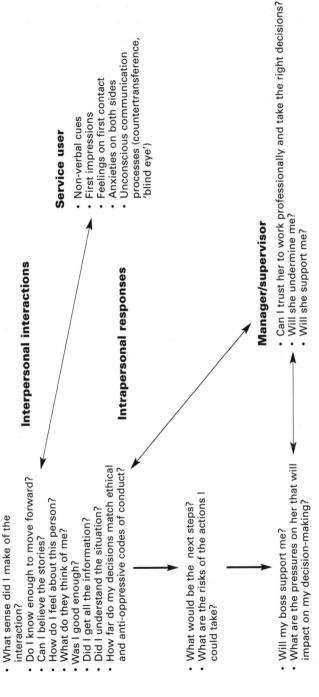

**Social worker**

- What sense did I make of the interaction?
- Do I know enough to move forward?
- Can I believe the stories?
- How do I feel about this person?
- What do they think of me?
- Was I good enough?
- Did I get all the information?
- Did I understand the situation?
- How far do my decisions match ethical and anti-oppressive codes of conduct?

**Interpersonal interactions**

**Service user**

- Non-verbal cues
- First impressions
- Feelings on first contact
- Anxieties on both sides
- Unconscious communication processes (countertransference, 'blind eye')

**Intrapersonal responses**

- What would be the next steps?
- What are the risks of the actions I could take?

**Manager/supervisor**

- Can I trust her to work professionally and take the right decisions?
- Will she undermine me?
- Will she support me?

- Will my boss support me?
- What are the pressures on her that will impact on my decision-making?

**Figure I.1** Why study psychology?

2014; Nicolson et al., 2006; Sugarman, 2001). In what follows in this book we enable the reader to engage with these elements as well as develop a sophisticated understanding of human nature and behaviour.

## Contextualizing this book

The past forty years have witnessed a constant and continuing cycle of changes in the training of social workers and expectations about their role and practice. Social work is frequently said to be at a 'watershed' (Dickens, 2011) (perhaps) as a reaction to child care or mental health mistakes and mismanagement as well as economic pressure on public services (Munro, 2011; Stevenson, 1986). However each watershed appears to inspire structural and practice-related changes.

Since the publication of the first edition of this book in 1984 we have seen the rise and fall of the post-Seebohm, generic, university-educated social worker in the 1970s/1980s through a period of 'de-professionalization' whereby social work training took place along the lines of an apprenticeship. By the end of the 1990s, and even more so by the end of the 2000s, the public image of the British social worker had suffered a series of blows, based on widespread ignorance of what social workers do, which the DoH specifically identified as a major barrier to entering the profession. This led to rethinking the way social workers were trained and the UK government at the time put extra money into recruitment and training, providing funding for students to study on postgraduate and undergraduate university courses. This led to a new professional qualification – the Diploma in Social Work (DipSW) to be followed up with post-qualifying specialist courses, in childcare and mental health.

In 2010 the government introduced 'Step Up to Social Work', a part-time conversion programme for professionals and/or graduates with at least a 2.1 degree wanting to change career and become social workers. This is run by local authorities in partnership with higher education institutions, successful completion of which leads to a postgraduate diploma in social work. It includes a core course on human growth and development that requires students to have all the skills and knowledge reflected in our book.

Social workers now specialize in either adult or children's services. The adult services include working with vulnerable people, including those with mental health problems, learning difficulties or older adults. The consequent resurgence of demand for greater professionalism and specialism led to the final report of the Social Work Task Force (2009) and the Social Work Reform Board (SWRB) established in its wake. You can read about this on the website: https://www.education.gov.uk/publications/standard/ publicationdetail/page1/DCSF-01114-2009.

Further, some of the previous and more recent human and professional misjudgements, or failures of judgement and practice (such as in the cases of Peter Connelly and Victoria Climbie) have contributed to policy committed to raising the standards of social work provision (Munro, 2011). Lord Laming's report has now been archived by the DoH on their website at: https://www. education.gov.uk/publications/standard/publicationDetail/Page1/ CM%205730 and it makes an informative and interesting read.

Social workers are now regulated by the Health and Care Professions Council, a generic regulatory body covering health professions (such as occupational therapy, clinical and health psychology). This replaced the General Social Care Council in 2012. However further changes since 2012 have left most post-qualifying training to Continuing Professional Development (CPD) and local authorities with reduced training budgets.

Working in children's services requires a focus on working with families, managing adoption, fostering and residential care for looked after children as well as working with adolescents leaving home or care, where they might be at risk of becoming victims of crime (including involvement as perpetrators), through being unemployed, vulnerable to abusing drugs and being abused in other ways by adults such as sexual exploitation. Children's services also include working alongside those in the education services and with the probation services. For social workers in adult services, working alongside National Health Service (NHS) colleagues (for example, psychiatric nurses, psychiatrists, general practitioners, psychologists and others) is integrated into the team structure, particularly in mental health work. For all, then, inter-professional working (IPW) has become a routine expectation.

Other changes have taken place at a broader organizational and policy level in the UK. The DoH is now responsible for organizing and monitoring the delivery of services, which include social work and health care services. Political and organizational changes have also meant varying levels of joint working with NHS organizations and increased attention is paid to inter-professional working across agencies and disciplines aiming to improve services users' experiences of social and health care as well as outcomes of service delivery (Lymbery, 2006; Reese and Sontag, 2001). An important innovation during the 2000s also included an increased role for service users in both social work and health and social care and closer integration of service user representatives in the selection and training of social work students (Heffernan, 2006).

Further, changes in delivery of NHS services during 2013, particularly in public health, have once again impacted on the management structures in social work, potentially increasing inter-professional working. Whatever the policy and economically driven changes in the organization and practice of social work, human interaction and emotional health remain major components and it would be difficult to imagine that psychology and social work could be wrenched apart fundamentally.

## How this book will help you understand psychology for social work

None of the policy, structural or organizational changes to the profession has diminished the need for social workers to have a personal repertoire of psychological knowledge to enable the best practice and emotional survival. Psychology for social workers requires both a basic understanding of the discipline, and the knowledge and ability to pull out a theory, approach or relevant set of skills for each occasion.

*Psychology for Social Work Theory and Practice* integrates psychological knowledge with social work practice across the spectrum of knowledge needed to work with children, families and vulnerable adults. Examples used to illustrate psychological research and theories are directly relevant to social workers' ongoing experiences and as such facilitate answers to the daily challenges that face practitioners. What would the long-term psychological risks be in taking a particular child into care? How can I help this person face up to their family difficulties? How do I give bad news to a child or their family? What is this person *not* telling me? How can I change this man's violent behaviour? How can I ensure that my team is well supported and able to function effectively? These and many of the other questions faced by social workers at different stages of their professional life are addressed here. Moreover this book equips readers with practical information and the means to identify solutions for themselves.

Both Rowan Bayne and Paula Nicolson are committed to making psychology accessible to students and practitioners of social work and show a variety of psychology's applications to social work practice and practitioners' well-being. With this in mind, we have updated and reorganized our original individual chapters. Paula, while attending to the important role that psychology plays as it applies to understanding human growth and development across the life-span, also emphasizes how psychology informs reflective-relational practice, the organization of social work services and leadership and management of social work. Rowan, drawing effectively on his ongoing expertise from teaching and researching over many years, has revised his contributions on interviewing and counselling skills, to focus upon current research and practice-related to 'strengths' and communication. We continually draw attention to the relationship of theory to everyday practice and particularly take account of self-care as an integral part of practice. By this we don't only mean paying attention on a practical and emotional level to one's own well-being, although as you will see, particularly in Chapters 4 and 5, we do take this most seriously. We also see the importance of remaining up-to-date with theory as it relates to practice and the relevance of CPD to best practice. Feeling confident that you are making the most of your skills as well as understanding theory related to your work will enable you to develop your decision-making and practice.

In this book we also remain keenly aware of the increasing emphasis on research-influenced or evidence-based practice (Regehr et al., 2007; Sheldon, 2001; Webb, 2001). Social workers need to be able to assess the validity of 'evidence' and make the best of use of contemporary cutting-edge research – which does not mean swallowing it all whole but making informed and effective judgements. Following the lead from North America, research-led practice and teaching has gained such a foothold that no university department that trains social workers can afford to do so without a strong (or aspiring) research base among those who pass on the knowledge (Fook, 2002).

Since 1984 when the first edition of this book was published, the world itself has become a very different place. Mobility has been encouraged by greater access to various means of travel. There have been shifts in populations brought about by socio-economic and political factors including famine, wars, persecution of minority ethnic and religious groupings and changes in the distribution and structure of international trade and industrial revolution. This has had an impact on social work in several ways. For example, in the developed countries around Europe, the UK, North America, New Zealand and Australia, demographic changes and improved health status have increased the need to take account of older adults, while politico-economic change has meant a shift towards older adults and the physically and mentally disabled being cared for in the family rather than in institutions. This impacts on family dynamics, health and gender-power relations. Former taboo issues such as child sexual abuse in the family, in care homes, day nurseries and from some of the most trusted members of society such as priests, have become recognized in the twenty-first century more than previously and evidence of its widespread and pervasive nature has meant rethinking much of what was formerly identified as good practice (Craven et al., 2007; Dube et al., 2001; Macdonald and Macdonald, 2010).

Social workers are frequently the professionals who pick up the long-term pieces. Family violence is now recognized as frequent, transcending socio-economic and social class boundaries, although migration and cultural differences among some minority groups have highlighted the need for rigorous, informed and sensitive practice in order to prevent abuse of women and children. Recognition of the rights of individuals who are not seen to conform to the white, middle-class, protestant and heterosexual image of the 'norm' has impacted positively on psychological research and theory and social work practice (Nicolson, 2010).

Finally, social work in relation to health has changed particularly in the context of epidemics such as HIV/AIDS and developments in psychotropic medication that have changed aspects of practice and values in relation to mental illness.

While many changes in the backdrop to psychology and social work have occurred for better and worse over the last twenty years, what remains the same is the importance that applied psychology still has for social work practice.

# PART I

# Theory for Practice

The first part of the book explores the role of a variety of psychological theories in social work practice. It begins, in Chapter 1, by examining exactly what psychology as an academic, clinical and otherwise applied discipline really is. What do psychoanalytic ideas, behaviourism and cognitive neuroscience practices have in common? Is psychology more like biology or sociology? The answers might surprise you – so read on. To demonstrate the full extent of psychological research and practice we describe the different *methodological* approaches (from the experiment to the interview, from statistical to qualitative) and also the *tools* at the psychologist's disposal. These include magnetic resonance imaging (MRI) scanners for in-depth exploration of the human brain, attitudes scales, surveys, standardized tests (for such things as personality, motivation and intelligence) as well as open-ended interviews. What do social workers need to know about these methods and tools? As social work becomes more *evidence-driven* you will need to have a reasonably sophisticated knowledge of what counts as good and bad or indifferent research to make decisions about what might be relevant to your practice.

In Chapter 2 you will see a more detailed focus on the individual life-span which draws upon some of the theory outlined previously while adding greater depth to your understanding of its application. That chapter specifically explores attachment relationships and styles as well as the impact of trauma and grief on the course of human development.

The third chapter in Part I moves the focus from the individual to the group and the organization, looking at psychological approaches to understanding teams and organizations. We all work in teams and sometimes these teams work well focusing on the task of delivering for service users. Unfortunately some teams are dysfunctional and don't manage to effectively engage with the tasks that are its reason for existing. This suggests that somewhere along the line the service user is disadvantaged, not from ill will but from poor practice within the system.

To look forward briefly, in Part II, Chapters 4 and 5, you will see how personality testing can be applied to the development of interpersonal and interviewing skills as well as self-care. Some of the theory introduced in Chapter 3 is developed further in Chapter 6 where we look at groupwork skills.

# CHAPTER 1

# Psychological theories

## CHAPTER OVERVIEW

In this chapter we cover:

- The scope of the discipline of psychology with selected relevant examples.
- The variety of ways it continues to be studied, including through experiments, surveys, biological indicators, attitude scales, psychodynamic clinical case examples and in-depth interviews.

Psychology comprises a range of approaches to its subject matter and the methods it uses to make sense of the brain, social interaction, behaviour, development and emotions. Generally research findings across the discipline come together to make a coherent picture of the whole person, although research activities are frequently in separate spheres. Some evidence comes from neuro-imaging of brain activity and some comes from the associations made by listening and watching closely while people talk about their lives. All of this comes under the heading of psychology and all can claim a degree of influence over social work knowledge.

## Introduction

Psychology itself has never been a unified discipline but combines different approaches and theoretical orientations to the study of the individual and the individual in a social context. Its origins as an academic subject area, the science of mind and behaviour, go back well over a hundred years, although the study of psychology is not as old as some other sciences. In its relatively brief history, however, there have been a number of crises or turning points, and although Western academic psychology is now well established, there are a number of areas of contention that have increased, exacerbated by competition for research funding. These include whether emotions are social or biological in origin and which methods are more likely to demonstrate an enduring truth about human nature.

The greatest acclamation that during the early years of the twenty-first century has been awarded to discoveries from cognitive neuroscience, evolutionary psychology and genetics has been criticized by many whose interest is in the social nature of human thinking and behaviour (Bentall, 2006; Bjorklund and Pellegrini, 2000). The UK Coalition Government has expressed an interest in understanding 'happiness', which some psychologists have argued is political and used to mask the effect of the economic recession and austerity measures (Layard, 2006). It is perhaps noteworthy that Richard Layard, who conducted the government study of happiness, is an economist rather than a psychologist. There is a current interest in *positive psychology*, emphasizing happiness rather than mental ill-health and depression, which has traditionally been of greater concern across the discipline.

Studies of happiness, for example, may be accomplished in several ways (questionnaires, interviews) but there are possible technological methods of identifying people's 'happy' brains through using a MRI scanner, and one group of researchers at Harvard University have suggested that they discovered that a mind or mental state that lacks the ability to adapt to change is typically an unhappy one (Diener, 2000). We shall consider adaptation and responses to change in Chapter 2 when we look at the life-span in detail.

A debate currently rages around the so-called 'hard-wiring' of sex differences. This has been based on experiments with people on the autism spectrum, where discoveries by cognitive neuroscientists suggest clear differences in brain activity between female and male participants (e.g., Baron-Cohen, 2004).

The remit of psychology is so fundamental to all aspects of human life and society that it informs the theory and practice of several other diverse disciplines and professions as well as social work. These include neurophysiology, medicine, health care, psychiatry and broader mental health studies, nursing and midwifery, anthropology, sociology, town and urban planning, architecture, driver behaviour, communication studies as well as aspects of media and public relations work. The list is long and the increased recognition of the role psychology can play in understanding everyday life has come to the fore through reality television programmes, involving interpersonal competition and cooperation, which have reached a pinnacle in popularity. Psychologists, however, are divided as to how far this type of esteem for their subject is helpful to its development, but whatever their opinions, popular psychology has never been more popular!

In the following chapters we demonstrate that psychological knowledge complements intuition in making judgements during face-to-face encounters with service users and in long-term assessments of service provision. It is also valuable in the self-assessment and personal growth of the practitioner and for an understanding of social work organizations.

We want to stress that there is a world of difference between a socially competent human being, the friend with concern for others, and the professional social worker required to make judgements about someone's behaviour based on previous knowledge of that person and a valid prediction of how they will cope in the future. Social workers have to do more than get along with other people – they seek to make objective assessments, interventions and take decisions that radically affect the course of other people's lives.

## The development of psychological theories for social workers

Academic psychology (the substance of research and teaching) draws upon several perspectives, although broadly speaking the focus is upon the individual. Social psychology is to some extent an exception to this rule, as it concentrates on the interaction between individuals and the impact of the social context on the individual. Academic psychology research favours the study of mental mechanisms and processes such as thinking (cognition) and perception, and how these processes relate to and are influenced by behaviour. Social work, emerging as a profession after World War II, increasingly identified itself with psychoanalytic psychology, and while this approach to understanding human thought, emotion and behaviour is invaluable, only exceptionally is it seen by academic psychologists as integral to their discipline.

Academic psychology prides itself on being a scientific discipline. This means that its theory and practice are based upon empirical evidence that is derived from observations rather than on opinions, beliefs, prejudice or argument. Scientific observations are reliable and repeatable according to a fairly strict set of rules. Measurement is crucial, and the data (generated by observations) have to be compiled in a systematic way. There are, though, inevitable problems for a discipline like psychology that requires the assessment of people by other people, and in order to meet the constraints imposed by the scientific method, the focus of energies has been upon the study and analysis of behaviour, often using the experimental method. Although this has ensured the rigour which science demands, it has also meant that the scope of the discipline has been limited in certain ways, at the expense of studying emotions and feelings in everyday situations. How does this benefit social work practitioners?

In the remainder of this chapter we identify selective issues from psychology theory that have relevance to practice.

## Research on memory and eye-witness testimony

There is a tradition in experimental psychology of studying human memory and, more recently, its application to eye-witness testimony. Concern with prosecution in child abuse and child sexual abuse cases has led to a positive relationship between experimental cognitive psychology and the practical and emotional problems and benefits for children giving evidence against their abusers (Castelli et al., 2005; Goodman, 2006).

The pioneering work of Graham Davies and colleagues, begun in the 1980s, on the psychological processes connected with witness reports, memory and testimonies, demonstrated important ways in which experimentally based psychology has enhanced the procedures surrounding giving evidence in court, particularly for children who are victims of alleged abuse. Understanding the efficacy of children's memories under stressful conditions (such as recalling abuse in detail when appearing in court) has had an important practical effect within the legal system where changes to the way children's evidence is received have been of immediate practical importance to both psychologists and social workers. The data derived from this psychological research led to the Home Office's commitment to the closed-circuit TV link to the courtroom. Without the child's testimony there are problems in securing convictions against abusers and it becomes more difficult to make plans for the future of the child. Research demonstrated that the trauma of a courtroom appearance is potentially damaging as the original experience of abuse is re-created and the ensuing stress is likely to hinder memory as well as precipitate emotional disturbance (Davies, 1988; Boon et al., 1993). Thus giving evidence outside the court via closed-circuit cameras is not just something that is 'more pleasant' for children. It is demonstrably more effective in obtaining truth and accuracy of recall. Additional recommendations based on psychological research indicate the importance of a 'trusted intermediary' (probably a social worker known to the child) to be employed to assist in the questioning procedure rather than an unknown court official (Boon et al., 1993).

Helen Westcott (Westcott, 2003; Westcott and Kynan, 2004) has taken the evidence from this research further. She examined ways in which social workers apply methods of interviewing children through a story-telling framework. Westcott and colleagues are clear though that caution needs to be applied – you cannot just tell children a story and get them to complete or comment on it. They may not be able to distinguish between what is true, what is untrue and what they believe the questioner wants to hear. On the other hand it isn't appropriate to use the same techniques on children as with adults.

## Applying psychology to the impact of disasters, accidents and their aftermath

In addition to experimental techniques, academic psychology has developed a sophisticated approach to validated, reliable psychometric testing, which is using tests that compare the results of individuals with established norms developed through statistical testing. Victims of disasters react in a number of ways to their experiences, depending on their personalities, previous histories and the event itself. Psychologists have developed assessment methods to identify people who might be classified as having PTSD (post-traumatic stress disorder) and varying degrees of related stress (Bisson, 2007; Busuttil, 2004) including domestic violence (Israel and Stover, 2009; Jones et al., 2001).

In work with victims of disasters, which could include a variety of harrowing events, expertise has grown to both identify and to help individuals who have survived traumatic experiences overcome them, minimizing subsequent psychological disturbance (see Clegg, 1988; Ehlers et al., 2003). Expertise in this kind of work has developed exponentially over the past thirty years as a consequence of the spread of conflict across Europe (in the Balkan States), the Middle East (in Iraq and Afghanistan), the 'Arab Spring' and Africa (in Somalia and Ruanda) in particular. A series of disasters that relates to technological and human failures on a large scale including motorway and aircraft crashes, and football stadium collapses have also been too apparent. Also there have been unexpected and devastating terrorist attacks such as those on the World Trade Center in New York City in 2001, the '7/7' attacks on the transport system in London or the Omagh bombing in Northern Ireland in 1998 (Bonanno et al., 2006). People involved in each and every one of these different types of disaster experience fear for their own safety and lives, loss of loved ones, friends and colleagues and are inevitably the witnesses to horrific sights of suffering and consequent feelings of helplessness and guilt. Stories told by survivors of the Nazi Holocaust and death camps and of the atrocities in the Balkans have identified the different ways in which those who survived feel guilty for simply surviving and how some people cope by burying their experiences and others by telling the stories to themselves and others time and again. No one technique returns the person to the same psychological state as they were before any of the events they experienced took place. That is impossible – the trajectory of their life has already followed a pathway of no return. However, psychology and psychologically informed social care practice can support survivors in coming to terms with their multiple experiences, losses and fears in such a way that they can get on with the rest of their lives and not dwell forever on their traumas (see Bettelheim, 1979). This also applies to some aspects of grief, as you will see when you read Chapter 2 about the life-span.

Social workers may be faced with immediate emergencies, but commonly are tasked with the longer-term role of picking up the pieces. Psychological research has provided a 'profile' of the disaster victim's experience indicating a 'post-traumatic stress disorder' (PTSD) which may prevent someone from being able to lead a normal life for a period of years.

PTSD is a clinical disorder or a syndrome, which means the person suffers from a group of clinically recognized symptoms. Its symptoms are grouped into three types:

1. re-experiencing the traumatic event, through constantly re-enacting it in your mind and dreaming about it;

2. numbing or reduced involvement in the external world as if you are at a distance from things that are happening to you;

3. a diverse group of symptoms such as memory impairment, difficulty in concentrating, hyper-alertness (being over aware of what is going on – 'jumpy').

Some survivors experience a few of these symptoms all the time and others sometimes. Other people have a clearly defined PTSD. That means they experience most of these symptoms all or most of the time. People who have these symptoms are also likely to feel worse when faced with a situation that reminds them of the trauma. So if you have survived a train crash or suicide bomber attacks, you might be coping well and not thinking about the experience until you have to get on board a train or see a crash on television. That might make you break out in a sweat, tremble and have nightmares. This experience can last for a few hours or a few days. This disorder presents further problems for family members – both financial and emotional – including management of the grief process.

Outside of the dramatic trauma of events such as those identified above there is evidence that experiences less overtly dramatic, such as childbirth, separation, domestic violence and divorce might precipitate some degree of PTSD (Nicolson, 2010a). Asylum seekers who leave their homes after bloody conflicts, such as in the course of the civil war in Syria which began in 2011, have borne not only the immediate pain of witness and suffering, but also the separation from their families and familiar surroundings with the knowledge that they will be unable to return home and to normality either for many years or forever. Supporting people and families who have had this kind of experience and helping them fend off or recover from mental ill-health, requires specialist skills based on the psychology of multiple long-term loss. There is increasing concern with PTSD among children and research on children's experiences of road accidents makes a useful contribution. It was found that negative appraisal of the event itself increased the likelihood of chronic PTSD in children between 5 and 16 who had had road traffic accidents (Ehlers et al., 2003). This suggests that child victims of other types of trauma, including abuse or having to leave their homeland as asylum seekers or refugees following war or persecution, are most likely to need therapeutic intervention and support.

Leach (Leach 2004) and colleagues' work on memory and survival is noteworthy. He focused his efforts on why some people actually choose not to survive Leach and Ansell (2008). He contrasts survivorship, such as in cases where plane crash survivors ate the flesh of the dead passengers, the climber who cut off a limb in order to get free of the rock crevice, people who survived brutal concentration and prison camps, with those whose lives have been less documented but nevertheless have appeared to give up on life. Leach argues that there are many people who experience this and in fact die, perhaps of what we used to call a broken heart, and some of the unanswered questions are around the cognitive function of memory at the time of the disaster. During a threatening situation memory may not work as well as it should, so that some threatened individuals actually *forget* how to survive. They have difficulty retrieving the information in their memory store that enables them to escape and return to a sense of health and well-being. This is not just about the difficulties faced by disaster victims but applies to vulnerable people who seek social work help, or perhaps fail to seek help because they have given up on their situation. They might thus choose to remain institutionalized, give up the fight to keep their children, fail to come off drugs or alcohol, or engage in other equally self-abusive or neglectful behaviours.

This research, relating trauma to loss and grief, is relatively new, but founded on psychological theory and psychological methods of investigation that come originally from ideas advanced by Freud himself and which are now also the province of neuroscientists (e.g. Lehtonen, 2012). This work, its practice and research, also begs for cooperation between social work and psychologists in a joint effort to explore the parameters and consequences of disasters for individuals, families and communities from social, psychoanalytic and cognitive-neurological positions.

## Perspectives on psychology

What follows is an outline of some of the different perspectives on psychology that are most relevant to social work practice, including psychoanalytic, behavioural, social learning, cognitive-developmental, humanistic, social and evolutionary psychology (see also Nicolson, 2014). We explore the ways in which these different approaches tackle issues connected with the structure of the individual personality, development and how people relate to each other.

## Psychoanalytic psychology

We begin with psychoanalysis because pioneering social workers in the UK after World War II and more or less until the late 1970s adopted a psychoanalytic perspective on relationships, particularly those that, for whatever reason, were dysfunctional. This approach, unfortunately erroneously seen as equivalent to blaming the underprivileged, went through the doldrums for about twenty years, mostly because a more radical analysis of social deprivation and exclusion identified the impact of social inequalities and lack of opportunities on their service users' lives. However there is now something of a resurgence of psychoanalytic ideas in social work (Ruch, 2005), alongside the more sociological perspectives which are proving helpful to the lives of those in receipt of social work support and intervention (Borden, 2000; Bower, 2005).

Psychoanalysis, as most of you will be aware, had its origins in the work of Sigmund Freud in Vienna, a neurologist whose early work with hysterics led him to explore psychological techniques to probe the unconscious. These included *free association,* in which the person seeking help would tell the analyst everything that came into their mind trying not to censure what they said out loud. Freud also advocated the analysis of fantasies and dreams as an important point of access to the unconscious. This approach was further developed by others such as Erik Erikson, Melanie Klein, Alfred Adler and Carl Jung and in Chapter 2 we shall see some of the ways in which psychoanalysis has contributed to an understanding of the life-span while Chapters 3, 7 and 8 provide further information about the contribution of psychoanalysis to understanding organizations. For this reason we have chosen to dedicate significant space to describing Freud's work here.

This method and approach towards helping people change continued to be used in counselling and psychotherapy, which may be the reason new thinkers across the discipline of social work are considering its value afresh (e.g., Ruch, 2005).

Susie Orbach, well known for making psychoanalytic ideas accessible, has used her experience and understanding of psychoanalysis to explore problems faced by her patients which she describes as:

some of the most profound questions we have to encounter as human beings. The issues of how one can trust, how disappointment tears the psyche, how love and hate are related, what sexuality means to the individual, how betrayal closes us off to other people and how we can dare to open ourselves again are all dramatised within the therapeutic relationship. (1999, p.1)

Psychoanalytic theories concentrate on questions of adult personality and developmental problems and crises as they relate back to early development and will be discussed further in Chapter 2. Freud's theory of *psychosexual development* proposed that all behaviour is characterized by *instinctual drives* or motivating forces. These can be divided into the *libido*, which is the sexual drive; the life-preserving drives; and the aggressive drives. In Freud's view the sexual drives were the most important. Within each of us, he believed, is the need to seek gratification, and this process occurs throughout life.

Freud considered that there are three basic structures of personality that serve to help the gratification of the instincts. These are the *id, ego* and *superego*. The id is the original source of personality and contains everything that an individual inherits, the instinctual drives and the pleasure-seeking impulses. Like a young child, the id can be seen to operate according to the pleasure principle, avoiding pain and obtaining pleasure, regardless of external considerations. This basic push for gratification remains part of the personality, but with the experience that gratification can often be achieved better by a more considered approach to the external world.

By planning and negotiating, the child gradually transfers energy from the id to the ego which is the second structure to develop, acting as a go-between amongst the demands of the id and the realities of life expressed consciously. The ego also mediates between the id and the superego; the latter is known colloquially as the *conscience* and is the third structure to develop. The superego then enables individuals to decide between right and wrong and conflicts with the ego and the id acting as a control over the instinct to self-gratification.

The ego is the mainly conscious part of the mind, and the id and superego are unconscious. These parts of the personality are seen as being in conflict, and the result of this conflict is *anxiety*. Most people experience anxiety, a major principle of Freudian and post-Freudian psychoanalysis, which can often be directly handled by the ego. An example of this is the anxiety which surrounds the experience of being called out on an emergency duty visit to an unknown family, with the likelihood that a child will be taken into care or violence and aggression will be experienced. This is a situation which calls for judgement about the risk that the family will be hostile to the social worker, the problems of liaising with the emergency children's reception centre and so on. The ego can handle this by looking objectively at the situation, realizing its difficulties, recognizing other people's likely anxieties, and mustering all one's professional skills in order to do the work as well as possible, bearing the child's needs in mind, rather than being overwhelmed by anxiety.

However, sometimes there is too much anxiety to be handled by the ego, and individuals resort to *defence mechanisms*, Freud's term for unconscious strategies for reducing anxiety. These are clearly and comprehensively described in another book that we were involved with (see Smith et al., 2012). Because these mechanisms are unconscious they involve some self-deception, but they are quite normal, and part of everyone's experience. The defences can take the form of *denial, repression, rationalization, projection* and *displacement*. So, for instance, someone might repress the feelings surrounding a break-up of their relationship by insisting to themselves that nothing has gone wrong (denial). Alternatively, she/ he may rationalize that they never loved their partner anyway, and a break-up would be the sensible solution. Projecting the anxiety would mean experiencing the partner as uncaring and unworthy of love, when in fact they fear those particular qualities in themselves. Finally, anxiety about the break-up could be 'displaced' by having arguments at work or being irritable with the children, and thus focusing attention on these 'problems', and away from the source of the anxiety. Orbach (1999) highlighted how she struggled to make sense of feelings and emotions that a patient had aroused in her which appeared to have no conscious or objective explanation. As she describes it, the therapist is drawn into the emotions experienced by their client: 'the therapist bobs in and out of the emotional turmoil that is at the heart of the human condition ... [and] offered a special kind of opportunity to enter into the emotional experiences of another' (1999, p. 2). We discuss this process, called countertransference, in Chapter 7.

## Psychosexual development

In the course of development a child goes through a series of what Freud called psychosexual stages. The ego and superego develop during the course of these stages. Also the goals of gratification change according to the focus of the libido, which centres upon a particular part of the body, which he calls the erogenous zone, at each stage. These are the mouth, the anus and the genitals.

Freud proposed five stages. Between 0 and 1 years of age, the infant goes through the oral stage, when the libidinal focus is on the mouth, tongue and lips. The major source of pleasure surrounds this area, and attachment to the mother is related to her being a source of oral pleasure. The anal stage occurs between the ages of 1 and 3. During this stage the baby is sensitive to the anal region of its body, which corresponds to the parents' efforts in toilet training. If toilet training becomes fraught, which it often does, Freud considered that a child might suffer to some extent for the rest of its life. The phallic stage takes place between the ages of 3 and 5. It is characterized by a shift away from the anal region towards the genital erogenous zone. At this stage both boys and girls may begin quite naturally to masturbate.

Freud considered that an important event occurs during the phallic stage, which he calls the *Oedipal conflict* (see Nicolson, 2012, for a discussion of how this plays out in adulthood in relation to competition in organizations). Freud himself put more emphasis on the events related to boys' development than that of girls, but parallel occurrences, he believed, take place for girls. He suggested that the boy becomes intuitively aware of his mother's sexuality, and at about the age of 4 begins to have a (sort of) sexual attraction to his mother, regarding his father as a sexual rival. He sees his father as having the ultimate power to castrate him as a punishment and thus the boy is caught between desire for his mother and fear of his father's power to achieve his revenge. The result of this conflict is anxiety, which he responds to with a process Freud calls identification. Thus he tries to make himself as much like his father as possible so that he is taking on some of his father's powers too.

The related process which according to psychoanalytic theory occurs for girls is not described very well by Freud, who asserts that the girl sees her mother as a rival for her father's sexual attentions although he argues she will not fear her mother's power so much as the boy fears his father's – perhaps because she assumes she has already been castrated. This means her anxiety is weaker and so is her identification.

Freud considered successful resolution of the Oedipal crisis by identification with the appropriate parent to be decisive for healthy development and any disruption of the identification process to be severely problematic. An example where a mother is more powerful than the father could create problems for boys in the family. However for most of us the model family as described by Freud is rare. It is important, therefore, for social workers to accept and understand the relevant aspects of a theory about competition and accepting difference, while able to modify and reject theories or parts of theories that are not applicable. The paper referred to above (Nicolson, 2012) about Oedipus at work is an example of ways in which unresolved and *un-nameable* rivalry, competition and anxiety can hinder development and decision-making at work.

Between the ages of 5 and 12, Freud says that children go through a period of latency without any major developmental changes. During these years the child's friends are almost exclusively of the same sex and there is further development of the defence mechanisms, particularly those of denial (for instance, the child says that she/he is not tired when clearly unable to keep awake!), and repression, in which unacceptable thoughts and feelings are forced out of consciousness, particularly those about sexuality.

Between the ages of 12 and 18, and beyond, the adolescent's psychosexual stage corresponds with hormonal and biological changes, with the focus of interest on the genitals. The child is now interested in people of the other sex with, according to Freud, mature heterosexual love being the maturational goal. Other psychoanalytic psychologists (e.g., Dinnerstein, 1976; Mitchell, 2000; Sayers, 1982) have challenged Freud's developmental theory in this respect and shown gay relationships as one perspective on normal development.

Freud's work is a major attempt to explain human development, human relationships and emotions and explore the different ways in which we are (apparently) irrational. However it is difficult to prove many of his assertions which are value-laden and partial. Freud's studies of developmental psychology led him to believe that structural reorganization of the personality occurs at certain crucial points in development, and that these stages are universal features in the development of all human beings. Children want their wishes fulfilled immediately and flare up in anger if frustrated. They also show strong sexual passion. He considered that during socialization antisocial impulses were brought under control so that a process of internalization through which children moved from external behavioural controls (rewards and punishments) to internal self-controls occurred. This transition linked with children's feelings towards their parents. Parental pressure towards socialization makes children angry, and the thought of expressing this anger arouses their anxiety, partly because they might lose their parents if they were to express their anger too fervently. Children therefore repress their anger and turn it in on themselves. This is the foundation of 'guilt' – a powerful motivating force in development. The internalization of the parents' (and thus society's) rules are embodied in the superego which is a harsh, punitive and inflexible psychological mechanism.

## Behavioural psychology

Many social workers are now familiar with behaviour modification and more recently cognitive behaviour therapy (CBT) therapeutic techniques based upon knowledge derived from the behavioural school of psychology. This is one of the earliest approaches to understanding human behaviour, developed initially by Thorndike, Watson, Pavlov and Skinner in the late nineteenth and early twentieth centuries. Behaviourists are interested in questions relating to the conditions and events surrounding behaviour, for example, what actually happened before someone broke into tears, and what events took place in response to this. Psychologists taking this perspective limit themselves to observable events, and the ways in which behaviour is influenced by the environment. This is directly in contrast to the psychoanalytic approach that concentrates on the inner and unconscious life of individuals, and stresses the significance of biology in determining development. Behaviourism is concerned with how individuals learn about the way in which they can best exist within their environment, including emotional development, perceptions of the external world, social behaviour and personality. Individuals learn by making connections between events in the environment. Two particular theories have been developed to explain learning. These are *classical conditioning* and *operant conditioning*.

Studies of classical conditioning derive from the work of Pavlov who noticed that dogs salivated when they saw and smelled the food being brought to them. A bell was sounded just before the time that the food arrived, and Pavlov noticed that the dogs would eventually salivate on hearing the bell, even when there was no food to be seen or smelled. People learn to anticipate relationships among *stimuli* in order to make sense of the world. A child might learn that when her father has had too much to drink he hits her, and the pain makes her cry. Thus, when she hears her father returning from the pub she responds by bursting into tears before he has a chance to be violent. She has learnt that the combination of her father returning home and the place that he has been to indicate punishment for her. This is an example of classical conditioning.

Operant conditioning, described by Skinner (1953), occurs when an individual learns that some behaviour of his/her own leads to a particular consequence. A boy may take part in a range of activities at home, but when he plays with guns, and behaves in a typically 'masculine' way, his mother smiles at him. He therefore learns to behave in this way more frequently, as it gains his mother's approval. This process was studied by Skinner who demonstrated that behaviour in rats and pigeons can be conditioned if responses are followed by *reinforcement*, the reward or punishment following particular manifestations of behaviour. The mother smiling at the little boy's games is the reinforcement. Conversely, a little girl playing with guns may have them taken from her, or be told with a frown that her behaviour is 'unladylike'. This acts as a punishment, and the child learns not to behave in that particular way. Skinner, in direct contrast to Freud, challenged the idea of human agency, or self-determination, believing that human states of mind do not cause behaviour. For Skinner inner processes such as thinking and feeling are simply responses to the external world.

Behaviour modification based on the theory of operant condition is a method of helping someone change undesirable and antisocial behaviour by offering rewards or punishments. For instance children with learning disabilities often respond favourably to being cuddled or given sweets, and if they wash themselves or go to the toilet at the right time, they can be rewarded in that way. They learn to modify and adapt their behaviour as a means of obtaining the reward. CBT represents a more sophisticated approach to behavioural and cognitive change and works through enabling the individual to unlearn patterns of depressive or negative thoughts. This is particularly useful for changing the way depressed people see their lives and the world around them and adopt a more optimistic or hopeful outlook.

Behavioural psychologists are concerned with the way people act rather than the way they reason about their behaviour, ethics and morality. They propose that a person's obedience to a culture's moral rules depends on the consequences of doing so, or not doing so, that is, the punishments or rewards that ensue. They consider that behaviour that provides rewards in a given situation is likely to be repeated in a similar situation, and behaviour that is punished is less likely to be repeated. Thus individuals who are punished for breaking the law are less likely to do so again. However psychologists (e.g., Thorndike, Watson, Skinner and others) have argued that if acceptable ways of behaviour are to be learnt, it is important for the rewards or punishments to be administered immediately after and clearly related to the behaviour.

Psychologists would consider that reward is preferable to punishment in child rearing, because punishment merely suppresses behaviour. It does not provide long-term inner control. Studies have also demonstrated that it is likely to create hostility, which may well increase antisocial activities in those who receive too much punishment.

Changing children's behaviour has found its way into popular 'reality' television where techniques of behaviourism are put on display. Aggressive, hyperactive and anxious children who won't go to bed, to school, or eat for example, and thereby cause distress to their parents are subjected to change in parental response under the tutorship of the celebrity psychologist. Where, when and how negative behaviours have previously been reinforced is demonstrated to parents and these reinforcements are withdrawn in favour of positive reinforcement for acceptable behaviour – frequently with impressive results.

## Social learning theory

Innovations in social work, such as the work in Hackney documented by Goodman and Trowler (2012) in their book *Social Work Reclaimed*, have combined systemic approaches to families with social learning theory. Thus, as with psychoanalytic ideas, social learning theory has become relevant once again to contemporary practice despite its major developments having taken place half a century ago. The Hackney team identified its relevance to combating child abuse and domestic violence in particular as well as for working with others who have signs of PTSD.

During the 1960s and beyond, Bandura (1977) developed social learning theory combining behavioural and cognitive psychology. Social learning theory explores how people learn their social behaviour. Social learning in developing children is accomplished through the influence of models (usually adults) whose behaviour is imitated by the children for whom that particular adult is important. It has been suggested that children model the behaviour of people who are warm and caring, which would include their parents, perhaps their favourite nursery teacher, or relatives. However psychologists have shown that this is not always the case, and that perhaps it is the qualities possessed by models rather than their place in the child's early life that makes them effective. Another important aspect of social learning theory and one which conflicts with psychoanalytic theory is that it is observing the model that is crucial, not necessarily interaction between the child and model. In one famous set of experiments, Bandura identified the importance of modelling behaviour in young children's development. The psychologists used nursery school children as participants, and divided them into experimental and control groups. The children in the experimental group watched an adult spend several minutes mistreating a doll – punching it, standing on it, pulling its hair, and eventually banging it with a mallet. Then the groups of children were allowed to play with some attractive toys. These were soon taken away and the children were told that some other children were going to play with them instead. This was clearly and intentionally a very frustrating situation, during which the children were expected to initiate aggression.

At this stage, all the children were given a doll and a mallet to play with, as well as aggressive toys such as darts and guns. Both the experimental group and the control group were observed through a one-way mirror for 20 minutes. The experimental group expressed their aggression on the whole by an imitation of the adult: by mistreating the doll. The control group were also aggressive, but did not adopt this behaviour: they made more varied use of the guns and the darts.

This explanation of behaviour may well be important in practice for breaking the pattern of aggressive parenting by individuals who themselves were physically abused by their own parents. According to the social learning theorists, they would have learned a particular style of parenting which is aggressive, and to react to personal frustrations by hitting their children. By providing day-care for children who have been attacked by their parents, it should be possible to give a stronger alternative model for parenting behaviour. It might be the qualities possessed by the model rather than their importance in a child's life which makes them effective. A warm, caring nursery teacher or residential worker may be more influential than an aggressive parent.

Bandura also suggested that individuals do not learn about moral rules in response to their exposure to reward or punishment, but by observation of other people's behaviour. By watching other people, individuals witness the consequences of their actions and the behaviour that they assess to be appropriate under certain conditions. It is worth noting that although the results of these and similar experiments remain valid, the methodologies, using trickery and deception, are no longer permissible for ethical reasons. Nicolson (2014) includes further discussion of social learning theory and its role in moral development.

## Cognitive-developmental psychology

Cognitive-developmental psychology, an offshoot of cognitive psychology, developed as a reaction to behaviourism which, its advocates believed, ignored 'what goes on inside the heads' of human beings. Cognitive-developmental psychology therefore attempts to explore the maturational changes in mental structures as well as the changes in capacities which occur as the infant becomes the child and then the adult. This is a particularly relevant approach when considering aspects of socialization (the way culture is transmitted from one generation to the next) as well as psychological development. Cognitive-developmental psychology is concerned with the way people process information derived from both their internal world and the external world, and the way in which changes in the processing mechanisms occur.

The most influential psychologist in the area of cognitive development was Jean Piaget, the Swiss research biologist who, because he was writing in French from the 1930s, was not taken seriously until his work was translated into English in the 1950s. Piaget demonstrated that a child's behaviour alone did not present a complete picture and that the quality of the thought processes behind that behaviour needed equal consideration. Also he found that children of different ages had different ways of thinking and solving problems from each other. Piaget's approach challenged thinking which at the time had been geared to intelligence testing and quantifying changes in development (Piaget, 1972, 1990).

The central idea of Piaget's work, and that of subsequent cognitive-developmental psychologists, is that every child is born with certain strategies for interacting with the environment. These strategies, which enable babies to make sense of their world in a particular way, are the starting points for the development of thinking. As children develop, so do their strategies – partly as a result of maturation, and partly as a result of the child's encounters with the external world. The discoveries the child makes about the world come about during the processes of development and exploration and occur in particular sequences. Thus there are certain things children are unable to do until they have grasped concepts which precede them (for example, a child cannot grasp the idea of adding and subtracting until she has realized that objects are constant).

Piaget considered that the environment in which the child lives may affect the rate at which she goes through this developmental sequence, because the quality of experience is an important source of stimulation and mental exercise. However, as far as he was able to demonstrate, the environment does not enable children to miss out or skip stages in cognitive development. An understanding of the concept of children's cognitive structure is especially important for residential workers faced with the task of ensuring that the children in their care make sense of their worlds, and the reasons why they are in care. It also provides a means of assessing children's responses to particular situations, as in the case of 'good' and 'bad' behaviour and moral reasoning.

Piaget's interest in moral rules has a resonance with contemporary concerns about respect for others and unruly or disruptive behaviour of children and adolescents in schools and in public places. Typical assumptions are that young people who are disruptive will change their behaviour if they are threatened with punishments such as community service orders where they might have to clean streets and public toilets under the supervision of probation workers or work on older people's gardens. This may not necessarily be the most helpful means of changing 'antisocial' behaviours. Piaget (1965) and Lawrence Kohlberg (1969) worked on this aspect of moral development. Piaget had based his research on younger children's thinking about intent in moral issues. He worked with children aged between 6 and 12 and told them pairs of stories about childish transgressions, asking them which action was the naughtier and why. The pairs of stories might be as follows:

1. There was a little boy called John, who thought he would help his mummy by cleaning the kitchen. While he was doing this he knocked a pile of plates over, and they all broke.
2. William's mummy told him never to play in the kitchen when she was not there, but one day he did, and knocked over a cup and cracked it.

Piaget asked: 'Who was the naughtier and why?' Younger children usually insisted that John was the naughtier because the consequences of his action were more severe. Piaget found that they did understand that he was trying to help, but were still more concerned about the amount of damage. He calls this type of reasoning *objective responsibility*, meaning that actions are judged on the basis of their material outcome rather than their intent. He also demonstrated that children's first views grow out of their relationship to adults as authority figures. They are subordinate to adults, and believe that rules emanate from sources outside themselves, which adults recognize and thus forbid and punish. He refers to this stage as *heteronomous morality*. When children grow older, free themselves from adult authority and mix more with their peer group, they begin to understand that rules are social agreements, accepted by all members of a group as a basis for co-operative action. This stage he refers to as one of *autonomous morality*. This suggests therefore that simply punishing young people for antisocial transgressions will not change their behaviours because they still think in the same way.

In the late 1960s Kohlberg built upon Piaget's work on moral development. He aimed to show that if cognitive development in human beings had a natural and normal development course, then moral reasoning may also demonstrate a normal pattern of development. This was based on the premise that if the development of moral reasoning demonstrates a standard or universal form of development with increasing maturity, then the mature form of moral thinking can be considered to be better or more desirable than earlier forms of moral thought. Kohlberg attempted to describe the changes in children's moral thinking systematically as they occur with development, through a series of comparison studies of children of different ages, and a longitudinal study of a group of children as they grew up. The consistencies between these two studies gave him a firm basis for claiming that age group differences do reflect individual development in moral reasoning.

Kohlberg presented his participants with a moral dilemma which presented a conflict between competing claims for justice. Their task was to choose a solution and explain their choice. After analysing the statements of children at various stages of development, he constructed a model of growth in moral reasoning. This consisted of three levels of morality, each of which could be divided into two stages (see Table 1.1).

**Table 1.1** Kohlberg's levels of moral reasoning

| Level 1: Pre-conventional morality Most children under the age of nine reach this level of reasoning. | *Stage 1* The individual conforms after punishment or through fear of punishment by authority that he or she accepts<br>*Stage 2* Self-interested exchanges – the individual conforms to get the most advantage for themselves. |
|---|---|
| Level 2: Conventional morality Most adolescents and adults are at this level. The individual now understands, accepts, and upholds social rules and expectations, especially those that emanate from authorities. | *Stage 3* Maintaining good interpersonal relationships – the individual wants to be seen as good.<br>*Stage 4* Maintaining the social system – the individual agrees to a set of rules and obligations that are seen as socially justified. |
| Level 3: Post-conventional morality Only a minority of people reach this level of reasoning, usually in adulthood. They have their own rules that guide them. | *Stage 5* At this stage a social contract and a sense of individual rights are paramount in thinking.<br>*Stage 6* The individual recognizes universal ethical principles that they themselves adhere to. |

Kohlberg suggested that these levels of morality reflect three different social orientations. Pre-conventional people have a concrete individual perspective on society; conventional people have a member of society's view; and post-conventional people take a 'prior to society' perspective. Only post-conventional people ask themselves what kind of social regulations a society would have to develop if it were to start from scratch. It is likely that the majority of social workers see themselves as operating at a post-conventional level of moral reasoning which is necessary for working with people with very different moral rules, behaviours and experiences from their own. Social workers need to be more than tolerant 'liberals'. If they are going to work successfully with service users of all ages and backgrounds to help them change their behaviours, then they need to be confident in their own, independent judgements of morality beyond those of popular rhetoric, policy and law enforcement. This does not mean that psychologists are advocating challenges to the current policy, law and social structures. It simply means that social workers, to do their work with service users effectively, need to be able to think beyond the popular imagination. Kohlberg predicted that moral reasoning was related to behaviour. He did a series of experiments to show that people at a high level of moral reasoning are less likely to administer shocks in experiments like Milgram's (Milgram, 1963; see Chapter 6). Another piece of work which used Kohlberg's stages showed that children at Stage 3 are more likely to give way to group pressure than when they are at a higher stage. Also, that people at Stages 5 and 6 were seen to be more likely to cheat than those at 3 and 4. Another study showed that university teachers of science and university administrators tended to employ law and order reasoning more than social science and humanities teachers.

Carol Gilligan (1982/1993) provided a challenge to this view on moral reasoning, arguing that Kohlberg's model was 'gendered'. Through her own examination of moral stories which focused on matters like abortion, clearly of more immediate concern to girls and women, she found clear gender differences in the processes of reasoning, with decisions made along lines reflecting the interests of each gender group. That is not to say she found that women and men came down on separate sides, or even the same sides as each other when addressing issues around 'a woman's right to choose' an abortion. It was that they based their judgements on different premises.

## Social psychology

Social psychology has origins in sociology as well as psychology, with Auguste Comte in France and Charles Cooley in America (at the turn of the twentieth century) both making reference to social psychology. The 1930s and 1940s were another period of growth with studies of industrial management and army leadership inspiring researchers. Social psychology is different from the approaches described so far, partly because it incorporates a variety of psychological theories, but especially because it focuses upon the study of more than one person, and of individuals within the context of wider social groupings. Most recently it has identified itself overtly with critical approaches to the discipline (Gough and McFadden, 2001). Social psychology is important for social workers, most obviously because of mutual concern for social networks. In Chapter 6, aspects of group behaviour relevant to understanding family patterns and institutional life are examined, while in Chapter 7 there is a discussion of the social psychology relevant to social work organizations.

Social psychology is both responsive to and initiates change in conceptual and methodological issues. In other words, social psychology is the critical wing of the discipline with some, although not all, advocates challenging the experimental orthodoxies of psychology overall.

In the 1970s there was a direct challenge to the positivist model of research (i.e. that measured and observed behaviour leads to the establishment of rules or the truths about human psychology). Harré and Secord (1972) argued that an understanding of the deeper levels of human encounter could only be gained through analysis of subjective accounts of actions rather than objective measurement of interpersonal behaviour. This line of attack upon mainstream psychology has been maintained and indeed strengthened through the work of social constructionists who argue for the understanding of human behaviour through the way individuals position themselves within existing discourses. This approach attempts to explain human experience (subjectivity) as an ideological venture rather than an essentially biological one, and so human social and individual actions might be understood as deriving from dominant social values rather than individual desires (see Gough and McFadden, 2001). This perspective is particularly important for social work practitioners grappling with the reasons why particular people appear to persist in what appear to be inappropriate behaviours. Unsurprisingly, then, social psychology, and in particular ideas about *social construction* of knowledge have also developed in contemporary social work discussion (see Nicolson, 2014).

## The phenomenological or humanistic approach

Humanistic psychology was initially rooted in the optimism of the 1960s and the work of Abraham Maslow, George Kelly and Carl Rogers. Rogers' work in particular was derived from his therapeutic/counselling work and, like Freud, he developed a theory of personality and human development based on his clinical experience. Unlike psychoanalysis, however, humanistic psychology emphasizes the positive nature of human beings and their efforts towards growth and self-actualization or self-fulfilment (see Chapter 4 for a discussion of how this theoretical approach applies to concepts such as 'strengths'). Smith et al. (2012) discuss applications of humanistic and phenomenological psychology extensively and in depth.

Humanistic psychology stresses the importance of freeing individuals from any barriers within themselves and between the self and the external reality. It also differs from other approaches in psychology, because of the value it attaches to subjective experience – that the individual's own view of the world is reality. The main concern therefore is how people perceive themselves and their surroundings, rather than with behaviour. The central component of Rogers' theory is the self-concept. Someone with a positive self-concept views the world quite differently from someone whose self-concept is weak. The self-concept does not necessarily reflect reality – someone may be successful in the eyes of others, but see themselves as a failure. Rogers suggests that individuals have an 'ideal self, the person they would like to be, and that self-concepts of 'fully functioning' people are consistent or congruent with their thoughts, experience and behaviour (Rogers, 1961/2002).

## Evolutionary psychology

Evolutionary psychology has gained an enthusiastic response from the popular press over recent years because it appears to provide a watertight and scientifically based rationale for gender-power differences and differences in gender-typed behaviours, although as with most theories the strength of the arguments is contested (Bjorklund and Pellegrini, 2000; Gannon, 2002). The ideas of evolutionary psychology are based on the premise that human behaviour originates from natural selection. That is, that the desire and behaviour by both males and females to maximize their reproductive potential leads to strategies that both sexes apply to their social and sexual relationship behaviours. Evolutionary psychologists suggest that these are by definition distinct from each other because women have greater investment in an individual offspring (since each infant has a nine-month gestation period). By contrast, men can produce children each time they have sexual intercourse with a different woman. Thus it is argued that women have evolved to become sexually/socially shy and choosy, while men have to compete with each other through aggression in order to impregnate the 'best' female they are able. Hence, they argue, the evolution of sex-typed personality traits. This work, usually developed through experimental means with humans (mainly students) is controversial within psychology and among feminist scholars, with its emphasis on sex differences in mating behaviour being seen as a limitation. It owes its contemporary significance, though, at least in part to developments in understanding the structure and influences of genetics on behaviour but the ethos of evolutionary psychology contrasts sharply with many of the values underlying social work practice.

For social workers, though, evolutionary psychology has raised important questions. For example, what would make an individual care for members of their family who no longer have reproductive potential, such as parents or grandparents? Is altruism in general an evolved behaviour? Why do so many men appear to physically and sexually abuse their female partners and/or their children? These questions are beyond the scope of this book but are socially and politically important and require consideration (see Nicolson, 2014). There is an ongoing debate (Rose and Rose, 2000; Campbell, 2002; Baron-Cohen, 2004) about the relevance and validity of evolutionary psychology which may be interesting to follow up.

## Social work and psychology in practice

Knowledge of psychology and the ways it can be applied are integral to effective social work practice. What therefore do social workers need to know and where might it be found in this book?

1. Social workers need to know how to develop, reflect on and improve the *psychological skills* most useful in interviewing, providing therapeutically based support and in assessing service users' needs. We shall be covering these issues in depth in Chapters 4, 5 and 6. In Chapter 4 we look at the role of personality theories and the development of people's strengths and preferences, exploring how personal development might increase resilience and respect for others. In Chapter 5, this theme is developed focusing particularly on skills versus personal qualities underlying communication skills, styles of communication and counselling techniques that help social workers develop their practice. In Chapter 6, the development

of listening, communicating and understanding what happens both above and below the surface of groups is developed.

2. Social workers need a thorough knowledge of human behaviour, including its relationship to motivation, personality and development in order to understand service users, colleagues and themselves. Personality is discussed in Chapter 4 in relation to personal development. In Chapter 2, psychological development including the role of attachment in early life and consequent attachment styles across the life-span are discussed. You will also recall some of these issues identified in the chapter you have just been reading!

3. Similarly social workers need to be able to make sense of social work, social care and allied organizations in order to cope with their own career or professional development and training requirements. This will be discussed in Chapter 3 where we examine roles and relationships across organizations in which social workers practice. In Chapter 7, we take up this theme again and following on from work such as that of the Hackney reclaiming social work group, we identify the role that psychology has in informing practitioners about their relationships within social work systems.

4. Many social workers achieve leadership management status in their organizations and the profession overall. In Chapter 8 the experiences of leadership and management are discussed and analysed using recently developed ideas from systemic and psychoanalytic theory which help us to survive in an emotionally intelligent way as leaders, managers, supervisors and practitioners (Howe, 2008; Nicolson 2014).

## Conclusions

Psychological knowledge is high on the agenda for both students and practitioners of social work. This involves the understanding of a variety of theoretical approaches and translating them into practice. The theories range from cognitive neuroscience which engages with magnetic resonance imaging of the brain and its relation to emotion and behaviour. This focus links with other branches of psychology, particularly psychoanalysis, attachment experiences, attachment styles, loss and grief and behaviourism. The other end of the spectrum relates to social-psychological ideas which propose that the social world is mostly subjective and that our own interpretation of what is going on may not be any nearer to an objective reality to that of any other individual or group.

Psychology also makes a major contribution to understanding how to communicate effectively between individuals, groups of individuals and within organizations. These skills are particularly important in practice with service users and in leadership and management. Clearly social work needs psychology – although we hope that as individuals you, the reader, will also be able to choose what areas are most useful to you.

## Putting it into practice 1

1a. Make a checklist of psychological considerations that need to be taken into account before meeting an asylum seeker, the only survivor from their family of a massacre in the home country.

1b. Write a brief account of how you would write up a report of a meeting with the survivor who is suffering from PTSD from a) a psychoanalytic perspective and b) a social learning perspective.

1c. Which approach do you find more useful for practice at this stage?

## Further reading

Baron-Cohen, S. (2004) *The Essential Difference*, Harmondsworth, Penguin.

Orbach, S. (1999) *The Impossibility of Sex*, Harmondsworth, Penguin.

These two books are both easy to read and each author has been courted and feted by the media. However each demonstrates a very different perspective on the psychology of human behaviour. Orbach concentrates on the application of intuition, feelings and emotion to understand interaction. Baron-Cohen, applies the day-to-day relevance of experimental psychology from an evolutionary perspective to looking at gender relations, particularly the differences in behaviours and attitudes of women and men.

## CHAPTER 2

# Life-span development

## CHAPTER OVERVIEW
In this chapter we:

- Explore key aspects of human development across the life-span using Erik Erikson's approach as a template.
- Consider the concepts of 'identity', reflexivity', 'biography' and 'narrative' as 'guides' to making sense of the transitions from birth to old age.
- Look in detail at attachment, loss and bereavement as key transitions in the life-span.

This chapter is concerned with psychological development across the life-span and although the emphasis is on *psychological* development, the links between psychology, biology and the social context need to be kept in mind because none happens without some interaction with the other. Many psychologists writing about life-span development take the work of Erik Erikson as a useful template (see also Sugarman, 2001; Nicolson 2014) very particularly because he takes this approach in his theory of *psychosocial* development. His work is age, stage, psychologically and socially sensitive based on a psychoanalytic perspective and underpinned by Freud's work, described and discussed in Chapter 1. Despite the obvious strengths of Erikson's framework it lacks consideration of attachment, reflexivity and narrative which we add here below.

## Introduction

Human development comes about through a mixture of biological, psychological, emotional, cognitive, social and cultural influences. Until relatively recently psychologists concerned themselves more with the developmental stages from infancy to adolescence than on phases of adulthood, but this has changed and there is an increasing interest in the life-span and ageing (Baltes et al., 2007; Sugarman, 2001; Windle, 2012). Research studies of adulthood tended to be studies of 'ageing' exploring the loss of memory and intellectual functioning conceptualized as deterioration rather than development. However, as evidence increasingly failed to demonstrate significant decline of intellect and memory in older people for reasons of age alone, there has been a shift towards seeing adulthood and ageing as part of a life-span trajectory through which development and change occur (Holland, 1995; Holland et al., 1996; Windle, 2012). Other psychologists, similarly, have written about the female menopause and women's ageing as a phase of life rather than as a clinical condition, the 'end' of fertility (see Gannon, 1992; 1999; Ussher, 2006). Men's experiences and perceptions of mid-life have also been explored as developmental phases rather than examples of decline (Boul, 2003) and sexual health and sexuality have been discussed as normal characteristics of growing older (Gott, 2005).

Here we explore the contributions of psychology to understanding the human life-span using the work of Erik Erikson on psychosocial development as a template. We do this selectively to provide key illustrations for social work intervention. We begin with key concepts such as 'identity', 'reflexivity', 'biography' and 'narrative' as 'guides' to development transitions.

Then we examine the role of attachment behaviours and the quality of early relationships to show how these represent the need we have for emotional relationships all through our lives. We then examine crises in development and finally integrate theories of attachment, loss and life crises to a model of psychological development that integrates multiple perspectives on psychology (see Chapter 1) and is of value to social work theory and practice.

## The life-span approach: integrating perspectives

Psychologists and other social scientists increasingly refer to theories of the life cycle, life-course and life-span. The term 'life cycle' is less frequently used in contemporary scholarship because of the implication that nothing changes – that one generation replicates the patterns of the previous ones, although evidence suggests that to deny this may be wishful thinking. However these terms may be used interchangeably in many texts, and models that show change through life and indicate the relationship of particular biological ages or stages of life to psychological and social changes and development are perennially useful for practitioners. Erik Erikson's (1963) model of the life-span (frequently referred to by the title he gives the work in which he first describes it as the Eight Ages of Man) explores change through a series of crises which move people from one stage of psychosocial development to the next (see Table 2.1). Successfully overcoming these crises equips an individual with the skills and knowledge to cope with the subsequent demands of the next stage of life. Central to his theory is the negotiation of a viable identity that enables the individual to progress towards forming mature intimate relationships. Erikson believed that provided a

**Table 2.1** Erik Erikson's Eight Ages of Man adapted for twenty-first-century life-spans

| Age (approximate) | Stage description | Emotional tasks |
| --- | --- | --- |
| 0–1 years | Basic trust versus mistrust | Will the infant be able to trust their care-giver and therefore themselves? |
| 2–4 years | Autonomy versus shame and doubt | Gaining mastery of bodily functions or failing |
| 4–5 years | Initiative versus guilt | Will the child's new skills lead to too many mistakes or failures or will they gain a sense of success? |
| 6–12 years | Industry versus inferiority | Will the child cope with entering school? |
| 13–18 years | Identity versus role confusion | Adolescence – who am I? |
| 19–25 years | Intimacy versus isolation | Can I have successful relationships? |
| 26–55 years | Generativity versus stagnation | Can I be creative at work and at home? |
| 56+ | Ego integrity versus despair | Does my life make sense? Have I achieved anything worthwhile? |

person is aware and reconciled to the strengths they have gained through the challenges throughout their life they will be able to face old age and death without fear (Erikson, 1950/1963, 1959/1980).

Psychologists now consider the whole of life as a platform for development, while continuing to concentrate research and theory on specific processes (for example, cognitive development, sociability) and from different perspectives (for example, evolutionary psychology, psychobiology) (Sugarman, 2001).

Contemporary developmental psychologists considering the experience of getting older have taken up debates about more general aspects of adulthood and ageing such as personality and maturity and their impact on the thinking and behaviour of older people (e.g. Sheldon and Kasser, 2001). Whether people continue to develop (that is, in positive ways) throughout their lives is now the focus of attention, although some researchers still argue that older people's perspectives on life shrink with age (Herzog et al., 1996). However this may be more to do with the social and physical context of their lives, involving losses and the physical limitations that older life presents, rather than the psychology of growing older per se (Pfeiffer, 1977). This indicates policy and practice implications for challenging social isolation and limitations in day-care and health facilities. As a general rule contemporary psychologists consider adulthood through the lens of individual differences rather than highlighting correlations of age and function as was more generally the case twenty years ago (for example, Belsky, 1997).

## Identity

A helpful way to understand and explore human development, changes and crises through the life-span is that of 'identity'. Identity is the means through which we understand our past life and integrate experiences into our sense of who we are or 'self' and through this integration we can also have expectations of our futures. Identity also enables us to bring together our gender, ethnicity, socio-economic status, relationships and unconscious elements of experience into the strengths individuals can build upon to survive. As Ferguson (2001) makes clear, it has become important for social work practitioners to move beyond the legacy of 'radical' social work that challenged the individualization agenda – that service users were the ones with the problems – towards a more nuanced understanding of human organizations and culture and the experience of living in society.

Symptoms of PTSD described in Chapter 1, for example, are exacerbated because the trauma has in some way disrupted our sense of who we are (Colic-Peisker and Walker, 2003; Lev-Wiesel and Amir, 2003; Lev-Wiesel et al., 2004). People who have become traumatized have fewer personal resources to survive emotionally if they have no memories of the events. The controversial debate about recovered memories has hindered mental health practitioners working to enable victims of abuse or accident to recover memories of their experiences. It is important for people to be able to draw on their sense of identity, particularly in times of crisis, as integration of experience provides the chance for healing, as we discussed in Chapter 1.

## Reflexivity and the 'self'

Social work theorists are increasingly interested in the concept of 'reflexivity' (D'Cruz et al., 2007) to enable an understanding of 'identity' and the roles of others in its construction and ongoing negotiation. Social developmental psychologists suggest a wider view that embraces theories from sociology, including socialization and the transmission of culture across generations, symbolic interactionism and the more recent emphasis on (auto)biography as both an approach to understanding ideas like identity and as a research method (Roberts, 2000). Symbolic interactionism, initially based on the work of G.H. Mead in the 1930s, regards the role of 'others', including both those with whom we have close contact and our sense of 'society' (other people, social norms and so on) as crucial to our development. They are symbolized and given a meaning.

How do we come to understand our 'self' at any moment in time? How do we (as social workers or service users) account to our self for who we are and what we do and thus to other people? In order to address this we move away from psychology itself to the recently developed links between sociology and psychology to explore the ways that individuals make sense of themselves in a social and biographical context (Sheppard et al., 2000). We all conceive of our (developing) self through the process of 'reflexivity' which Mead explains as the ability to think about ourselves in an objective way – as if we were making sense of who we are from the perspective of others – or at least from the perspective of how we understand and give meaning to those others, and envision how they make sense of the world. The reflexive process enables human beings to make sense of their actions and the context in which these actions occur – the immediate context and the context of the individual's life history. According to Mead (1934/67) reflexivity is 'the turning back of the experience of the individual upon himself [*sic*]' and thus the individual is able 'to take the attitude of the other toward himself … consciously to adjust himself to that process, and to modify the resultant of that process in any given social act in terms of his adjustment to it'.' This is akin to 'having a conversation' with your self. So for example, the unnamed feeling someone might have, where they lack energy and see their life and the world pessimistically, is also experienced by that individual, in the attempt to make sense of the experience, as if through the eyes of another. This means the individual can in some way 'witness' their own actions/feelings and identify them (perhaps) as 'depression'. A young person who wants to 'come out' to his parents as gay will have a conversation with himself based on his experience of presenting himself in the world and presenting himself to his parents and how he thinks his parents see him and will then see him in this potentially different way. He will be coming out in the context of who he is and who he has related to – it will be part of his life, albeit a 'crisis' point in his developing identity and in his biographical context.

This series of conscious actions relies upon (auto)biography and past experience and also upon an understanding of social institutions and the cultural context in which a person lives and has lived. It is through reflexivity in this way that biography and self are created and re-created. Peter Ashworth (1979) suggested that there were two fundamental elements to the self in Mead's work: the knower and the known. This distinction recognizes this structure of the conscious self. Mead equates these terms to the 'I' and the 'me'.

Mead (1934/67) drew a distinction between consciousness and self-consciousness in human experience which is useful for understanding internal 'conversation' and reflexivity. He was particularly interested in the way social interaction and the internalization of how we see significant others evaluating our behaviour and beliefs, influenced our self-conscious thoughts, and how those in turn were produced as a result of reflecting upon our consciousness. Thus:

I talk to myself, and I remember what I said and perhaps the emotional content that went with it. The 'I' of this moment is present in the 'me' of the next moment. There again I cannot turn around quick enough to catch myself. I become a 'me' in so far as I remember what I said. The 'I' can be given, however, this functional relationship. It is because of the 'I' that we say that we are never fully aware of what we are, that we surprise ourselves by our own action. (Mead, 1934/1967, p. 174)

In other words in order to be reflexive, we need to see our self as the 'object' of thought (i.e. 'me') but the seeing is done by 'I', the subject. The 'I' is impulsive and unorganized and equates to Freud's id, while the 'me' having come under social constraints enables us to experience ourselves 'objectively' and account for our feelings and behaviour in a socially recognized way. Thus we can experience ourselves 'objectively' (the me/known) by the part of ourselves that is doing the experiencing 'subjectively' (the I/knower).

Pure experience is impulsive, but via a process of reflexivity, the self as object becomes socialized. This cursory consideration of the composition of the self does not explain continuity of experience which is important for understanding how the self/identity develops and how actions and events (such as divorce, having a baby, experiencing a bereavement or personal trauma) take on a meaning within the context of self.

Symbolic interactionists, following Mead, saw self and society as interrelated, in that 'society' pre-dated 'mind', and 'mind' was the result of interaction between the individual and the social world. It is not relevant here to develop a critique of that view. Here we draw attention to the indivisibility of the social and the self to develop an explanation for why a crisis in a person's life cannot be separated from either the individual experience or the cultural experience.

### Biography and the life-span

The phenomenological sociologists and psychologists of the 1960s were concerned to explain human experience in terms of the individual making their own sense of the world through the experience of constant interaction.

Experiences at each stage of our lives are given subjective meaning, and the meaning itself will have been interpreted and incorporated into our accumulated biography, that is 'The common-sense view … that we live through a certain sequence of events, some more and some less important, the sum of which is our biography'

(Berger, 1966, p. 68). Thus the biography is experienced and understood within a prescribed social context:

> The socially constructed world must be continually mediated to and actualized by the individual, so that it can become and remain indeed his world as well. The individual is given by his society certain decisive cornerstones for his everyday experience and conduct. Most importantly, the individual is supplied with specific sets of typifications and criteria for relevance, predefined for him by the society and made available to him for the ordering of his everyday life. This ordering ... is biographically cumulative. It begins to be formed in the individual from the earliest stages of socialization on, and then keeps on being enlarged and modified by himself throughout his biography. (Berger and Kellner, 1964, in Anderson, 1982, p. 303)

The notion of biography therefore enables researchers and practitioners drawing upon theory and research to take account of present and past considerations of how people account for their lives, while individuals give meaning to their lives within a socially prescribed framework, which includes a sense of social organization and structure, including gender.

As illustration we draw on a case study of Sally, a mother of 27 who was the victim/survivor of physical abuse from her partner and father of her baby. She had left him after following up on a prosecution (resulting in a fine) and was now receiving threats from him via his friends in the neighbourhood. During her initial interview it was clear that Sally had had two previous abusive partners, and although this did not prevent her being fearful it did make her feel more confident that she knew what to do by way of seeking assistance and what her rights were in a criminal justice and legal framework. There was some sense in which Sally knew she had a place in the world as a survivor in the context of domestic abuse. It also emerged that her father had regularly attacked her mother when she and her siblings were children, resulting in them being taken into care and her mother admitted for psychiatric care. She went to live with her maternal grandparents when she was eleven and during the five years she was there she was sexually abused by her grandfather who beat up her grandmother relatively regularly – something that had apparently taken place throughout their lives together. At sixteen she went to live with her first violent boyfriend. Sally recognized that she was attractive to men, and often men who were 'alpha males' – this made her feel very powerful. However, they also made her feel trapped, vulnerable and depressed in the longer term because of the violence, although she managed to muster enough self-esteem to leave each one eventually. Sally believed that men were violent and that women had to put up with it or leave the man but that the next man would be similar. To hold on to a man you had to be attractive but you also had to expect violence, abuse and jealousy. That was women's experience – at least it was Sally's and she could see no other way than that.

How could Sally make sense of her life enough to make changes and move forward? This complex biography is not so unusual. Sally was experiencing herself as a sexual being, an attractive one but also as a vulnerable victim as she was separating from the adults who had brought her up at around the age of sixteen. She was, though, living in a social/cultural context in which she was a victim of abuse and unable to break away as the abuse had been perpetrated by the very adult(s) in charge of her care. Her mother and grandmother had also been abused, and Sally had witnessed this. Her vision of femininity and women's lives was one in which you could only survive through not putting up with this type of behaviour, although paradoxically it was men of violence who were potential protectors. For Sally to be supported to change her sense of self, she had to move beyond being sexually attractive and the object of a man's desire and attention (positive and negative). She needed to move beyond her sense of accumulated experience that provided the cues and symbols through which she assessed her identity and future life prospects. She also had to re-examine her biography through the eyes of someone other than herself or those to whom she had related up until the time of her initial interview. She also had to re-examine her early experiences of trust, shame, autonomy and sense of identity (see Nicolson, 2010a).

Here we draw attention to the value of applying integrated approaches to understanding service users at various stages of the life-span. The framework for this approach is Erikson's model of psychosocial development, which brings in both the unconscious and the role of biology, biography and adaptation. Erikson took Freud's model of psychosexual development, described in Chapter 1, for granted and built his theoretical framework accordingly. This approach is set against the social context of the immediate family and socio-economic and cultural influences as well as the 'body'. Through the body as mediator we gain a sense of identity that embraces gender and ethnicity.

As each individual matures biologically, cognitively, intellectually and emotionally, they experience and make sense of the world around them. Developmental crises occur at different life-span stages as Erikson indicates. So, for example, a woman in her thirties will be looking for a 'generative' experience which might be to have a baby, or it might be for career development. A thirteen-year-old boy will be struggling to understand who he is as his body rapidly changes and his parents or carers no longer offer the stability or the hostility and source of anxiety that they had done before. While crises are age/stage-related each one comes with a particular characteristic based on earlier biographical features. For the child who had had a disrupted early life and failed to gain any sense of trust in other people, each crisis might result in an increased sense of failure. This might lead to them becoming violent in later life, an addiction to drugs or alcohol or psychiatric difficulties. For someone like Sally the crisis was more complex as it seemed unrelated to a particular age or stage but more to a recognition of accumulated failures to resolve developmental crises.

For some, despite a poor start in life, it is possible to regain a sense of security from subsequent relationships – either personal or professional with a therapist or social worker who enables the person to recognize and address the issues that remain in their life but originate from unresolved crises from an earlier time.

## Narrative and the self

As part of being a reflexive social human being making sense of our biographies in their social and historical contexts, we tell 'stories' (narratives) to ourselves and others in order to maintain and 'negotiate' our 'selves'. This is particularly relevant for understanding how a service user presents themselves to social services and also to themselves (Riessman and Quinney, 2005). 'Narrative' as a concept is not so easily defined and has been used by social scientists, including social work academics, in different ways. Essentially, it is about how we all tell a story in order to make sense of our lives at any one time and as part of that activity we develop a plot, characters and contexts for the stories (Crossley, 2003). Researchers and scholars have focused on questions about how and why and for whom particular stories are constructed suggesting the evolutionary and dynamic nature of the narrative of the self for all of us. In memories of abuse, accounts of illness, bereavement and of other important life experiences, narratives can change and may give comfort or increase feelings of trauma. Sometimes these stories help us to bring things together so we ourselves can gain a clear picture of who we are, but at other times they are used to avoid who we are and what we might have failed to do (Andrews et al., 2007).

Walter Mitty, a character invented by James Thurber, was timid and insignificant but in his secret life, the one he chose to tell himself (and others) was real, he was brave and interesting. A more contemporary version is Geoff, 'The Oracle', in ITV's *Benidorm*. This character, played by the comedian Johny Vegas, lives with his mother (whom he tells others is his 'PA'), describes himself as the champion of general knowledge competitions and as having achieved various accolades in body-building and sport. The problem is that no one believes his account of himself (including his mother, although she colludes, at least sometimes) and when he dates a young woman he is interested in, she humiliates him by calling his bluff, leaving him nothing to fall back on. It is the latter point, the location of the 'reality' in each of our lives that is at stake through invention. As presented in Chapters 4 and 7 in particular, there is an important role for social workers to make sure that people they work with, service users and they themselves are supported to be authentic in order to manage their lives and relationships effectively.

## Attachment in infancy

We now explore the detail of how relationships form and are given meaning and provide meaning to our lives at different times and stages.

The first means of gaining a sense of identity is through our relationships with others and early relationships between infants and their carers often set a pattern for the types of relationships someone has through their life (Holmes, 2010). Moreover these early relationships equip individuals with their sense of self-worth, emotional stability and the ability to love and care for other people. The way we understand the social and emotional world around us therefore is part of a continual dynamic based upon the interaction between our selves, others and the way we make sense of ourselves in relation to others. Early relationships in life are referred to as 'attachments'.

Attachment relationships occur when an infant learns to, or experiences love and trust with another human being (usually the mother, father or a main carer) who in turn attends to his/her needs with warmth and affection (Marris et al., 1996). Understanding attachment is central to understanding the powerful influences of love and loss throughout our lives. Human beings are capable of forming strong emotional bonds with each other and indeed throughout our lives we seek such attachments and work to maintain them (Bowlby, 1988).

There is, however, strong evidence that when a baby is not able to form a relationship with a caring adult for some reason (perhaps because the adult is absent, is unable to express affection or the care is shared by a number of emotionally distant adults as with a children's home) then the child becomes emotionally withdrawn and depressed (Shemmings and Shemmings, 2011). There appears to be a consistent need to seek physical comfort among human infants, and research with monkeys has demonstrated how the lack of physical contact leads to emotional deficit and/or disturbance in infancy and in later life (Harlow, 1961).

Humans, primates and many other species are social in nature and there is evidence of a drive to seek close and secure company. Attachments across the life-span have been explored through empirical studies (see, for example, the work of Ainsworth, 1996) and through observational and clinical studies (Bowlby, 1969/1982; Marris, 1986; 1996). There is evidence that human infants thrive the best the more secure their initial emotional attachments. There is also evidence that older children, adolescents and adults whose early experiences were characterized by failed attachments (of varying kinds) suffered psychological consequences (Shemmings and Shemmings, 2011; Harris and Bifulco, 1996; Parkes et al., 1996).

Bowlby's (1969/1982) work on attachment and loss has also contributed to knowledge of the psychological effects of insecurity derived from social impoverishment in infancy. Although there are real concerns about the validity and reliability of the empirical source of Bowlby's theory, concepts of 'attachment', 'loss' and 'change' are important for understanding lifelong human development and a crucial component of psychology for social workers.

Since Bowlby's early work in the 1940s, there has been a growing interest in infant attachment behaviour. Schaffer and Emerson's (1964) longitudinal study of 60 infants in Scotland showed that by the age of eighteen months they were each attached to about three people. In the very early days the infants demonstrate what they call 'indiscriminate attachment', although by the age of around six months they become wary of strangers. Rutter (1972) produced similar evidence and stressed that infants can form attachments to men. Tizard's (1975) study of children in their adoptive families demonstrated that it is frequently possible to overcome early emotional disturbance and separation with a stable, loving environment.

## Attachment in adulthood: attachment styles

Research on attachment identified the existence of different *styles of attachment* (Bifulco and Thomas, 2013; Bowlby, 1988). Following Ainsworth, who talked about secure and insecure attachments, Bowlby described the following:

- **Secure attachment** in which the individual is confident that the parent figure will be available, responsive and helpful in adverse and frightening situations. This individual feels emboldened to explore the world.
- **An anxious, resistant attachment** pattern that reflects the experience of the individual who is uncertain whether his parent will be responsive or available. They tend to be prone to separation anxiety, be clingy and cautious about exploring the world.
- **An anxious, avoidant attachment** when the individual has no confidence that he will receive a helpful response and instead expects to be rebuffed. (See Bowlby, 1988, p. 124.)

Since then work on defining, describing and applying attachment styles to social work and clinical practice has expanded (Shemmings and Shemmings, 2011).

### Separation

Ainsworth (1960s and 1970s) used a series of observations of children of various ages to demonstrate the ways in which a mother's presence or absence can affect a child's behaviour and emotional security. She created a series of 'strange situations' where an infant and mother were in a room filled with toys. A stranger would enter, and the mother left shortly afterwards, having allowed time for the stranger to be introduced. It appeared that children stayed close to their mothers in the strange room, but soon moved to the toys, returning intermittently to establish contact. When the stranger entered, the child moved towards the mother, perhaps even hiding behind her, but most children warmed to the new person and responded to her efforts to play. When the mother left, however, most children showed distress and became less involved with play. Ainsworth (1964) suggested that once children have been exposed to separation, they become sensitized in such a way that similar experiences are likely to be especially traumatic for them. Douglas and Bloomfield (1958), however, had found that long-term ill effects generally followed separation only when it was accompanied by a change of environment. Their study was related to hospitalization of children, which indicates that the ill effects may be associated with the context of the environment rather than the change itself.

The 'strange situation' procedure and consequent classifications (see below) are seen as the gold standard for clinical assessment of attachment patterns (Zeanah et al., 2011) and the style of most concern to clinicians and social workers has been the *disorganized attachment style* (Hesse and Main, 2000).

## Assessing attachment styles in adults

During the 1980 and 1990s there was an increased awareness in the USA of the significance of attachment for understanding adult responses to loss and trauma (Hesse and Main, 2000; Main, 1995). This work led to the development of the Adult Attachment Interview at Berkeley (Main, 1995) which taps into the narrative style of the respondent demonstrating how the relationship is talked about and is 'represented' in their own mind. This enabled Main and colleagues to identify the insecure disorganized style described above as well as understand how individuals are able to make sense of their lives despite poorly supported early lives.

Antonia Bifulco and her team at the Lifespan Research Group at Royal Holloway, University of London developed a series of attachment style interviews that assesses characteristics of current adult attachment style in relation to a person's ability to access and utilize social support, an approach of particular value to social workers. The Attachment Style Interview (ASI) provides a categorization of attachment style for individuals, as well as assessing their specific support context and quality of close relationships. The attachment profile that results from the data collected not only determines which style best characterizes the respondent (Secure, Enmeshed, Fearful, Angry-dismissive or Withdrawn), but also the extent to which the insecure styles are dysfunctional in terms of whether the person is 'markedly', 'moderately' or 'mildly' insecure. This is important, given evidence that 'mildly insecure' styles carry a lesser risk of mental health problems.

The styles identified by Bifulco and colleagues (Bifulco, 2004; Bifulco et al., 2008) are:

- **Clearly secure:** This is the most stable and flexible style with comfort and closeness and appropriate levels of autonomy. This style enables ongoing ability to make and maintain relationships with at least two others. This would also suggest that an infant and mother who manage this stage will also produce a sense of basic trust over mistrust.
- **Enmeshed:** This style is dependent and the individual infant and later the adult will have a high desire for company and low self-reliance. Bifulco et al. predict this style is represented by superficiality across many relationships. It is positively characterized by sociability and warmth but there is also the tendency to anger and 'push-pull' relationships.
- **Fearful:** This style is characterized by anxiety about rejection or being let down. Early life experiences of rejection may be generalized to all others. There is frequently the desire for closeness coupled with fear of becoming close to someone. The positive characteristics might be sensitivity to others.
- **Angry-dismissive:** This is the angry avoidance of others with high levels of mistrust and self-reliance as well as a low desire for company. The key characteristic is anger. Individuals with this style are self-reliant but in conflict with those around them and frequently need a high level of control over their lives.
- **Withdrawn:** This is characterized by high self-reliance and high constraints on closeness, perhaps expressed as a desire for privacy with clear boundaries and with a closed style of relating.

To date two versions of the ASI have been developed: the ASI for Research, Clinical and Practice Use (ASI-RCP), tailored towards psychologists and psychiatrists working in research and clinical and forensic practice fields, and the ASI for Children's Services, tailored towards practice requirements of Adoption and Fostering and Child Care services.

## Loss

Marris (1986) developed Bowlby's ideas while also borrowing concepts from Piaget. He sees grief as a response to loss of meaning, suggesting that it is provoked by all situations of loss, including social changes and any conditions which disrupt an individual's ability to make sense of their life.

Loss is a core concept in the development of the human psyche and closely related to work on attachment which is connected to human emotional strength. Freud's work on bereavement led him to argue that the expression of grief following bereavement was not only natural and acceptable, but highly desirable. It was important to cry. It was important not to maintain the Victorian stiff upper lip. To bury such fundamental feelings of anguish would distort recovery and prevent emotional healing. The loss would be buried in the unconscious and never resolved. Some of the after-effects would be similar to what we now think of as PTSD (see Chapter 1). There is a difference between looking back at a period of mourning with sadness and even shedding a tear for the lost person, and having intrusive thoughts and dreams which cause anxiety. The latter is symptomatic of unresolved grief.

It is not only bereavement that leads to grief. Peter Marris (1986) has shown that moving away from home and changes in the structure of a community can lead to a grief reaction. The experience of being burgled also can, in some cases, lead to a severe grief reaction particularly if someone has lost items of great sentimental value or feel their once-loved house has 'let them down' (Nicolson, 1994).

The healthy grief reaction involves the recognition of the losses – some people deny their loss even when it involves the break-up of a marriage, for instance, or children leaving home – because they feel it helps them 'deal' with the problem. Many people do not want to acknowledge their emotional responses even to themselves because they see them as a sign of weakness. These people bury their feelings, but feelings so fundamental as the response to loss do not go away that easily.

In order to look at this more closely, we shall consider a traditional model of bereavement and the grief reaction.

## Bereavement

Bereavement most frequently occurs from late middle age onwards. This kind of bereavement is usually concerned with the loss of a long-term partner, but clearly the distress and grief are also acute for a child who loses a parent or sibling, for parents who lose a child, or for anyone who loses a close friend. Although most social workers are involved with the elderly bereaved, and the major studies are concerned with this group, it is not a condition exclusive to the elderly. Similarly many of the reactions in bereavement are similar to those originally described by Bowlby, who was concerned with loss and separation between parents and young children.

### The grief reaction

Psychologists and psychiatrists have long been interested in bereavement and grief. As early as 1917 Freud stressed the psychological importance of mourning after bereavement. Grief and loss produce a mixture of physiological and psychological reactions which are closely bound up with the social pressures concerning a change in status. These are often accompanied by financial problems, particularly in the case of a widow whose husband was breadwinner, who may well not be adequately insured or able to earn a living.

Evolutionary psychologists have suggested that grief has adaptive origins and is a means of maximizing reproductive fitness (Archer, 1999). Bowlby (1980) and Parkes (1972) also favoured this perspective, pointing out that a successful and healthy grief reaction enables the bereaved individual to engage in another relationship, which is not the case with the person who remains absorbed in and attached to the dead person.

Thus it is understandable that Colin Murray Parkes (1972), who made a famous study of twenty-two London widows, and has taken a special interest in the concept of bereavement, suggests that grief is an illness. He justifies this by saying that the emotional and physiological symptoms cause people to go to their doctors for help because they experience physical discomfort and disturbance of function. Also, he says that newly bereaved people are often treated as sick by the rest of society. They are expected to miss work, to be visited by relatives, and have others take responsibility for major decisions. However, Parkes says that bereavement can also bring strength and maturity, and if a person copes with the 'challenge' of bereavement they may well change their view of the world and themselves. He described the stages of grief reaction, but shows that at each stage people are subject to a series of emotional conflicts and a variety of psychological reactions which have also been replicated by other researchers and clinicians (Archer, 1999):

*Searching.* People experience 'pangs' of grief rather than prolonged pain, and will often cry out for their loved one. This reaction can begin within a few hours or days of the bereavement, and usually reaches a peak of severity within 5 to 14 days. Bowlby has called this the phase of yearning and protest. The bereaved person shows a lack of interest in normal life, and experiences a persistent, obtrusive search for the person who has gone. Most normal adults are fully aware that there is no point in searching for the dead person, but this does not prevent a strong impulse to search. Many experience illusions in which they see the dead person, or they will look for them in a crowd of people. Some people frequently return to the locations that were the favourite places of the dead to check whether or not they have really gone from them.

*Mitigation.* When people experience intense pining, something often happens to mitigate the grief and pain. Parkes says that this consists of a sight or sound to give the impression that the 'search' is at an end. The commonest experience is that the dead person is nearby, and this provides a very comforting sensation for the bereaved. This experience was reported by fifteen of the twenty-two individuals in Parkes' study. Also, many people experience hallucinations and dreams which include the dead person. They are often happy, but include the feeling that something is 'not quite well'. Other forms of mitigation include the bereaved person not believing the loss has occurred: waiting for the dead person to come home, or disagreeing with doctors and other relatives that the death has actually occurred. Several people report a 'numbness' on receiving the news of death, and feelings of unreality, but these reactions tend to be transient. Many will try to avoid thoughts of the lost person, and avoid meeting people who might discuss them, or getting into situations which might be connected with the dead person. Two-thirds of Parkes' sample found themselves putting away photographs, and trying to fill their lives with new experiences. However, bereaved people do tend to be occupied by the thoughts of their loss, and are unable to sustain this avoidance. With the passing of time it becomes less necessary to deliberately avoid memories of the lost person.

*Anger and guilt.* Anger is a normal component of grief, but it changes its form and expression as time passes. During the first month after bereavement anger appears greatest, with a great deal of emotion expressed concerning why the dead person actually died. The people who are most angry are often those who are the most socially isolated. The recognition of the irrationality of their anger leads bereaved people to feel guilty at the way they have behaved. Freud suggested that individuals frequently experience feelings of ambivalence towards a partner, which gives rise to a wish for the other's death. This is tolerable provided it is only a fantasy, but an individual needs a defence against this emotion once the wish has been fulfilled. Thus the bereaved person turns the anger inwards. Naturally, very few relationships are without a certain ambivalence, and Parkes found a high proportion of guilt due to these feelings in the people he studied.

*Gaining a new identity.* Part of the process of maturity through bereavement and coming to terms with grief, is the gaining of a new identity. Initially the bereaved person might adopt the values and attitudes of the dead person. This is particularly common if the bereaved person inherits certain of the dead person's roles – for instance, a man who has lost his wife might adopt her attitudes towards child rearing. This becomes less important as the bereaved person grows in confidence and gains a new identity in his/her new role.

Bereavement cannot be expressed as a simple stress reaction. It includes psychological and physiological reactions, such as insomnia, anxiety, nervousness, loss of weight and appetite, despair and depression, but it also includes the process by which a person regains a status and role in society. The death of a spouse causes a change in social circumstances due to 'stigmatizing'. Western society is still not accustomed to dealing with the bereaved, particularly after the initial shock and the funeral arrangements, so the person who continues to suffer is seen as not quite normal or acceptable; they do not fit in. Another source of stress for the recently bereaved is that most couples have pooled financial, emotional and social resources, and so the person who is left alone is without all the functions provided by the dead person. During the process of bereavement an individual has to counteract stigmatizing and return to 'normality'.

## Problems of bereavement

The side-effects of grief and mourning are related to the social disapproval directed against people who cannot join in with everyday life. Although, as Parkes suggests, grief can be seen as an illness, and is indirectly recognized as such in terms of time taken off work and extra help being provided, the pain of loss for most people extends beyond the normal time allowed for mourning. Many bereaved people feel unable to talk about their memories for a few weeks after the death, by which time friends and relatives are trying to persuade them to take a fresh view of life and look to the future, but mourning will probably not cease until they have been able to express grief and talk about the dead person from the distance that time can provide.

Self-help groups have come into existence over the last few years which enable bereaved people to meet others, compare experiences, and support each other, but it is often necessary for the bereaved person to be able to talk to someone exclusively about their loss, and by doing so set a pattern for re-establishing a life for themselves without the pain or guilt of an unresolved loss. Carole Smith (1982) has reviewed the research studies which looked at the scope for identifying vulnerable individuals and groups, and outlined those responses which may or may not facilitate recovery from the impact of the loss. The issues raised from these studies have led to a consideration of whether professionals should intervene (Currer, 2001).

It is effective mourning for any loss leading to integration and change, which leads to psychological well-being, which is where social work intervention can help. For people to move successfully through the conscious and unconscious crisis points in their lives they need to be reflexive and enabled to reflect on their self in the context of their biology, biography and experiences in an objective way.

## Conclusions

This chapter provided a (very) broad-brush introduction to psychology's contribution to understanding the life-span. The life-span, as will be clear, is a complex set of biological, social and psychological processes and social workers have to take account of these factors in their work with service users at all stages of the life-span. Social inequalities and exclusion frame the experience of human growth and development and impact on physical and mental health outcomes for us all. Life chances in which social and community exclusion, poverty, lack of educational opportunity, unemployment, disabilities and discrimination occur are central to psychological experience. Social work training facilitates anti-oppressive practice intended to militate (as far as possible) against social exclusion (Dominelli, 1996; Strier, 2007; Wilson and Beresford, 2000).

This chapter covered a great deal of ground – to introduce the reader to glimpses of ways in which understanding the life-span can be applied in practice with both service users and in self-awareness. It serves as an introduction to some ideas about development and attachment but cannot serve to replace the excellent textbooks, all of which come from differing perspectives, currently available on human growth and development.

---

### Putting it into practice 2

2a. Observation study of a young baby and her mother or father (or other main carer). Noting the age of the baby, describe how the baby reacts, or doesn't react when the parent or carer picks her up, talks to her, plays with her. Make a list of what you think is relevant evidence to assess the quality of the infant/adult relationship. For example does the adult make eye contact? How long for? Does the baby respond?

2b. What significance do you attribute to these actions and others you identified and observed?

2c. Reminiscence work. Interview a person living in a care home or attending a day centre with a view to helping them recall their past. How important is reminiscence for the mental health of an individual coming to terms with their 'biography' and evaluating their life?

# Further reading

Nicolson, P. (2014) *A Critical Approach to Human Growth and Development: A Textbook for Social Work Students and Practitioners*, Basingstoke, Palgrave Macmillan.

In this book Nicolson explores approaches to human growth and development in depth using case examples and within a material-discursive-intrapsychic framework. She shows how human growth and development share common features but also emphasize diversity and difference.

Parkes, C.M., Steveson-Hinde, J., and Marris, P. (eds) (1996) *Attachment Across the Life Cycle*, London, Routledge.

This book includes a series of related chapters by different authors about the way that our relationships at different stages of our lives are influenced by our early attachment experiences. It demonstrates the need we have for attachment and the problems we face when attachments are broken.

Archer, J. (1999) *The Nature of Grief: The Evolutional and Psychology of Reactions to Loss*, London, Routledge.

This book looks at bereavement and loss showing universal and biologically based responses to losses. Both are easy to read and informative.

Two informative and clearly written books look in detail at research and practice around attachment theories:

Bifulco, A., and Thomas, G. (2013) *Understanding Adult Attachment in Family Relationships: Research, Assessment and Intervention*, London, Routledge.

This book explores adult attachment styles based upon the findings from using the Adult Attachment Style Interview (described above in this chapter) which is now widely used by social workers to identify appropriate intervention strategies for vulnerable adults and their families.

Shemmings, D., and Shemmings, Y. (2011) *Understanding Disorganized Attachment: Theory and Practice for Working with Children and Adult*, London, Jessica Kingsley.

Here the authors look at the main causes of disorganized attachments – psychological, social and biological – and explore the consequences for individuals and social work practitioners.

## CHAPTER 3

# Psychological perspectives on social work organizations

**CHAPTER OVERVIEW**

In this chapter we introduce and explore:

- The way that social workers themselves are subject to the influence of psychological forces in the organization of their daily working lives with colleagues.
- How we apply psychological knowledge to social work settings and contexts of practice with colleagues and service users.
- Systemic and psychoanalytic thinking about organizations that will be developed further in Chapter 7.

Although social work is a highly individual experience for most practitioners, social work agencies arrange their staff in teams, all of which are structured hierarchically. Over the years since this book was first published much has been written about team working across statutory, voluntary and private sector organizations with the emphasis upon ways that a well-functioning team is able to deliver (Ellemers et al., 2004; Foster, 2001). Furthermore, policy-driven inter-professional working (IPW) has drawn social work into multi-disciplinary and multi-agency work and consequent complex psychological relationships within and between groups, teams and organizations. Research, particularly across business organizations, has been upon leadership, group structures, 'groupthink', leader selection, decision-making and dysfunctional teams and almost all studies indicate that a successful team can benefit both the employer and employees and vice versa (Glassop, 2002). However there are many potential pitfalls to be negotiated on the way.

## Introduction: staff relationships and the role of teams

The approach to teams as the context of social work practice here relies most heavily on the theory related to the social psychology of groups, psychodynamic and systemic theories of groups and organizations which highlight the impact of unconscious as well as conscious processes on how groups behave internally and with other groups.

What is important is thus:

1. Understanding the consequences of the team's dynamics for its effectiveness, and the well-being and productivity/effectiveness of the individual worker.
2. Understanding the role of the leader and the boundaries of responsibility. This will be discussed fully in Chapter 8.
3. That teams and organizations learn from their own histories and identify positive and negative practices.
4. Anxiety and other emotional experiences which occur when working with others may be best understood via an explication of the unconscious processes (Menzies Lyth, 1992; Obholzer and Zagier Roberts, 1994; Zagier Roberts, 1994).
5. The identification of team and organizational cultures – for instance what constitutes 'acceptable behaviour' and pressures to conformity. This has become increasingly important because of the impact of a series of mistakes in coping with child care, hospital and mental health cases where the outcome of inquiries has suggested that some organizations operate a code of silence and 'turn a blind eye' to misdeeds, negligence and incompetent leadership, as for example in the case of Victoria Climbie, described in the report of the inquiry headed by Lord Laming in 2003, which can be downloaded at: http://webarchive.nationalarchives.gov.uk/20130107105354/ http://www.dh.gov.uk/en/Publicationsandstatistics/Publication/ PublicationsPolicyAndGuidance/DH_4008654 and Staffordshire Foundation Trust Hospital, described in the Francis Report in 2013 (and to read this see: http://webarchive.nationalarchives. gov.uk/20130107105354/http://www.dh.gov.uk/en/ Publicationsandstatistics/Publications/PublicationsPolicyAnd Guidance/DH_113018).

There is more discussion of these issues in Chapter 7.

The processes involved in decision-making groups which are an integral part of the work of social work agencies and once again issues of leadership and culture are implicated in decision-making as well as anxiety and power issues (Ayre, 1998; Kerr and Tindale, 2004).

## The dynamics of the team

There are four major sources of influence affecting the dynamics of the social work team, the first three being mainly conscious processes – group membership, group cohesiveness and social facilitation – and the fourth being the role of unconscious processes (Bion, 1961; Maines, 1989).

*Group membership.* This refers to the nature of the group in terms of how well members relate to one another, share common goals, identify with their colleagues, or whether they merely see themselves as sharing the same office accommodation. Group membership inevitably affects a person's beliefs and activities. As we shall see in Chapter 6, groups exert pressure on their members to conform to particular points of view and ways of doing things, and if individuals do not or cannot share the same values as the other members of the group, they are likely to leave or withdraw emotionally. Membership of the team is important, because it is a source of support to workers who are otherwise quite isolated. If this support is not available it will reduce the quality of the service to consumers: incompatible and unsatisfying work groups have been shown to be a major source of dissatisfaction to workers, and to adversely affect the quality of their work.

*Group cohesiveness.* This is the term used by social psychologists to refer to the degree to which members are attracted to one another and the group as a whole. A high degree of attraction between members means that value is placed on group membership, and that group is said to be cohesive. Early studies in industrial psychology were concerned with improving the efficiency and the discipline of the workforce. By the 1930s it had become clear to psychologists that the workplace was a social setting, and that relationships at work were very important. Cohesiveness in a work group was found to benefit the workers in so far as their morale increased and they reported a higher level of job satisfaction. However since then the study of organizational psychology has highlighted the centrality of power struggles and conflict (Kolb and Barturek, 1992; Kipnis, 2001) in all groups and organizations. The way conflicts and power are managed and the quality of leadership in any team influences the quality of work life (QWL) (Glassop, 2002).

Although it may be argued that social work itself can be a satisfying occupation, it is also stressful for much of the time, potentially reducing the QWL, because many service users are likely to be on the brink of a crisis or experiencing chronic suffering. Cohesive work groups enable workers to cope better with stressful situations and improve QWL. It has been found that in a cohesive group, workers confide in one another, and as a result there is less absenteeism and less job turnover. In terms of dealing with the 'bureaucratic' aspects of social work, it has been shown that in cohesive groups the level and degree of communication is enhanced, making for greater efficiency.

There are, however, intrinsic forces which prevent groups from becoming cohesive. For example, the more people there are in a team, the more likely it is that only a few will take on responsibility. It is fairly common for teams to include a mix of skills, qualifications and experience which have their impact upon the learning culture, as each person will be an equal team member on one level, but on another have a different degree of responsibility and power. A hierarchy (both official and unofficial) will form. In an hierarchical structure, attraction and friendship patterns are affected, so there may be problems for a group when junior and senior members are friends: junior staff may see the senior person as patronizing, senior members are censured by other senior people for 'fraternizing', and may distrust overtures of friendship from junior group members, seeing these as flattery or other attempts at manipulation. In addition the impact of gender, ethnicity, age and class on power relations may prevent change and privilege traditional groups, militating against development and innovation (Nicolson, 1996). However there is also evidence that if managed effectively diversity is an asset to a team or organization (Cummings, 2004; Pelled, 1996; van Knippenberg and Schippers, 2007).

Promotion of individuals within cohesive teams exacerbates these difficulties, particularly if they resemble the existing leadership. If a team increases its membership it is also likely that subgroups or cliques will form. As we see in Chapter 6, groups tend to compete against one another, and membership of one clique increases hostility and suspicion towards another. The existence of cliques is likely to increase secrecy and gossip, reducing the effectiveness of communication. Secrecy may reduce friction, because if knowledge is restricted, those who benefit are less likely to be challenged by those who do not, as they do not know! However, secrecy derogates those from whom the information is kept. Thus large groups are not likely to be cohesive, which may reduce QWL and increase stress because of the lack of transparency clearing a way for fantasies to take hold.

Group cohesiveness is increased by any factor which enhances the value of the group to an individual member, such as success in achieving goals. Outside threats tend to increase the group's value to its members. This is particularly noticeable in the face of threatened cutbacks to the budgets of various social work agencies. The staff group becomes much more united in purpose, and attraction and communication levels are higher. The result is also prejudice and hostility towards those outside your own team or clique (see, for example, Dovidio et al., 2005, for a discussion of the social psychology of group conflict and prejudice).

Individuals working in the presence of others frequently experience an improved level of work from when they work alone. This is referred to as *social facilitation*, and has proved to be universal. Social workers who experience themselves as members of a team may well work more effectively than if they were unaware of the presence of other team members. This effect was first noted in the 1920s, when it was observed that cyclists who were trying to beat the clock on their own improved their performance when competing against others. Subsequent work by psychologists in the laboratory and in field studies has confirmed that when people perform in the presence of others their own performance improves. The social facilitation effect has been explained in terms of higher psychological arousal experienced in the presence of others, and concern with receiving positive or negative reactions to one's performance. But it may be affected most by the diffusion of responsibility that often takes place in groups. This occurs on occasions when a group effort is to be evaluated, and a contribution expected from everyone. The output is frequently less than would be expected from individual members' contributions. It has been proposed that some members engage in 'social loafing' and do not contribute much as their efforts will not be recognized as emanating from them. This may be reflected in the consequence of team projects, for example, a reorganization of an intake system, which makes the team rather than the individual worker responsible for the assessment done prior to allocation to individual workers: less work may be put into the assessment than if an individual had sole responsibility.

## Conformity and obedience

The degree of pressure to which individual social workers are subject is an important consideration when trying to understand staff relationships in fieldwork. The theory relevant to this is discussed in Chapter 6.

## Decision-making in groups

Decisions in work organizations frequently evolve from group decision-making. Psychologists have examined the way in which groups actually reach their decisions, that is, the group performance and whether this performance demonstrates group effectiveness. That is achieved according to how well the information had been processed, how relevant the decision was to the circumstances. It seems that certain biases are common in decision-making groups and awareness enables these to be avoided. These relate to:

1. The predispositions of the individual members. In an ideal group, each member's attitudes, opinions and beliefs would be discussed openly, and evaluated by the group. Each member would try to understand her colleagues, and reach a balanced outcome. Research into decision-making in juries has highlighted the impact that predisposition has upon final voting patterns, and has shown that in many cases, evidence presented after one has made up one's mind has little impact on final voting, despite persuasive discussion.
2. If a group reaches a minimally acceptable solution to a problem, then group members frequently develop a bias in favour of that solution. So in a committee meeting to consider financial cuts, the solution of reducing the number of administrative staff may be floated, and accepted by the most talkative members. This isolation then becomes the one which group members become biased towards and argue to defend, even though they did not necessarily start out by believing this to be the best solution to the problem. There is a general failure among group members to accept criticisms and new ideas, and researchers have found that this is a widespread pattern in groups solving complex problems, like many of those relevant to social work. The actual processes involved in these cases are that several ideas are put forward until a solution meets with some positive response from the most

active members. Once there is a minimal agreement, there is a shift in the quality of the discussion with a search towards justification rather than criticism. If new solutions are offered, it is these that are criticized.

Not only are there biases in decision-making groups, but groups also tend to reach polarized decisions. It has been shown that groups will frequently take risky decisions to which individual members themselves are not privately committed. This has been called the 'risky shift' phenomenon. A group of social workers and related professionals might decide to send a child home from residential care to his parents, or decide not to renew a statutory treatment section on a psychiatric patient although privately each individual member of the group might not be prepared to take such a risk alone. Reasons for this might be diffusion of responsibility, or a cultural norm which favours risk, or at least rejects 'overprotectiveness'. Also, group discussions release members from certain inhibitions which they experience when alone. Research into the 'risky shift' effect has also demonstrated that sometimes groups favour decisions which are more conservative than those that individuals might have made. The main conclusion must be that group decisions tend to be polarized, more extreme than individual members' decisions might be outside the group.Finally, returning to the effect of cohesiveness in groups, we will focus on the work of Irving Janis. He did research into group decision-making in the late 1960s, when he suggested that cohesive groups are impaired in their effectiveness by 'groupthink'. This occurs when the group's need for consensus overwhelms the members' realistic appraisal of alternative courses of action. Groups of close friends are under a great deal of pressure to agree and do not want to criticize or challenge the ideas of people they like. Janis argues that this may well be disastrous because it limits the number of alternatives, prevents the group from fully examining the action it is taking and avoids seeking expert opinion to support one particular line of argument against another.

There are thus a great many characteristics of social work teams that affect the nature and quality of individual workers' efforts for their service users, and the way policy and practical decisions are made. Despite the apparently individual nature of social work, it is clearly influenced by group dynamics, and an understanding of these processes is useful for professional survival among social workers.

## Conscious and unconscious processes in organizations

Residential or day-care staff work as part of a team, and the same dynamics apply to their inter-relationships as to social workers but the residential and day-care experience is usually a more intensive one, with the emphasis on group development and the effects of organizational stress.

## The nature of the residential task

Residential workers in general do not have the opportunity to remove themselves from residents' lives by doing bureaucratic tasks, as do community-based social workers. Residential work involves constant confrontation with service users' needs and problems. Often the workers see themselves as the cause of some of these problems. Some studies have made significant contributions towards understanding how people deal with these immediately stressful situations. They have been based on the hypothesis proposed by Elliot Jaques concerning social defence systems, which has been developed from the psychoanalytic approach to psychology outlined in Chapter 1 and below in Chapter 7. Knowledge of group dynamics and unconscious processes has been developed from studies of hospitals and care homes which have become classic case studies. Jaques considered that in an organization the defence against anxiety is one of the primary elements which bind individuals together. In other words, he suggested that within an organization maladaptive behaviours such as hostility and suspicion will be exhibited, and these are the social counterparts of the symptoms that an individual might exhibit through projection (a concept in psychodynamic theory dealt with in Chapter 1, a defence mechanism which occurs when someone attributes to another person a characteristic which is in fact their own). Thus Jaques sees individuals as externalizing impulses which would otherwise give rise to anxiety, and 'pooling' them in the life of the social institutions in which they associate. One classic study undertaken at a teaching hospital (Menzies, 1970; Menzies Lyth, 1992) illustrates this clearly. This was a study of the way that nurses cope, or fail to cope, with their job, but is relevant to residential workers. Menzies found that the nurses in her study experienced a great deal of anxiety, and set out to understand how they managed to tolerate it. She found that there were two mechanisms for dealing with anxiety: the personal and the institutional. Individual nurses, by the nature of their jobs, were faced with coping with stress and emotions surrounding the physical care of patients, comforting relatives, comforting patients who were sometimes hostile, and having intimate contact with patients that they might find distressing or even repugnant. In addition, patients and relatives experienced a great many conflicting emotions concerning the nurses: gratitude for the care and attention, envy of their skills and health, and hostility because of their forced dependence. Menzies claims that the nurses project their anxieties into their work situation; because this was unsupportive the nurses were unable to develop coping mechanisms, and so they regressed. This was exacerbated by the 'social defence system' of the organization, which is the result of each member of the nursing staff's collusion as they operate their own defence mechanisms.Menzies provides several examples to explain and illustrate this. One of the most important is the way the nurses attempted to minimize their anxiety regarding individual responsibility. Each nurse experienced a powerful internal conflict between the responsibility demanded by her work, and her wishes to avoid this heavy and continuous burden of acting responsibly. This conflict was partially avoided by the processes of splitting, denial and projection, which converted this intrapersonal struggle into an interpersonal one. In Menzies' words, 'Each nurse tends to split off aspects of herself from her conscious personality, and to project them into other nurses'. Thus the irresponsible impulses were split off and projected into a nurse's subordinate, who was then treated with the severity which that part of the split-off self deserved. The stern and harsh aspects of herself were split off and projected on to her superiors so that she expected harsh disciplinary treatment from them. It could be observed that nurses frequently claimed that other nurses were careless, irresponsible and in need of continual supervision and discipline.

Defences against anxiety are also defences against reality, when situations become too stressful to bear. However, operating defence systems like the ones that Menzies described requires energy which is deflected from the primary task of caring for the inmates of the institution. Thus residential staff may actually become 'institutionalized' themselves, a phenomenon which is frequently observed. This means that they are less open to new ideas, less responsive to individual needs, and unlikely to create an environment which enables the residents to operate as individuals

(Lokman et al., 2011). Miller and Gwynne (1972), in their study of residential institutions for people with disabilities and young people with disabling chronic illnesses, used a similar theoretical base. They looked at the primary task of the institution and concluded that society assigns the staff the task of catering for people treated as the 'socially dead' during the interval between this social death and physical death. When people cross the boundary into such an institution, they show that they have failed to occupy or retain any role which, according to the norms of society, confers social status on the individual. However, most staff do not consider the notion of social death as significant, probably because it is too painful. The staff are there because of advances in medicine, prolonging life of the chronically and terminally ill, because families fail to cope with disabled members and because of cultural changes in society which have deprived it of adequate cultural mechanisms for coping with death (Chapter 2). In contemporary society, death is still a taboo subject despite efforts to change this. Most residential staff in long-stay institutions are committed to caring and probably see themselves as taking on a task with which most people are unable to cope. However this will raise their levels of anxiety and stress. As Zagier Roberts (1994) proposed, the workers had made conscious choices based on idealism although unconsciously have assigned themselves impossible tasks. Miller and Gwynne demonstrated two models of defence systems which these staff might operate:

*The humanitarian defence.* Despite social death, there is a pressure of humanitarian values to ensure that the interval between social and physical death is as long as possible: sick people in old people's homes are given medical treatment, even if their life will be reduced in quality afterwards, and staff are not prepared to hear complaints about lack of fulfilment and unhappiness, or their wishes to die.

*The liberal defence.* Superficially the liberal defence is at odds with the humanitarian defence. The abnormalities of the inmates are denied, and hopes of physical and social rehabilitation are encouraged. However, the truth is soon realized by residents who venture back across the boundary and find they do not easily fit into 'normal' society. Miller and Gwynne found that staff who profess liberal values also tend to 'infantalize' their inmates by claiming they are really normal, but in much the way that babies and children are:

they refer to the inmates' activities in a patronizing way, realizing that they are not normal, but refusing to admit it openly.

Goffman (1961) draws attention to the fact that in long-stay hospitals for people with mental health problems, staff have roles and statuses which are not only recognized internally, but have external meaning: they are not only in the institution to serve the needs of the inmates, and serve society by providing care for its rejects, but are often there to gain professional experience in order to move on to other positions. This is another way individual staff can prevent themselves from becoming overwhelmed by the suffering of the people in their care.

Residential workers, then, appear to face an impossible task, made worse by their own staff and professional networks seeming to deny the reality of the anxiety this type of work produces. The extent to which people are drawn to this work is related to their need to work through their own unresolved issues (Bion, 1961; Zagier Roberts, 1994). In the next section, the *therapeutic community* model of residential care will be examined.

## Residential and day-care from the service user's perspective

There are a variety of factors in residential and day-care which inhibit or encourage emotional development in consumers for whom they are provided and once again, evidence has evolved from a series of classic studies. The physical facilities and resources obviously affect the scope of the experience, but probably more significant are the attitudes and behaviour of the staff.The problematic relationships faced by the staff are experienced at first hand by the consumers. The extremes of regime which are possible greatly affect the quality of life experienced by the consumer. The different models of residential and day-care, and their effects, will be discussed in this section. If we are to accept Miller and Gwynne's notion of 'social death', then it can be applied to a greater or lesser extent to most residential and day-care institutions. Certainly, people attending day nurseries and luncheon clubs are still very much part of wider society, but there is also evidence that children in residential care suffer permanent emotional damage from their experiences. It is not 'social death' in the sense of being a state of suspension between being a full member of society and being physically dead, but it does *impair* all these individuals' capacity to live. This impairment may be in the form of 'institutional neurosis' as described by Barton (1976), who showed how people who spend a long period in psychiatric hospital adopt certain bizarre characteristics such as strange ways of walking, a lack of interest in their surroundings and a general mood of passivity; all of these to a greater or lesser extent can be seen in consumers for whom attending a day centre is the main focus of their lives, or who live permanently or temporarily in institutions. This is true for children, but studies in residential nurseries have shown a retardation effect in learning and a lack of facility for forming relationships. Reports of older children in residential institutions have demonstrated passivity and dependence in addition to an inability to form lasting relationships. Scott (1992), discussing care for older people in the USA, traces the roots of 'anti-institutionalization' sentiment to the 1950s, arguing that for some user groups it is important to change the nature of the institutional context rather than simply dismantle the institution. Smaller residential care facilities have developed through the private sector in both the USA and the UK which are preferable to many in terms of emotional and physical care than either being in their own homes or in large state-funded institutions.

## Models of institutions

Miller and Gwynne describe two models of large-scale residential care which correspond with the humanitarian and liberal values previously described. They call these models the 'warehousing model' and the 'horticultural model'. In the warehousing model, the primary task is to prolong physical life, and it translates the model of the hospital into the setting of the residential home. The new resident is defined in terms of physical malfunctioning and is provided with medical and nursing care. The horticultural model caters for an inmate who is perceived as deprived, with unsatisfied drives and unfulfilled capacities. The primary task of the institution is to develop these capacities. The staff provide the residents with opportunities for growth. Miller and Gwynne admit that the horticultural model is an aspiration rather than a reality.

Cardonna (1994) used the same models as Miller and Gwynne to explore Green Lodge, a residential care centre for adolescents with severe behavioural problems. She observed how the warehousing model applied to those who wanted the children to be dependent, well-behaved, contained and containable, which they expressed as a need for more discipline and formal organization. This group of staff saw children as dangerous. Alternatively the horticultural model was employed by those staff wanting to explore and support the emotional needs of the children.

## Therapeutic communities

The therapeutic community model has now been bypassed in mental health settings in favour of expediency and cost-effectiveness. However, this model of social care and rehabilitation for people with severe and complex mental health difficulties actually made some inroads into tackling the problems of institutionalization and dependence. Studies of therapeutic communities still have much to offer those concerned with successful caring organizations. The original therapeutic community was the Social Rehabilitation Unit in Surrey, which became known as the Henderson. It was closed in 2007 amidst widespread controversy (details can be found on the website http://news.bbc.co.uk/ 1/hi/health/7144686.stm). It had originally catered for ex-prisoners of war who were unable to maintain themselves in society because of social inadequacies. Maxwell Jones, who was the medical superintendent of the unit, felt that the social relationships of these people needed to be developed, rather than that they should receive medical treatment. He involved staff and residents in the task of providing social feedback on how each of them coped with their work and social routines, which were part of a strict regime.

The therapeutic community model developed by Jones enabled all staff and residents to participate in treatment and policy making. The 'therapeutic' component related to rehabilitation to a role in society which was the primary aim, via the 'community', which was the sum of all the people who lived and worked there. The hierarchy was flattened, and responsibility diffused, and thus a sense of community or joint decision-making could arise. In this model everyone is aware of what is happening to everyone else, and is free to comment accordingly. A 'twenty-four hour living learning experience' is what Jones claimed for this approach, and it meant that all interactions between community members had therapeutic potential. The therapeutic community represents a social microcosm, a miniature society, where individuals can practise new roles, and be made aware of their social and interpersonal impact. Residents also had administrative responsibility. All this was done through a rigid network of policy and psychotherapeutic groups, which everyone had to attend, and where they exposed themselves to situations from which they could receive feedback on their behaviour.This is potentially stressful for staff and residents, but does counter passivity and apathy, and makes people aware of their potential and ability to contribute to their own and other people's treatment, improving QWL. This mechanism, called sociotherapy, involves the treatment and reinforcement of a person's ability to perform roles within the microcosmic society. It is of course difficult to provide any kind of therapy or treatment which does not include an element of coercion. By definition the person who needs therapy does so in order to be accepted by society, which only happens if a 'deviant' learns to conform. However, it is the broader use of this model which is of most interest to social workers especially those working in drug, crime and alcohol rehabilitation (Ashley et al., 2003; Inciardi et al., 2004; Leon et al., 2000). However most work via the therapeutic community model now takes place in the United States rather than the UK.

## Wider applications of the therapeutic community approach

It has been suggested that there is a difference between the therapeutic community proper, and the therapeutic community approach. The Henderson represented the therapeutic community proper, but other institutions can adopt the important characteristics such as regular group meetings, and a flattening of the hierarchy. It is the opportunity to participate in community decisions, and provide feedback on people's behaviour, that enables most experiences of dependence and passivity to be reversed. Powerful hierarchies can only exist if communication and information are exclusive to particular groups of people. The transparency of information provides fairly rapid changes in the nature of institutions.

Martin (1962), describing the therapeutic community approach as it was introduced to a ward of long-stay female psychiatric patients, records how many of the nurses and junior doctors resisted the move to redistribute power. However, the most striking demonstration in his work is the change in the behaviour and emotional responses of the women who had been 'written off' by society. They had developed an interest in their fate and surroundings in the course of a few months. Adult day centres and residential institutions offered scope for sociotherapy which happened in a variety of settings (Day and Howells, 2002; Dobson et al., 2002; Jainchill et al., 2005). The psychiatric profession has neglected to make use of the model, but on the whole social work and specialist educational agencies have been more flexible in finding ways to improve their users' experiences of life. The basis of this model is that it is not so much the individual in need of treatment, but the residential or day-care setting itself, which is in need of change. The only change that is to the advantage of the consumers is one which enables them to express their opinions and views and have them acted on where appropriate.

Work with children and young people presents conceptual difficulties as well as practical ones although surprisingly it is in this sector where the idea of therapeutic institutions has been taken up more enthusiastically than with other groups of service users (Obholzer and Zagier Roberts, 1992). Statutory limitations impose restrictions on the degree of democracy which can be introduced in institutions for children, but it is still possible for children to be informed of the circumstances surrounding their lives in care and the fate of the other children they are living with, and to have an equal say in decisions crucial to their own lives. Naturally the aims and objectives of residential and day-care settings vary, but most would achieve at least some of their aims by increasing the emphasis on sociotherapy, which entails the use of all the consumers' experiences in assisting emotional growth.

## Supervision, emotion and contexts of practice

How do social workers manage their anxiety in these contexts that are potentially hostile, volatile and unsupportive ? Fineman (1993) argued that descriptions of organizations, even those which take the unconscious seriously, suggest 'emotional anorexia'. Organizations are treated as if they are rational places where decisions, leaders, goals and functions make sense and follow clear trajectories (Huffington et al., 2007). The day-to-day reality is that emotions play an important, perhaps even a central role, in decision-making, strategy and leadership (Gabriel, 2004). The role of managers, if they are to improve QWL and to ensure the best provision for the service users, is to support staff and help them manage the emotional content of their daily working lives, and in the case of social work, manage their anxieties (see also Chapters 7 and 8) (Fineman et al., 2010).

This is traditionally accomplished through the process of supervision in the work teams. Clulow (1994), using the case of the probation service to explore the dilemmas in managing organizational anxiety for people conflicted about their roles of 'care' and 'control', suggests how that same conflict enters the managerial/supervisory relationship. Being managed and supervised has connotations of not being trusted and setting up a system of surveillance, and there is evidence that abusive supervision damages not only the individual social worker but the team and organization (Tepper, 2000).

Staff need help and advice with complex decision-making about service users and their own careers (Lloyd et al., 2002). Clulow argues that a profound distrust of other people exacerbates anxiety about disclosure which can impede learning, progress of practice skills and services to clients. It is therefore incumbent on the manager to enable the social worker to understand and consequently explore the ways in which their work and discussion of their emotions and how these impact upon relationships are direct parallels to their work with service users. In a supervisory role the manager should be able to access the 'big picture' as well so that the social worker can relate interpersonal practices, emotions and organizational dynamics (Holloway, 1995). For this reason supervision needs to be explicitly about learning and the manager/supervisor also needs both to benefit from a similar experience and to recognize the value of being a supervisor for their own development.

## Conclusions

The relationships between team members with their peers, juniors and managers are in constant need of attention in all organizations but never more overtly than in one which works to support and change people. The workers need to acknowledge the same ethos in order to build and maintain the effectiveness of their teams. This requires both honesty and a degree of bravery because for all of us this demands challenging our own resistance and facing the anxieties within ourselves that are brought out in the context of a social care organization.

## Putting it into practice 3

3a. Do an observation of a team meeting or case discussion. How do you feel about being in the room? Who is doing most of the talking and what purpose does it serve (giving information, persuading, 'flannelling' and so on)?

3b. What defences are there against the anxieties related to the job? For instance is there an overemphasis on bureaucracy? Scapegoating of a particular group of colleagues (for example, quality control managers) or service users or people living in a particular area?

3c. What might be done to shift the defences and face anxieties in a thoughtful and calm manner (see also Chapter 7)?

## Further reading

Fineman, S., Gabriel, Y., and Sims, D. (2010) *Organizing and Organizations* (4th edn) London, Sage.

Menzies, I. E. P. (1970) *The Functioning of Social Systems as a Defence against Anxiety*, London, Tavistock Institute of Human Relations.

Menzies Lyth, I. (1992) *Containing Anxiety in Institutions: Selected Essays*, Volume 1, London, Free Associations Press.

Fineman's book highlights the fact that organizations are not rational although their overt aim is to ensure that the employees work effectively to ensure the development of the 'product'. However, when people work together either cooperatively or in competition it is impossible to achieve the outcome of a successful product without distress, greed, vanity, anxiety, fear and conflicts of various kinds being part of the process. Menzies' classic works which investigated the reasons that trainee nurses left their jobs either during or shortly after their training identified various unconscious defences used by the individual and the organization which were the result of a highly stressful occupational role.

Perhaps the most enduring edited volume is that edited by Obholzer, A. and Roberts, V.Z., *The Unconscious at Work*, published in 1994 by Routledge.

Each chapter is based upon a case example of consultancy work with a social care, educational or health care organization and demonstrates social defences and how they might act to prevent effective practice. Each chapter shows how the defences were identified and the groups worked with in order to change practices and relationships.

# Skills for Practice

Part II of the book, as the title suggests, brings practical knowledge drawn from the theoretical issues discussed in Part I to the fore. We begin with two chapters by Rowan Bayne, who has become an international expert on psychological type and preference theory. You will see reference to his work on this, particularly in the context of the Myers-Briggs Type Indicator (MBTI) over the next two chapters. The MBTI has become a standard tool for training with many professional groups including social workers, especially at the management level, and the detailed information it engages with provides further data for team development, effectiveness and well-being. Chapters 4 and 5, then, shift slightly away from the kind of literature that social workers are usually expected to read. It is more common for counselling students to learn about the relationship of personality, strengths, resilience and respect to skills necessary for best practice than it is for social work students and practitioners to do so. The neglect of counselling-type skills in social work training is to be regretted, however, although we know that social workers have many other things to learn about! We hope though that by taking time to read Chapters 4 and 5, and taking up the offer to participate in the exercises and tests which appear in these chapters, you will gain insight into your own personality and motivations from a different perspective from those with which you have become familiar. Moving just out of your comfort zone always brings challenges and rewards.

Chapter 6 will potentially return many of you to your comfort zone, but will nonetheless, we hope, challenge you to think about your practice and the ways in which you set about relating to others, especially when you are in a minority of one or two. However group-work practice went through a practice doldrum in social work during the early twenty-first century as it was seen rather like a luxury – a kind of therapy – rather than as fulfilling some of the high-profile statutory obligations. It is now returning and is recognized as a serious, effective and highly skilled means of prevention for those working with vulnerable adults of all kinds and in child protection services. We hope that reading the next three chapters will inspire you all to try something a little bit different.

## CHAPTER 4

# Working with strengths

**CHAPTER OVERVIEW**
In this chapter we discuss:

- Respect for oneself and others as a fundamental value.
- Focusing on people's strengths as well as their problems as a practical expression of respect.
- Psychological type (MBTI) or preference theory as a second practical expression of respect.
- Observing the preferences sufficiently accurately to be useful.
- Increasing resilience (managing stress) as a third practical expression of respect

The idea of respect, also called acceptance, non-possessive warmth and positive regard, is central to some major theories of helping (for example, Rogers, 1961; Egan, 2010) and social work texts (Ross, 2011). Moreover, along with 'disrespect', it is frequently used in everyday and professional conversations, as in 'No disrespect …' and 'With all due respect' (though these phrases can of course be said in very different tones). Primarily, it refers to respecting people as individuals but not necessarily accepting their behaviour or some aspects of it. It is not about liking someone or being nice to them; as Gerard Egan suggests, it is 'both gracious and tough-minded' (2010, p.42).

A review of research on positive regard concluded that it was related to effective therapy (and by implication to good communication in relationships generally) as one of several 'relational factors' (Farber and Doolin, 2011). (Other relational factors, including empathy and a collaborative approach, are discussed in Chapter 5). Farber and Doolin noted too that Carl Rogers and others have struggled to be clear about what positive regard or respect means and to give clear examples of it. In this chapter and in Chapter 5, respect is defined as a focus on strengths in oneself and others, and more specifically as the appropriate application of several sets of skills. The sets of skills are: ways of identifying strengths including some personality differences; increasing resilience; listening well; and being more assertive.

## Introduction: strengths

Strengths are defined by Alex Linley (2008) as ways of behaving, thinking or feeling that are 'authentic or energizing to the user, and enable optimal functioning, development and performance' (p.9). Thus, they are each of us at our best and potential best, and everyone has some strengths.

For social workers, three practical aspects of this view of strengths are that it:

- directly encourages respect for oneself and others (you are more likely to be positive about a person and they are more likely to feel more respected and better understood);
- does not mean neglecting or underestimating problems but rather provides balance;
- can suggest possible ways of managing or solving problems.

### Exercise

What are your strengths? You may at this point like to make a list, before reading the next paragraph. If so, please remember that enjoyment is an essential quality of a strength – you can be very good at something but if you don't enjoy it, then, in Linley's definition, it is not a strength. There is a comment on this exercise after the box. Please read it and the box after your first try at the exercise.

### Box 4.1 Some ways of identifying strengths in yourself and others

- notice what a person (X) looks forward to;
- notice what X misses doing;

- complete one or more of the free questionnaires at viastrengths.org, authentichappiness.org and the Center for Applied Positive Psychology (CAPP) at cappeu.com;
- reflect on X's early childhood and what X enjoyed then;
- reflect on who X admires and why;
- ask people who know X well. In particular, they may suggest strengths that X takes for granted;
- reflect on the strengths that are associated with X's psychological type;
- consider if X's weaknesses imply corresponding strengths.

Linley suggests two problems in describing a person's strengths. First, we're generally not used to talking or writing about our strengths. You may have observed a difference in your approach to describing your strengths versus your weaknesses. Second, in many cases we don't yet have the words; although sixty strengths are named in Linley et al. (2010), Linley thinks there are likely to be hundreds more.

Strengths are developed through lots of practice. Linley and others argue that to achieve excellence in a strength so much practice is needed that it is usually feasible to fully develop only about five strengths at the most. Part of the philosophy inherent in this principle is echoed in the next approach considered here: psychological type or preference theory. It is that 'No one has to be good at everything' (Myers with Myers, 1980, p. 210).

## Psychological type or preference theory

### Exercise

Think of three people you know and a way in which two of them are alike in personality and different to the other. Do this until you have stated at least three personality characteristics. Then compare these characteristics with those in Tables 4.2 and 4.3 later in this section.

Social workers often need to understand other people's personalities and motives, to predict behaviour and to communicate more effectively. This section discusses the most widely used applied personality theory: psychological type or preference theory in the Myers-Briggs Type Indicator (MBTI) sense (Myers with Myers, 1980; Bayne, 2004; 2013). The validity of the basic level of preference theory is strongly supported by the relationships between scores on the MBTI and on measures of the 'Big Five', the personality theory that has dominated mainstream personality research for several years (Bayne, 2013). There is much more, and generally more sophisticated, research on the Big Five than on preference theory and most of it is equally relevant to both theories.

Preference theory's general aims are to help us understand and respect ourselves more, and to help us understand and respect others more. There is a major emphasis on strengths and potential strengths and on the 'constructive use of differences', as opposed to judging people with different preferences to ourselves to be stupid, inefficient, awkward, weird or even as having a personality disorder. Thus, preference theory is a constructive, anti-oppressive approach to people's remarkable diversity of personality.

The sustained success of this theory can be explained by its positive tone and its versatility. It can help us make peace with ourselves, identify our natural strengths, clarify how others tend to see us and where we may choose to develop, explain some difficulties in communication and suggest strategies for managing or resolving them, and explain why we're energized by some activities and drained by others. Other areas of application include bringing up children, health, education, team building, leadership training, career development and relationship counselling.

This section is in three parts: first, an outline of the theory, emphasizing the central concept of preference and the core motives associated with four combinations of preferences, called the 'temperaments' (Keirsey, 1998). Often the most effective way of understanding and communicating with someone is to understand their main motives. Second, the preferences and the related motives are illustrated in four areas of life which can be problematic for many people: choice of what to do (work or interests), learning styles, making decisions and dealing with money. Third, the theory is useful at two levels of understanding: that people differ so profoundly (general level) and the nature of those differences (more specific level). Application at the specific level is most effective when accurate judgements of the preferences are made. This part of the chapter therefore outlines current knowledge about improving accuracy of judgements of the preferences and other personality characteristics.

## The concept of preference

A broad definition of preference is 'feeling most natural and comfortable with a particular way of behaving and experiencing'. For example, someone with a preference for Introversion will, given normal development and the opportunities, behave introvertedly most of the time and extravertedly some of the time, and Introversion will feel more comfortable and natural to them. For someone with a preference for Extraversion the opposite is the case. Thus the preferences provide stability, coherence and continuity and at the same time allow for flexibility in behaviour.

---

### Box 4.2  Some criticisms of preference (MBTI) theory

The theory is sometimes criticized for putting people in rigid boxes and therefore for being too simple. The concept of preference is one argument against this criticism. Another argument is the model of development in the theory which assumes that most people's early experience encourages, or at least does not greatly discourage, development of their preferences (Myers and Kirby, 1994; Bayne, 2005; 2013). 'Development' here primarily means trusting and using your own preferences more and more skilfully than your non-preferences, as in the example of Extraversion–Introversion above, but it also means developing the non-preferences, though usually to a lesser extent and with less sense of fulfilment.

The theory is also criticized from time to time, by people who haven't read earlier critiques and replies, for being unscientific. This criticism is briefly answered at the beginning of this section, although Big Five theory naturally has its critics too.

---

This development of both preferences and non-preferences is seen as happening throughout a person's life (K. Myers and Kirby, 1994) and the theory is optimistic about people in general developing their preferences most and 'being themselves' in this sense. However, some people develop one or more of their non-preferences most – like a left-handed person taught to be right-handed – and according to the theory don't 'feel right'. They can recover their real selves through experience or therapeutic (professional or personal) relationships (Myers and Kirby, 1994; Bayne, 2005).

### Descriptions of the eight preferences in current preference theory

The following descriptions allow you to clarify or discover your own preferences if you wish. If so, please choose in a *provisional* way, behaving like a good detective (Bayne, 2013). Your aim is to isolate your basic enduring preferences from other influences on your behaviour and these 'other influences' include culture, upbringing, roles, other personality characteristics, stress, self-image (such as ideal woman, man or social worker) and how developed your preferences and non-preferences are, hence the need to gather clues and interpret them carefully. This may sound a formidable task but in everyday life people are generally quite accurate in their judgements of personality, though with scope for improvement (Vazire, 2010; Funder, 2013).

The standard terms for and meanings of each preference are indicated in Tables 4.1 and 4.2, but please note that their names have a particular, technical meaning, so that, for example, Thinking does *not* mean 'without feelings' and Judging does *not* mean judgemental.

There are many other ways of clarifying preferences, including reading descriptions of the types (see for example Appendix III, p. 214; and Myers, with Kirby and Myers, 1998); asking someone

**Table 4.1** Eight preferences

| Extraversion (E) or Introversion (I) |
| --- |
| Sensing (S) or Intuition (N) |
| Thinking (T) or Feeling (F) |
| Judging (J) or Perceiving (P) |

**Table 4.2** Some general characteristics associated with each preference

| E | More outgoing and active | More reflective and reserved | I |
| --- | --- | --- | --- |
| S | More practical and interested in facts and details | More interested in possibilities and overviews | N |
| T | More logical and reasoned | More agreeable and appreciative | F |
| J | More planning and coming to conclusions | More easy-going and flexible | P |

**Table 4.3** Four preference descriptions compared with the corresponding factors in Big Five theory

| Description | Preferences | Big Five theory |
|---|---|---|
| Introversion (low Extraversion) | Depth | Inhibited |
| Sensing (low Openness) | Observant | Unimaginative |
| Thinking (low Agreeableness) | Analytical | Unsympathetic |
| Perceiving (low Conscientiousness) | Flexible | Weak-willed |

who knows you well to read your choice of the closest descriptions; and observing your comfort with and energy for different ways of behaving (Carr, 1997; Bayne, 2004, 2013). MBTI results themselves are still only a clue, as the term 'Indicator' implies, though generally the single best clue. On average they are about 75 per cent accurate (Myers et al., 1998, p.116 ), which is good for such a complex task. However, using the MBTI or another questionnaire is often not practical or even desirable (Bayne, 2013).

Four of the personality characteristics central to type theory and Big Five theory are compared in Table 4.3. There is considerable agreement about the general nature of the main personality characteristics but a dramatic difference in tone. For example, 'flexible' and 'easy-going' (words used to describe a preference for P) may describe the same kind of behaviour as being low on Conscientiousness (the broadly parallel Big Five characteristic) but the words used in that theory include the rather less positive and respectful 'aimless' and 'weak-willed'.

A person's psychological type is one from each of the four pairs of preferences, for example, ISTP. There are sixteen combinations and therefore sixteen types. However, a few people seem, both to themselves and others who know them well, equally comfortable with both preferences in a pair and who therefore describe themselves as, say, an EFP, an EXFP or an ESNFP. Whether they are best described as two types or one type with excellent development of both preference and non-preference is arguable (Bayne, 2005) and may be trivial. Either way, it makes the theory more subtle and more realistic rather than reducing its practical value.

> ### Exercise
>
> If you make a provisional choice of preferences, look for the best fit rather than a perfect fit. If you don't find a best fit, it may mean that the theory or parts of it don't apply to you or alternatively that you need more time to clarify your preferences (Carr, 1997; Bayne, 2004; 2013). See also the activity at the end of this chapter related to the personality descriptions in Appendix III.

### Two new preferences: Calm (C) versus Worrying (W)

Until very recently, the Big Five characteristic of Anxiety seemed unlikely to be a preference. Being highly anxious in personality seemed not to be a strength in any way, more a quality to manage, and being calm or emotionally stable seemed to be a good thing with few if any associated weaknesses. However, Nettle's (2007) arguments, and events in banking and politics which vividly illustrate the catastrophic effects of some people not worrying enough, make Worrying much more credible as a preference.

Briefly, Calm (C) is associated with being more carefree and less likely to experience 'negative' emotions like anxiety and sadness, and Worrying (W) with being more sensitive to potential risks and threats and more likely to worry about things the person knows are minor. Nettle (2007) argues that W is associated with qualities which are strengths in some circumstances, for example being more cautious, avoiding potential dangers or preparing well for them, and feeling more intensely. People who prefer C also have qualities which are strengths in some circumstances but not others, for example taking risks and being optimistic. Bayne (2013) suggests a further link between Worrying and Elaine Aron's (2010) work on Highly Sensitive People, who also have strengths corresponding to their weaknesses.

How the possible preferences for C and W fit with the eight preferences of current preference theory is not yet clear. The standard type descriptions (see Appendix III, p. 214, for example) either assume C or ignore CW altogether. Moreover, thirty-two descriptions would be needed to include C and W, which might well be too cumbersome in practice. Further, there is no reported body of practical experience with CW's interactions with the other preferences to draw on. The best solution for now seems to be to think in terms of the current eight preferences most of the time but with CW in mind as two further preferences which will enrich the theory and its applications (Bayne, 2013).

## The concept of 'type'

In current psychological type theory, the term 'type' is a statement about personality structure as well as a set of four preferences. The central idea is that in each person one of the four preferences for S, N, T and F is dominant – the managing director of a personality – another is second in command, and so on. The characteristics associated with a person's dominant preference, given sufficiently normal development, are thus seen as the main elements of their personality. It 'dominates and unifies their life' (Myers with Myers, 1980, p. 10) and 'It plays by far the biggest role in the personality (Lawrence, 1997, p. 11). However, this level of the theory is much more speculative than the eight preferences (Reynierse, 2012; Bayne, 2013) and this chapter focuses on the preferences.

## The preferences and work/interests

There are strong relationships between the ten preferences and some kinds of work and interests but the theory recognizes that people with minority preferences in a particular activity can contribute to it in unusual and positive ways. They can also find and create niches, which implies that studies of job satisfaction need to focus on different aspects of a job as appealing to people with different preferences as well as on whole jobs (Myers et al., 1998; Bayne, 2004).

There is as yet no research on the preferences of UK social workers. In the USA, Sandra Chesborough found that in contrast to some occupations, for example, managers, counsellors and fine artists (data summarized in Bayne, 2004), social work students were similar to the general US population (Chesborough, 2009). The only significant difference was that more of the social work students were extraverted. Eighty-seven per cent of Chesborough's sample of two hundred and twenty-three students were female and so not surprisingly there were more people with a preference for Feeling than Thinking. (On current evidence, about 60 per cent of women prefer Feeling and about 60 per cent of men prefer Thinking).

Overall, the relationships between the preferences and choice of activity definitely do *not* mean that a person of the 'wrong' type for it should avoid it, rather that they should examine their motives with particular care and be prepared for most of their colleagues to have fundamentally different personalities from themselves. Tieger and Barron-Tieger (2007) suggest motives for career satisfaction for each type, as well as characteristic strategies and potential pitfalls in actually searching for a fulfilling career. Preference theory has also been applied to creating job descriptions, completing application forms and selection interviewing (Bayne, 2004).

### Eight preferences and learning styles

Aspects of the learning styles associated with eight of the preferences are listed in Table 4.4 (cf. DiTiberio and Hammer, 1993; Lawrence, 1997, 2009). They vary dramatically. For example, brainstorming is as natural as breathing for most people with some preferences, but pointless and threatening to those with the opposite preferences. Similarly, a student's preferred learning style or styles will almost inevitably match the preferences and therefore probable teaching styles of some tutors and clash with others. This is more likely to cause problems and injustices when tutors are not aware of their own biases.

The biases can be very persistent. For example, Jane Smith (1993) compared the comments on an essay made by six lecturers with a preference for Thinking (T) and six with a preference for Feeling (F). All the lecturers were experienced teachers of English. They all put comments in the margins of the essay and summarized

**Table 4.4** Eight preferences and aspects of learning styles

| | |
|---|---|
| E | Action, talk, trial and error, role play |
| I | Reflection, work privately |
| S | Close observation of what actually happens; starts with the concrete and specific, ideas and theory later |
| N | Theory first; links and possibilities; surges of interest |
| T | Analysis and logic; critiques |
| F | Harmonious atmosphere; need to care about the topic |
| J | More formal; organised; clear expectations and criteria |
| P | Flexible; not routine; bursts of energy; work as play |

strengths and weaknesses (or 'areas to develop') at the end. They all also agreed on the mark for the essay, wrote about the same amount of feedback and used similar numbers of questions and reactions. However, the differences were striking too, especially as their department had explicit guidelines on giving feedback on essays: the F lecturers praised the essay twice as much as the Ts and wrote twice as many suggestions.

Smith suggested that these differences illustrate different philosophies of teaching associated with preferences for T and F. The suggested T philosophy is that students should focus on their weaknesses, on 'What is the problem that needs solving?' (p. 40). In contrast, the F philosophy is to encourage students to develop their strengths first. Smith found greater concern on the part of the F lecturers about students' feelings and greater emphasis on the part of the T lecturers on essay content and potential learning. An obvious practical question is the impact of the different styles of feedback on students generally, and on T and F students respectively, but students' views on the two approaches to giving feedback have not yet been studied.

Chesborough (2009) included several suggestions for teaching methods based on preference theory which could work well on social work and other courses, for example, working on case studies in groups of people with the same or similar preferences first, and later in mixed groups; interviewing colleagues of opposite preferences; and students of opposite preferences comparing their notes on the same teaching session.

Another example of a marked difference in approach to an aspect of studying which is related to two of the preferences is reactions to deadlines. People with a preference for Judging (J) tend to start a piece of work early and, circumstances allowing, finish it well before the deadline. Their motives, according to theory, are enjoyment of closure and avoiding what they experience as the stress of an imminent deadline. (About 10 per cent of Js are exceptions: Quenk et al., 2001.) Conversely, people with a preference for Perceiving (P) tend to do their best work at the last minute; they like to keep things open and they enjoy an imminent deadline energy surge. (About 40 per cent of Ps are exceptions: Quenk et al., 2001.) Js and Ps produce equally good work, but in their contrasting styles and with characteristic strengths and weaknesses.

Development of non-preferences can compensate for these weaknesses. For example, Js tend to be more skilled than Ps at writing conclusions to essays and reports, and Ps at integrating more diverse material, but just as Js can learn to return to 'finished' essays and add another idea or more notes of caution, so Ps can learn to add considered and appropriately firm conclusions.

## Four preferences and making decisions

Preference theory assumes that we make our best decisions using both Thinking and Feeling but giving most weight to the one we prefer. Thus people who prefer F can use their non-preference for T to list points for and against, then their preference for F to say which of the points matter most, then F again to make the decision. Conversely, people who prefer T are likely to find the analytic listing of points and arguments most natural but can also include their emotional reactions to each point, then come back to their T again to make the decision.

Another framework for making decisions based on the theory is to use four preferences:

S: What are the relevant facts and details?
N: What are the possible ways, however speculative and unlikely, of interpreting these facts? Are any models or theories relevant?
T: What are the consequences of each choice, short and long-term? What are the arguments? What's logical?
F: What are the probable effects on each person involved? What are the priorities here?

The theory implies putting most effort into our non-preferences (because they are likely to be less developed) and applying our preferences last (because they are likely to be more trustworthy).

## Four 'temperaments', their core motives and money

Temperament theory assumes that four combinations of preferences are especially useful in understanding personality differences (Keirsey, 1998; Bayne, 2013). For example, people of each temperament have a natural approach to money, derived from core motives. Thus, SPs (a combination of Sensing and Perceiving) tend to spend money to feel free and excited; SJs to be careful with money, to try to achieve security and stability; NTs to spend it perfectly (competence is their core motive); and NFs to ignore it or at least give it less priority (because their core motive of 'self-actualization', though rather vague, is not materialistic).

In the theory, each of these approaches to money has strengths (Linder, 2000). However, the strengths can be taken too far and they can be modified as part of developing preferences and non-preferences. For example, an SP who wants to save more might find some excitement from other sources than spending money. Similarly, NTs, especially INTPs, might set a time limit on their detailed comparative analyses of a particular purchase, and develop their ability to make decisions in a Feeling way to supplement (not replace or equal) their Thinking decisions.

A fuller version of the core motives of the four temperaments is as follows:

SP: Excitement, solving practical problems, freedom (feeling unrestricted), variety.

SJ: Being responsible and useful, stability, planning in detail, seeing those plans through to completion.

NT: Creating new methods, theories and models, analysing, criticizing (to help the person improve).

NF: Self-development, supporting other people, harmony, authenticity.

### Exercise

Rank the motives central to each of the temperaments from most like you to least like you. You may find it easier to start with 'least like'. The core motives are seen as relatively important in each temperament; for example, everyone needs some excitement (SP) and some stability (SJ) but one of them is more characteristic of each person (Bayne, 2013).

## Observing the preferences more accurately

The general 'spirit' of preference theory is probably in itself a positive influence on respect (and communicating), but accurate observation of the preferences of those involved is likely to enhance this effect. There are a number of obstacles to accuracy and some strategies to counteract them. However, people's observations of personality are often quite accurate (Vazire, 2010; Funder, 2013) so it is a matter of improvement rather than major change. At the same time, the serious impact of many of the decisions made by social workers makes even small improvements in accuracy worthwhile.

The obstacles to accuracy include the nature of perception, the disproportionate power of stereotypes, first impressions, similarity and the ambiguity of nonverbal communication. The process of seeing, for example, includes upside-down images on our eyes and this information passing to the brain in the form of electrical impulses. When people have worn special glasses which invert the images – in a sense put them the right way up – they have adapted to the glasses in about a week, seeing things through them as they normally do (Kosslyn and Rosenberg, 2004). This phenomenon also illustrates what has been called the 'effort after meaning', which we habitually make to the extent of seeing meaning where there is very unlikely to be any. Perception seems like taking a series of photographs but is more like making a sketch or a cartoon. Selection is inevitable but it may mean missing crucial bits of information. It also makes prejudice possible.

Stereotypes are the extreme misuse of categories: a person is judged on the basis of one quality, such as age, sex, culture, occupation, when people of, for instance, the same culture vary considerably in personality (Myers et al., 1998). One stereotype that appears to be generally believed is that 'what is beautiful is good' (Baron and Byrne, 2004). It appears at an early age: even nursery school children tend to prefer their more beautiful peers. Similarly, people have been asked to judge reports of 'rather severe' classroom disturbances, apparently described by a teacher. Photographs of the child who caused the trouble were attached to the reports. The judges all saw the same reports but the photograph, of a physically attractive or unattractive child, varied. The effect was a tendency to place more blame on unattractive children – 'a real problem' – than attractive children – 'a bad day ... her cruelty ... need not be taken too seriously'. Such results are obviously unjust, but a human tendency which can be counteracted.

Impressions tend to be formed very quickly and almost automatically (Baron and Byrne, 2004). Just a name sometimes suggests a certain kind of person: expecting something from all people called Judith, for example, because of one Judith in your life. Gordon Allport suggested that if you merely glance at a stranger and then let yourself imagine what they are like, a wealth of associations will probably appear (Allport, 1961). This is probably more true of people with some preferences than others.

We also generally pay most attention to our first impressions, treating them as revealing the 'real person' and tending to see later, discrepant information as unrepresentative: 'Bipasha is very friendly normally, she was tired today', because she was friendly the first time we met her, or in the first few minutes of the first meeting. This effect (called the primacy effect) is easy to counter-act, with a simple warning enough for most people. However, there may then be a recency effect, which can be just as misleading.

The most direct way of countering the disproportionate power of first impressions is to notice them, to check the evidence on which they are based, and to look for further evidence. Less obviously, look for evidence supporting the *opposite* hypothesis too (Lord et al., 1984). A further strategy is to think of alternative interpretations of the evidence. These strategies all involve suspending belief in one's first impressions until sufficient information has been gathered. How much is 'sufficient'? It depends, but Epstein's (1979) research suggests finding three supporting pieces of evidence before accepting a particular judgement. The supervisor at a holiday camp who judged me as a 'surprisingly good worker for a student' on the basis of a surprise visit in which she found me polishing vigorously, would have been more accu-rate if she'd tried two more surprise visits, had observed me work-ing in other situations, and had considered alternative interpretations of her single observation, such as novelty of the task, energetic mood.

Strong liking or disliking at first meeting is particularly likely to be an inaccurate and unjust reaction, based on reacting to the person as if they are somebody else. The following six steps are developed from co-counselling. In co-counselling, or at least one approach to it, the steps are carried out openly in the relationship. In other situations they will generally be carried out privately, at the time or later.

1. Ask 'Who does this person remind me of?'
2. In what way is she/he (the new person) like X? Find as many specific similarities as possible, for example, 'the way he holds his head'.
3. What do I want to say to X?
4. Say it.
5. In what ways is the new person not like X? Again, look for specific differences.
6. Say 'This is Y, not X.'

The idea, of course, is to see the new person more clearly. It is also possible to suggest that this kind of confusion may be happening to someone who is reacting very strongly to you, and then, if appropriate, to take them through the six steps.

Similarity is another source of bias. Both small and large similarities tend to be attractive in another person, for example, their choice of newspaper, speed of thought, sense of humour. This may be because it feels good to have our views confirmed, because we anticipate that if someone agrees with us they are more likely to like us, because we feel more likely to be understood, etc. For accuracy of judgement, it means simply to beware of the 'like me' bias – of immediate positive judgements based on similarity.

## Increasing resilience

### Exercise

Do you accept – really accept – that it is professionally responsible for anyone whose work involves caring for others to take care of themselves too, both physically and psychologically? One argument is that you are then more likely to work well. Another is that you are less likely to be 'burnt out', 'caught up' or 'sucked in' – vivid metaphors.

Social work is both stressful and rewarding. There are always far more people to see and things to do than anyone could possibly manage, frequent changes of policy and practices, inadequate resources and decisions to make which profoundly affect people's lives. However, a review found high levels of job satisfaction of social workers compared with many other occupations (Collins, 2008). For example, a large majority of social workers reported feeling that they can make a real difference, enjoy their contact with service users and colleagues and enjoy the variety and challenge of their jobs.

Social work students too have been found to enjoy 'a high sense of personal accomplishment' in their work with service users (Collins et al., 2010). Nevertheless, most people, including social workers, social work students and service users, experience significant stress at times and would probably benefit from reviewing and improving their coping strategies.

Much has been written about how to manage or cope with stress, with a recent emphasis on interpreting the ideas and evidence more positively and preventively as 'developing resilience' – the capacity to persist in the face of stressful challenges and to recover well from them (see, for example, Skovholt and Trotter-Mathison, 2009; Reivich et al., 2011; Walsh, 2011).

There are numerous definitions of stress. Meg Bond's is 'the experience of unpleasant over or under stimulation as defined by the individual in question, that actually or potentially leads to ill-health' (Bond, 1986, p. 2). This definition emphasizes individual experience, and hints at feeling threatened and strained to the extent of being overwhelmed. It recognizes that both too much and too little to do are stressful.

There are many problematic aspects of stress, for example, the relative importance of external and internal factors in causing it; whether it is more effective to intervene at the level of organizational and social structures or at the level of individuals; motives for *not* looking after ourselves; which ways of coping with stress are most effective for which kinds of problems and/or people; how important stress is in various illnesses; when it is important in illness; and the processes involved.

How responsible are we for our own stress levels? Training courses on 'managing stress' and 'developing resilience' generally emphasize the role of individuals rather than their organizations, social contexts or cultures. However, if for example an organization expects employees to regularly have very large 'case loads' or does not deal effectively with bullying or harassment, then the organization is a major source of stress and providing stress management workshops won't tackle the real problem. On the other hand, we generally do contribute significantly to our own stress and working on ourselves is therefore helpful. It should also make well-considered and productive political action more likely.

The rest of this section outlines a three-stage model of coping with stress and then discusses several strategies for managing stress and increasing resilience: relaxation, sleep, exercise/physical activity, a new and very ambitious course on resilience training, expressive writing and peer support groups. The model is:

Stage 1:  Monitor your signs of too much or too little stimulation, especially *early* warnings.
Stage 2:  Choose one or more coping strategies.
Stage 3:  Try them out, monitoring the effects.

**Table 4.5** Some effects of stress

| On thoughts and emotions | On the body | On behaviour |
|---|---|---|
| Difficulty concentrating | Tight throat | Irritable |
| Anxious | Aches | Accidents |
| Tired | Dry mouth | Drug misuse |
| Bored | Tics | Critical |
| Depressed | Frequent urination | Difficulties in sleeping |

*Note:* Some of these signs of stress may be caused by *illness* and may therefore need medical attention.

Table 4.5 lists some signs of stress. Another sign, unfortunately, is ignoring such signs. Ideally, we would notice them early and take action to reduce or remove them, but being stressed is distracting. The advantages of early action are obvious: less energy wasted and less damage done. Working out the source(s) of stress, internal and external, may also be more feasible.

Choosing one or more coping strategies is currently a matter of personal experiment, although the strategies reviewed next are generally well supported by research (see, for example, Walsh, 2011). They work for most people and are therefore more likely to be worth trying.

## Relaxation

The coping strategy of physical relaxation illustrates some of the points above well. Physical relaxation is an obvious way of coping with stress, both immediately and preventively, and instructions/guidelines are widely available. Two ten-minute sessions of progressive relaxation a day seem to have a beneficial and cumulative effect (Seligman, 1995). However, sometimes attempting to relax is itself stressful. Several factors can make a difference: for example, some people prefer a well-lit room, others a dark one, some respond best to several two- or three-minute sessions, and so on (Lazarus and Mayne, 1990). Moreover, someone can try too hard to relax or may be afraid of losing control of certain images or emotions. Relaxation can also be boring and therefore stressful.

A simple relaxation technique is to:

1. Make yourself comfortable. Take two or three deep breaths through your nose. Then place one of your index fingers on the point between your eyebrows, with the thumb on one nostril, middle finger on the other.
2. Closing your left nostril, breathe in slowly and deeply through the right.
3. Closing your right nostril, breathe out slowly through the left.
4. Keeping right nostril closed, breathe in through the left.
5. Closing left nostril, breathe out through the right.

You can breathe in to (say) a count of three, hold for two, out to six – but ideally find your own rhythm. A further refinement of the instructions is that when you've breathed out, pause and wait until you want to breathe in – until it 'feels right'. Mindfulness is a related set of ideas and techniques. The basic idea is to become intentionally aware of thoughts and actions in a respectful way, and to find stillness. It can be practised at almost any time. For example, when eating, just eat. The Wise Brain website and Collard (2013) are good resources.

Having too much to do is stressful by definition and not relaxing. Of the numerous approaches to time management, the simplest – which manages tasks rather than attempting to manage time – may be enough. It is first to make lists of things to do, thus clearing your mind and helping you to focus. Then, either do an item on the list if it's quick and practical to do it, or write the next step that's needed to make progress with it. The obvious underlying principles are taking small steps and increasing sense of control. Any problems with it can be managed as described in the later section on expressive writing. On a particular day, you might make a sub-list of, say, four priority things to do that day and at night you might make a list of things 'on your mind' or things to do the next day, both of which can help with going to sleep. (You don't have to actually do the things that are on your list the next day or at all – things come up – for this method to work!)

## Sleep

Sleep is a form of relaxation and deserves to be taken seriously because poor quality sleep contributes to accidents, bad decisions, illness etc (Horne, 2006). Advice on sleep is readily available (see Horne, 2006; www.rcpsych.ac.uk; and www.raysahelian.com/sleep). Small changes to diet, bedroom, etc. can be very effective.

---

### Exercise

If you're not sleeping well, you may like to review your 'sleep hygiene' and experiment with changes. Some researchers think most people in Western society need more sleep. As a guideline, there is general agreement that most people need 7 to 9 hours' good quality sleep per night. Tiredness can be caused by other factors than not sleeping well.

---

## Exercise/physical activity

Guidelines on how much exercise is healthy are contentious (Biddle, 2010). A few years ago, the UK government's recommended minimum amount of exercise was being slightly out of breath for 30 minutes most days but the 2008 British Association of Sport and Exercise Sciences (BASES) guideline is 'vigorous exercise' for several minutes two or three times a week, with 'vigorous' defined as making it difficult to speak in sentences. Much more demanding! However, although the evidence for the benefits of vigorous exercise for health and reducing stress is strong, some people thrive with very little exercise.

General principles are to become more active gradually and comfortably in ways that you enjoy and to have rest days. Different kinds of exercise seem likely to suit people with different preferences. Suzanne Brue uses a colour system based on preference theory, and there is a brief quiz to indicate which colour represents you at www.the8colors.com. For example, people who prefer INTJ and INFJ are whites in her model and tend to enjoy exercising alone in a calm, familiar and pleasing setting and letting their minds drift – exercise as a 'moving meditation' – whereas ESTPs and ESFPs are reds and tend to want lots of stimulation, variety and quick responding – exercise as absorbing action. Thus motives may be the key to finding the form of exercise which suits you (Brue, 2008).

A general recommendation is to avoid sedentary behaviour such as prolonged sitting (Biddle, 2010). This could mean for example standing from time to time (say two or three times an hour) while watching TV, using a computer or reading etc.

### Resilience training

Several programmes for resilience training have been developed and evaluated; for example, the Penn Resilience Program, which is for teachers, has been shown to reduce anxiety and depression in their students. Reivich et al. (2011) drew on this programme and on positive psychology and CBT for their response to a request from the American army for help with record rates of suicide, depression, PTSD and divorce in their soldiers. The resulting resilience training programme is being experienced by over a million soldiers, their families and their civilian workforce for about ten years (up to 2020 or so) and, if the outcomes are sufficiently positive, could be used widely in the general population too.

---

#### Exercise

How do you react to this training being directed at the US army? You may like to write some notes or discuss your reactions and then compare them with the comment at the end of this section. (There are further, strongly worded critiques and a reply by Martin Seligman in *American Psychologist*, October, 2011, pp. 641–7.)

---

Many of the ideas, strategies and techniques in the programme will be familiar to social workers: self-awareness, strengths, empathy, thinking traps, 'icebergs' (deeply held and undermining beliefs such as 'Asking for help shows weakness'), energy management and assertiveness skills. Others may be less familiar, at least in their latest forms, for example, 'active constructive responding' (which sounds deceptively like empathy but is not empathy as defined in Chapter 5) and 'cultivating gratitude'. The programme emphasizes prevention and positive psychology. It seems not to be relentlessly and one-sidedly positive in the way some contributions to 'positive psychology' are; for example, it does seem to recognize the value and inevitability of 'negative emotions'. Considering what soldiers experience in wartime, and that their trainers are drill sergeants (the programme is initially being run to train the trainers), this is probably not surprising. However, its ideas, philosophy and tone do strike an optimistic note, and they reframe ideas about managing stress.

Seligman and Fowler (2011) recognized that some helping professionals will find working with the military in any way distasteful or unacceptable (p.85). They discussed three objections that might be raised. In 'unvarnished form', they are:

- Psychology should devote its scarce resources to helping those who are suffering, not those who are well.
- Psychology should do no harm. Aiding the military will make people who kill for a living feel better about killing and help them do a better job of it.
- Psychology should not aid the foreign policy of the United States.

Part of their response to these objections is that soldiers suffer from PTSD, depression, etc. and need help for humanitarian reasons and that it is not the military that sets policy but a democratically elected government. They argue further that a strong military was needed to overcome threats from fascism and communism and is needed to resist current threats.

### Expressive writing

The key researcher in this area is James Pennebaker. For example, Pennebaker et al. (1990) divided students who had just started their first year into two random groups. The experimental group were asked to write for 20 minutes on three consecutive days about their 'very deepest thoughts and feelings about coming to college'. The 'control' or comparison group wrote on what they'd done since they woke up that day. Therefore, thoughts and feelings were emphasized in the first group, and behaviour in the second. The main finding was that students in the experimental group went to the health centre less in the next six months than those in the control group.

In another study, unemployed professionals either wrote about their reactions to redundancy (experimental group) or to relatively superficial matters (control group). Those in the experimental group found new jobs more quickly but *not* because they applied for more jobs or wrote more letters (Spera et al., 1994). The basic finding and variations have been replicated several times, with some attention to explaining the positive effects of this form of writing on health (Frattaroli, 2006; Lyubomirsky et al., 2006).

## Box 4.3 An example of expressive writing in action

A model of coping consistent with Pennebaker's research and with the model of counselling discussed in Appendix I, p. 210, is outlined next with an example. It is in three steps and a key principle is to take both inner experience and action seriously.

*Step 1: Reflection*
Write as *freely* as you can about something that matters to you – not analysing, not concerned with literary merit, and for yourself only:

> Very angry about extra work, said to D: 'This sort of thing makes me feel like giving up.'

> I was furious and reacted at once, without thinking. The next few months are packed and I don't want to feel overworked. Hated feeling that way last week. Why me anyway? Is he trying to get at me anyway? Doubt it. Glad I did react strongly and quickly. Quite rare for me and it felt good being spontaneous.

(End of Step 1– reflection – at least on this occasion. Step 2 is a much more considered analysis.)

*Step 2: Analysis*
Analyse your reactions and perhaps challenge them:

Be specific: e.g. what was actually said?
What is the evidence for any interpretations, beliefs?
Is there a familiar feeling or pattern there?
What assumptions are you making?
Do your reactions tell you anything else about yourself, e.g. suggest important values that may explain them?
How realistic are you being?
What other ways (however unlikely) are there of looking at what happened?

> What I actually did was speak forcefully and briefly. I didn't throw or break anything. I then just shrugged and said something general. I don't know what he thought. I was most angry about first not being consulted and second becoming so stressed so

quickly. Actually, the extra work has some possibilities. It's not just a burden.

(End of Step 2 – a more considered analysis. It is meant to contrast with Step 1, which is written more freely, indeed as freely as possible.)

*Step 3: Action*
Consider possible actions:

Is there any action you want to take now?
Is there anything which you might do differently next time?

> I'll a) ask J's advice; b) think about whether it's worth saying something to D (my head of department) about consultation rather than being ordered, perhaps think about cutting back my work in another area; c) think about my reaction to sudden requests to take on new responsibilites; and d) plan the possibilities in the new work. Do (a) today.

(End of Step 3.)

**Evaluation of the example**
Analysis is relatively neglected but a useful start is made. The actions are relevant and promising, but could be expressed more specifically.

Other writing techniques include making lists, for example of things you're happy about, wants, problems; freewriting; writing about yourself in the third person; letters (probably not to send); and writing dialogues between part of you and another part of you, or with another person (Rainer, 1978; Thompson, 2010).

## Peer Support Groups

A peer support group usually consists of people in the same general situation who agree to support and challenge each other. If an overall aim and strategy are agreed, then anything that happens in the group can be evaluated on whether it is consistent with them or not, such as the amount of time any one person in the group speaks, whether to allow silent members or not, to practise new behaviours or not, when to allow new members, and so on.

It's not clear what social support is or how it protects (Baron and Kerr, 2003; Schwarzer and Knoll, 2010), but it seems to be powerful. Explanations currently include an increase in perceived control, increased self-esteem and self-disclosure (as in expressive writing). Sense of belonging and involvement is another possibility. On the other hand, groups can of course be undermining and destructive, for example, through being critical in a hostile way and being condescending.

Some suggestions for running a support group are: for each member of the group to have equal time; to negotiate the amount of structure – some effective groups are highly structured but others are free-wheeling; no discussion of any aspect of the group (process or content) outside the group; that the person speaking asks for the kind of support they'd like, for example, basic listening, empathy, challenging, sharing factual information, advice, encouragement (Bond, 1986); that you review your group after some (or all) meetings (What is working well? What could work better?); that you look out for 'games', such as 'Ain't it awful', in which the group reinforce each other's sense of gloom and powerlessness, 'Psychologist', and the three roles in the Drama Triangle – Victim, Persecutor and Rescuer – (Bayne et al., 2008); and that you notice and challenge any interfering beliefs about asking for or accepting support. Examples of interfering beliefs are:

I don't have time.
It's not fair on other people.
I'm not worth it.
It shows I can't cope.
Other people aren't interested.
Other people don't care.
I can cope on my own.
It may make me vulnerable.

Generally, these beliefs are unhelpful, and, for social workers and other practitioners in the helping professions, inconsistent and disrespectful of self and others.

## Conclusions

Social workers can show respect for service users, colleagues, themselves and others in serveral ways. You can focus more on identifying and developing strengths as defined by Alex Linley; you can understand your own and other people's preferences (in the MBTI sense) more deeply; and you can accept that it is professionally responsible to monitor your own levels of stress and work on increasing your resilience. Applications of preference theory include choice of work, making decisions, managing money and writing essays. Ways of increasing resilience include relaxation, sleep, exercise and peer support. These ideas about expressing and developing respect for oneself and others are built on and refined in the next chapter.

## Putting it into practice 4

Below are some additional exercises you might want to try.

4a. Try commenting more on the strengths you see in colleagues, service users and others. The skill of giving compliments as outlined in Chapter 5 may be helpful here.

4b. How well do the preferences (in the MBTI sense) and the associated core motives fit with your choice of socal work as a career? Are there any implications for you specializing within social work? (Bear in mind the principle that people with preferences that are not usually associated with a particular activity may contribute a valuable perspective for that reason.)

4c. Try an approach to coping with stress for, say, a week and monitor the effects systematically.

4d. In the section on learning styles, two philosophies of learning are discussed. Is either more true of you and if so is it related to your preference for T or F or to your upbringing? Are there any implications for you as a receiver or giver of feedback?

4e. Which of the descriptions in Appendix III is the most characteristic of you? A *perfect* fit is unlikely because the descriptions are of people of each 'type' with good development of their preferences and leave out their non-preferences. They are therefore rather glowing! The opposite descriptions for example, ISTJ if your preferences are ENFP and vice versa) indicate likely weaknesses.

Two other points about Gordon Lawrence's descriptions. First, they don't include the suggested new preferences for Calm and Worrying because these descriptions have not been developed yet, and may not be developed for reasons discussed earlier. Second, there is a phrase in each description for a suggested 'strongest mental process', e.g. 'Extraverted THINKING' in ENTJ. This phrase refers to a much more speculative level of MBTI theory which was touched on in the section on the concept of 'type'.

# Further reading

Linley, A. (2008) *Average to A+: Realizing your Strengths in Yourself and Others,* Coventry, CAPP Press.

Linley revives and refreshes the concept of strengths in a very practical way. His aim is to help people understand and make the most of their strengths.

Bayne, R. (2004) *Psychological Types at Work: An MBTI Perspective,* London, Thomson.

Chapter 1 of this book discusses the strengths and limits of preference theory, evidence-based practice and applying the theory ethically and effectively. The applications of theory which are discussed in these chapters are about the way these concepts can be used in careers, selection interviews, communication skills, health, coaching and counselling, and leading and managing others.

Bayne, R., and Jinks G. (2010) *How to Survive Counsellor Training: An A–Z Guide,* Basingstoke, Palgrave Macmillan.

This book provides practical reviews of many topics common to social work and counsellor training, including selection, assessment, emotional reactions, writing and critical thinking.

Rosenthal, T. (1993) 'To soothe the savage breast', *Behaviour Research and Therapy,* 31, 439–62.

Walsh, R. (2011) 'Lifestyle and mental health'. *American Psychologist,* 66, 579–92.

The Rosenthal paper is an entertaining review of ideas and research about several strategies for coping with stress such as visualization and having a pet. The Walsh paper is a drier and much more recent review. You may like to compare the two authors' ideas and interpretations of evidence.

Sapolsky, R.M. (2004) *Why Zebras Don't Get Ulcers* (3rd edn), New York, Henry Holt.

This is an optimistic and lively discussion of stress and stress-related illness but with only one chapter on managing stress.

## CHAPTER 5

# Communication skills

**CHAPTER OVERVIEW**

This chapter discusses:

- Skills versus personal qualities in communication skills training.
- Experimenting with your communication skills.
- Skills for listening and gathering information.
- Giving information.
- Aspects of interviewing which may be particularly difficult.
- Assertive skills.
- Personality and styles of communication.

This chapter reviews and applies some ideas and research about communicating more effectively. How helping relationships work has recently become much clearer and we now know in relatively specific terms more – though definitely not everything – about how to put that knowledge into practice. The respective subtitles of two editions of *The Heart and Soul of Change* illustrate this progress. The first edition's subtitle was 'What works in therapy' (Hubble et al., 1999), and the second edition's 'Delivering What Works in Therapy' (Duncan et al., 2010). The chapter draws on reviews of skills training (see, for example, Hill and Lent 2006) and ideas and research on many forms of interview, such as social work (Ross, 2011), investigative (Bull, 2010), counselling (Norcross and Wampold, 2011) and selection (Macan, 2010).

## Introduction

Social workers talk and listen to a wide variety of service users, colleagues and others. You may, for example, be gathering sensitive information from a service user with complicated needs one moment and liaising with a health or housing professional the next. One or more of the people involved may be anxious, upset or angry. Some of these conversations, meetings and interviews go well, but in others the outcome could have been better.

### Exercise

Think of a conversation at work, formal or informal, that went well and one that went badly. What aspects of the situation, the other person and you might explain the difference? What did you think, feel or want to do in these conversations? What did you actually do? What did the other person do? What would you rather have happened?

A model of interviewing consistent with the approach taken here is outlined in the box below.

### Box 5.1 The PEACE model of interviewing

This model of interviewing was introduced into police training in the UK in the mid-1990s (Bull, 2010; Walsh and Bull, 2010). The models it replaced were more manipulative and coercive and more likely to result in false confessions. The PEACE model is:

Preparation and Planning
Engage and Explain
Account
Clarify and Challenge
Evaluation

'Engage and Explain' is similar in meaning to the skill of 'negotiating a contract', which is discussed in this chapter in the section on skills for listening. 'Account' is encouraging the interviewee to talk about relevant topics. The final phase, Evaluation, is shown in Table 5.1, which also outlines the model of interviewing discussed in this chapter.

## Skills versus personal qualities

A skills approach to communication has been criticized as neglecting personal qualities when they are actually more important than skills. It is seen as too superficial. For example, Carl Rogers (1987) commented on training people to 'reflect feelings':

> It does not describe what I am trying to do when I work with a client. My responses are attempts to check my understanding of the client's internal world. I wish to keep an accurate up-to-the minute sensitivity to his or her inner searchings, and the response is an endeavour to find out if I am on course with my client. (p. 39)

Skills training is indeed sometimes superficial, and interviewing and counselling are in some respects mysterious and artistic. There's more to them, and the resulting behaviour can seem, and be, mechanical and hollow. A sense of timing, for example, is part of this artistic side.

On the other hand, the term 'timing' is more a question than an explanation. Moreover, the qualities most relevant to good communication are complex and hard to define and measure (for example, Gerdes et al., 2010). For example, *empathy* can be defined as 'showing that you understand the other person's feelings and see their point of view' – with the emphasis on 'showing', and in a specific way; *genuineness* as 'being yourself' – though 'appropriately' rather than bluntly or unflinchingly; and *respect* as 'warm acceptance of the other person' – though some people respond best to a matter-of-fact kind of warmth. The comments after each brief definition hint at some of the complexities of the qualities and of communicating them well.

Therefore, an alternative view is that skills training and personal development (of qualities underlying good communication) can complement each other, with the skills giving a more systematic framework for analysis, and the analysis helping the qualities to develop. This in turn allows a deeper analysis of the use of skills and so on. The skills discussed in this chapter can both communicate qualities like empathy and respect and help to develop them.

## An approach to developing your communication skills

This chapter is intended to help you analyse your own interviews and other conversations in a constructive way. There is lots of room for individual style, as the quality of genuineness implies. Indeed, improvising – the meta-skill of choosing when and how to use a particular skill – is essential. The approach taken assumes that although you will have developed at least some of the skills already, all helping professionals, whatever their training and experience, can usefully review their skills. It is also likely that working to improve your skills will involve feeling self-conscious and awkward for a while. However, as with developing other skills, they will usually feel and become more natural in time.

The central method is analysis plus experiment with changes plus feedback. The following principles for giving feedback are general guidelines, not absolute rules. Moreover, giving feedback is itself a skill, and therefore it too develops with appropriate practice.

- Comment on behaviour, and try to be specific, for example, 'I seemed very relaxed – I think it was the way I sat and my use of silence.' (The comment could be more specific still, but this is probably sufficient.)
- Include positive comments. Treat yourself kindly (for research supporting this principle, see Leary et al., 2007; Neff and Vonk, 2008).
- Express your feedback as an opinion. You may be wrong.
- Criticize behaviour that could be changed and try to say what you might do differently: one or two changes at a time only.

Receiving feedback (from yourself or others) can of course be threatening and demoralizing, even when the feedback is given skilfully. The following strategies may help:

- Try to see the feedback as potentially useful.
- Separate what is said from your reaction to it (this can be very difficult!).
- Consider asking for clarification, examples, details, but in a spirit of open-minded enquiry rather than defensively or accusingly.
- Notice if you have a tendency to dismiss *positive* feedback.

Table 5.1 includes the skills reviewed in the next three sections (plus other aspects of skilful interviewing) in the form of a checklist for analysing an interview. You may find it most helpful when used with both the guidelines on feedback and those on giving and receiving compliments and criticism from the section on assertiveness. Ideally, you will use it when reviewing a recording of an interview by you, but this may not be practical. Similarly, it is usually better to have feedback from others as well as yourself, especially and not surprisingly, expert interviewers.

**Table 5.1** Checklist for analysing your interviews

---

*Preparation*

*Did I:*

Plan the interview? (e.g. decide about aim(s), structure, look up
    procedures, legislation)
Prepare the seating, etc.?
Clear my mind?

---

*Did I:*

Welcome my interviewee?
If a first meeting, introduce myself?
If necessary, attempt to put my interviewee at ease?
Negotiate a contract and if necessary state boundaries?
Use immediacy, etc. if appropriate?
Set a collaborative tone?

---

*Did I:*

Attend (in the sense of *show* I was listening)?
Help my interviewee talk both freely and to the point?
Follow up leads?
Miss any leads?
Check my understanding?
Help my interviewee to focus?
End skilfully?

---

*Did I communicate:*

Respect?
Empathy?
Genuineness?

---

*Overall:*

What state is my interviewee in now compared with at the beginning?
What about my style, e.g. warm, abrasive, obscure, formal?
How well did my style match this interviewee's?
Did I overuse any skills and neglect others?
What about pace?
Mannerisms?
Posture?
What state am I in? Am I stressed? If so, what can I do about it?
What of value did this interview achieve?
Are there any changes (one or two at a time) in my approach to try
    next time?

Note that the checklist is a mixture of intentions and ways of trying to succeed in them. Your response to the checklist might combine evaluations – 'Yes, I did welcome my interviewee well' – and comments on behaviour/skills – 'I used my interviewee's name, I smiled (rather than beamed). I reflected the word 'better' in her first sentence well, but forgot to agree to a time in the 'contract' ...' Then, in your next interview, try to improve *one or two* aspects of your skills.

## Skills for listening and gathering information

### Preparation

Preparing for an interview can include thinking about the following aspects: the time available; what you hope to achieve; whether your aims conflict with those of others, for example, the service user's or an organization's; a broad structure for the interview; and what information, such as details of agencies or policies, it might be useful to have available.

A straightforward structure would be 'Introduce myself. Negotiate purpose of interview. Find out about X. Find out about Y. See if we agree on action.' A more specific structure would add a checklist of aims and topics, and perhaps an opening question for each topic. The aims could include gathering information (for one or more specific purposes), giving information, helping someone to make a decision or to behave differently.

There is also a 'public relations' element in many interviews. The term is perhaps unfortunate, but how social workers are seen by service users matters because it can affect whether they come to see you or a colleague in the first place, how much they trust you at the beginning, and whether they return or drop out.

Clearing your mind of distractions is another aspect of preparation, aiming for what Michael Argyle called an 'atmosphere of timeless calm'. This is usually an ideal to aim for more than a reality. Relaxation exercises are one possibility for approaching nearer to it, for example the breathing technique described in Chapter 4. Further aspects of preparation are (again, ideally) having a quiet room with no interruptions, and knowing that your interviewee has waited, if at all, in pleasant surroundings.

### Negotiating a 'contract'

The advantages of negotiating a contract are numerous. The interviewer is likely to become less mysterious and threatening. The ground is cleared and a purposeful, collaborative tone is set. If agreement is genuine, both people are more likely to take part wholeheartedly. If you do not reach agreement, at least some time is saved.

In outline the basic skill or rather set of skills is straightforward:

1. Say what you would like to achieve and how etc. and/or ask the other person to say what they would like to achieve and how.
2. Listen.
3. Reach agreement if possible. You or the interviewee may modify your perceptions or intentions in the light of the other person's intentions. The contract can be re-negotiated or clarified at any point in the interview.
4. Check the contract from time to time (either to yourself or with your interviewee) and be ready to renegotiate.

Done well, preparation and negotiating a contract will probably increase the interviewee's trust in you. Methods of developing trust and mutual respect vary widely and include revealing something personal, 'flexing' as in the later section of this chapter on personality and communication styles, and two skills called immediacy and using interviewee feedback.

### Immediacy

One form of immediacy is talking about your experience of what is happening at that very moment between you and your interviewee, and encouraging them to talk about their experience. It is 'direct, mutual talk', and you are both involved; the focus is on both of you and the relationship between you. For example, 'I feel stuck, as if we're going round in circles. What do you think?', or 'I see us as playing something of a game. I think that I'm suggesting solutions, which may be much too soon, and each time I do you point out why it won't work' (Bayne et al., 2008; Egan, 2010).

A variation of Immediacy, which is at the same time a particularly direct way of expressing respect, is to routinely discuss how things are going by asking your interviewee what they see as useful about the interview and especially what could be improved, as discussed in the next section.

## Collecting and using interviewee feedback

In research on counselling, routinely asking clients for feedback has been shown to be clearly related to positive outcomes, especially if the counsellor listens and, where appropriate, changes their approach accordingly (Duncan et al., 2010; Lambert and Shimokawa, 2011). Duncan et al. are very positive about the implications: 'Using formal client feedback to inform, guide and evaluate treatment is the strongest recommendation coming from this volume' (2010, p. 424). This effect seems likely to be true for helping relationships generally. Be especially alert to interviewees' negative feelings about any aspect of you, the interview or your organization and try to respond non-defensively to them.

A straightforward way to ask interviewees for their feedback, ideas, reactions and reflections is to use a brief questionnaire. For example:

Your views are very important in helping monitor and improve what we do together. Please return this questionnaire in the SAE. Your answers will be treated as strictly confidential.

1. What do you think of the room we used?

   *Very poor    poor    ok    good    very good*

2. Please comment on ... (titles of any written information provided).

3. How helpful did you find your social worker?

   *Very poor    poor    ok    good    very good*

4. Is there anything your social worker could have done differently that would have been helpful to you?

The following skills are listening skills. Like the skills already discussed, they show respect and make gathering good information more likely. They are not straightforward or easy as the research in the next box illustrates.

> ## Box 5.2 Some studies of interviewers and interviewer training
>
> A classic early study of how well senior medical students gathered information from patients found numerous deficiencies, including failure to pick up cues and asking leading questions: for example, 74 per cent of the medical students were rated as poor or very poor at picking up verbal leads and 24 per cent failed to discover their patient's main problems (Maguire and Rutter, 1976). 'Patients were often forced to repeat key phrases such as 'I was feeling very low' as many as ten times in order to try to get the students to acknowledge their mood disturbance' (p. 537). Similarly, in a study of 141 interviews by benefit fraud investigators, Walsh and Bull (2010) concluded that 'Shortcomings were particularly found in terms of rapport development, summarizing, flexibility and how investigators brought interviews to closure' (p. 99).
>
> On a more positive note, the training programme devised by Peter Maguire and his colleagues was effective: for example, the trained medical students obtained nearly three times as many relevant items of information (Rutter and Maguire, 1976). Training in the PEACE model described at the beginning of this chapter has also been quite effective (Walsh and Bull, 2010).

## Attending

Attending is partly a fairly straightforward nonverbal behaviour: looking at the other person but not staring; being fairly relaxed; nodding slowly; smiling (appropriately); not fidgeting. And it is partly internal: avoiding distractions and concentrating (cf. the relaxation exercise in Chapter 4). As well as listening, the interviewer can consider 'How is the relationship between us?', 'What is she or he not saying?', 'What about their nonverbal behaviour?', 'What about mine?', 'Where is the interview going at the moment?', 'Is this relevant to the aims?', 'Time to summarize?' and 'Support or challenge?'

## Asking questions

In interviewer training a distinction is often made between open and closed questions. Open questions invite the interviewee to talk at greater length if she or he wants to, for example, 'Tell me about

X', 'What's happened?', 'Mmmm …', and perhaps less obviously: 'In what way?' and 'Can you say how?' However, interviewees sometimes respond too briefly for your aims to be met.

Closed questions are easy to answer too briefly. A more serious problem with them, or rather with more than one or two in a row, is that they soon sound like an interrogation, with the interviewee more likely to leave information out because 'I wasn't asked'. In addition, by asking a series of closed questions (and to a lesser extent open questions) the interviewer is saying in effect, 'I know what is important and relevant. I will ask the questions. I will come up with a solution', which is obviously not a collaborative tone.

Similarly, 'Why' questions are relatively open but may lead to your interviewee feeling attacked, or making up an answer to please you. (Like all 'rules' of interviewing this is only generally true.) Consider the difference between 'Why are you scared of seeing a doctor?' and 'Can you say what scares you about seeing a doctor?'

Many other forms of question have been suggested, for example, leading questions like 'I suppose you're sorry now?', which are both closed and suggest the 'right' answer, and several questions at once, which is rarely if ever a good approach. Usually, either the first or last question is answered and the rest ignored.

General principles for interviewers are to:

- ask few questions
- prepare opening questions carefully
- have a balance between questions that are likely to be easy for your interviewee to answer and those that are probably sensitive
- let what the interviewee says influence strongly any follow-up questions
- use the skill of paraphrasing more – much more – than asking questions.

## Paraphrasing

All the skills outlined so far can have strong effects. This is particularly true of paraphrasing (sometimes called 'basic empathy', restating, reflecting or active listening). It is the single most powerful communication skill in most professional circumstances because it is the main way in which empathy is communicated and because it clears up more miscommunications than any other skill. It is described here in detail. The idea is to *gradually* try any aspects that are new and appealing.

A paraphrase is an attempt to restate, in a fresh way, the main part of what someone has said without adding any of your own ideas, feelings, interpretations, etc. Thus, it is not an attempt to guess what your interviewee is feeling, or even less to show how insightful or intuitive you are! That is a misuse of the skill and not empathic.

In skilful paraphrases, the tone is tentative – slightly questioning without being a question – and your aim, in Laura Rice's phrase, is 'to unfold rather than package experience' (Rice, 1974, p. 305). The most basic form of paraphrase is 'You feel ... [emotion] because ...' You therefore restate your understanding so far of your interviewee's emotions and his or her view of the causes of them, for example: 'You feel angry and frustrated about the council's treatment of you?' It is thus far more than saying 'Yes, I see what you mean', or 'I understand how you feel' (which may mean 'I know how I feel in that situation').

A key aspect of good paraphrasing is being both in close emotional contact with the other person and also clearly separate – neither over-identifying (sometimes called 'fusing') nor being coolly distant. Davenport and Pipes (1990) suggested the analogy of swimming close to a deep powerful whirlpool: 'the challenge is to be close enough to the emotional energy to understand what the client must be experiencing without getting swept down into the action oneself' (p. 139). Drowning with the other person is not helpful, nor is viewing from too far away. When you use a paraphrase of emotions, your intention is to help the other person clarify their feelings because of a) the destructive power of feelings or emotions that are not clear or resolved, and conversely, b) the positive energy that can result.

A key practical question is 'How often should I paraphrase?' The answer is that it depends, but Carl Rogers (for example, 1987) believed in frequent checks, and Eugene Gendlin (1981, p. 19) suggested an *average* of every five or ten sentences. Gendlin's suggestion can be treated too literally! It is a guideline, not a rule, and its merit lies in being concrete about the term 'frequent'. Gendlin made another specific suggestion about frequency: 'Don't let the person say more than you can take in and say back. Interrupt, say back, and let the person go on' (p. 20).

If you paraphrase well, the other person is more likely to either say more, and go further 'inside' (may become more focused and intent) or sit silently, relieved that they've been understood and accepted. If you paraphrase less well, the other person is more likely to try to paraphrase what you've said, or become tense, confused or annoyed ('I've just said that'), or agree in a desultory way.

Three subtle aspects of paraphrasing well are that if you've understood (or think you've understood) only part of what the other person has said, paraphrase that part, and add that you don't understand the rest; pause before you paraphrase or during a paraphrase, and trust yourself to find words which are good enough or better; and try including a *little* of their emotion or emotions in the way you say the paraphrase.

Generally the most difficult aspects of this skill are:

- judging when to paraphrase and when not to (and particularly to avoid sounding like a parrot);
- paraphrasing several times in a row, and thus keeping the focus on trying to help your interviewee clarify;
- paraphrasing emotions (paraphrasing ideas, thoughts and facts is generally easier).

Being accurate about depth or intensity of emotion is particularly difficult but vital. The following steps may help in developing this aspect of paraphrasing. First, you observe that one or more emotions has been expressed or clearly implied. Second, you decide this is an emotion that matters. Third, you choose an apt word. Fourth, you say it in such a way that the other person can readily check how accurate it is and refine and clarify e.g. 'furious and scared' rather than 'frustrated', or vice versa.

Four broad categories of emotion can be used as a first approximation and then refined (Yalom, 1989; Bayne et al., 2008). They are Sad, Mad, Bad and Glad. Although easy to remember in this form, two of the categories are open to misinterpretation, so Sad, Angry, Afraid and Happy are better alternative terms. Each of them can be refined: for example, Angry could mean furious, fed-up or frustrated. In addition, emotions are quite often mixed, with, say, jealousy being both bitter (a variation of Angry) and upset (Sad), or are about other emotions, for example, being afraid of anger.

Gendlin (1981) suggested that *gradually* getting closer to your interviewee's meaning and emotions is a realistic expectation – so expect to be *wrong* at first. ('Accuracy' is defined at this stage by the other person: it is whether the paraphrase feels right to him or her that matters.) Gendlin's emphasis here may well also contribute to a genuinely collaborative tone: you are both gradually working together towards clarity about your interviewee's thoughts and feelings rather than you being an authority figure or a therapeutic wizard.

A scale for giving feedback on paraphrasing of emotions is:

1. Communicated no awareness of even the most obvious emotions.
2. Slightly accurate about explicit emotions.
3. Often accurate about explicit emotions.
4. As level 3, plus slight accuracy about underlying, veiled emotions.
5. As 3, plus often accurate about underlying emotions.
6. Complete accuracy.

Paraphrasing at level 2 on this scale would probably be helpful to most interviewees, at least through the **attempt** to understand and listen without judging. Level 3 is reasonably empathic. Level 4 would be more helpful and level 5 a very high level of skill and an ideal to aim for. Level 6 is the aim of some interviewers, but is not realistic.

It can be helpful in developing the skill of paraphrasing to contrast it with other kinds of response. For example, suppose someone says 'I feel so hopeless. My children don't listen. I've no money. My wife is hardly here and when she is she just sits or we argue. We don't go anywhere. I used to like going out with her.'

### Exercise

You may like to pause here and imagine (a) a range of responses to this person and (b) how you might respond.

The responses listed below are examples of non-paraphrasing:

1. To move quickly on to another subject.
2. To say 'Nonsense', or 'You don't really mean that.'
3. To offer advice: 'If I were you ...' or 'What you could do is ...'
4. To sympathize: 'I know just how you feel ...', or 'I feel hopeless sometimes too ...', or 'Lots of people feel like that ...'
5. To offer practical help.
6. To blame someone or something.
7. To diagnose: 'When do you feel this way?' or 'How long have you been married?' or 'Your problem is ...'

An example of a paraphrase is: 'You feel despairing, and deeply sad about the way your life has changed so much' (in a tentative and serious tone).

What the non-paraphrase responses have in common is that they do not encourage people toexplore their thoughts and emotions further from **their** point of view. On some occasions each of these responses can be helpful but in a fundamentally different way from paraphrasing which says, in effect, 'I want to see your point of view, as a first step'. With enough practice, paraphrasing will seem at least as natural as offering opinions and advice, asking questions, or other responses. It is also natural in the sense that some people paraphrase without formal training.

### Exercise

You may like to think of a similar range of responses – non-paraphrases and paraphrases – to someone saying: 'The baby cried all night. I came close to hitting him. I want to have a life of my own. I'm so fed-up', or: 'You're a lot of pompous do-gooders. I despise you. You're no use to anyone except your own kind. I don't know how you can live with yourselves, why don't you do a proper job?'

## Reflecting

There are no generally agreed terms or definitions for the skills in the interviewing literature. A useful definition of reflecting is that it's to say back a word or phrase that your interviewee has used, for example, 'Hopeless?' The skill lies in choosing the word or phrase, in the timing and how you speak, and in using it only occasionally. Used well, it is obviously economical and can be very effective. Used often, you sound like a parrot.

A variation is the delayed reflection, when you remember a phrase or word the person used earlier, and tie it in with something they have just said, but again relatively gently and tentatively rather than as an interrogation.

## Silence

Interviewers are sometimes afraid of silence and rush to fill the gap. Generally it is more skilful to wait, and try to assess (silently) why your interviewee has stopped talking. Reasons for an interviewee's silence include:

- because there is nothing more they wish to say about a particular topic;
- to organize thoughts/look for the right word;
- to remember something;
- because they are feeling angry, defensive, confused, etc.

The kind of silence (productive, peaceful, rejecting and so on) suggests which skill to employ: silence, a paraphrase or reflection, an open question, a summary or immediacy. The main skill is distinguishing between working silences, natural breaks, and hostile, bored and stuck silences. If your interviewee seems deep in thought – working on clarifying a thought or feeling – then a silence is very skilful and likely to be helpful. If it's a natural break, a lull, again silence is skilful. For the other kinds of silence, it is probably best to say something like 'I'm not sure what's going on here ...' or 'I notice you're very quiet'.

## Summarizing

Summarizing can help your interviewee (and you) clarify what they mean, feel and think. It may also increase their sense of control and hope. Summaries, like paraphrases and reflections, need to be expressed tentatively and followed by a pause. The implicit question is: 'How accurate is this?' and if the relationship is good enough, your interviewee will probably tell you. When the summary is or becomes sufficiently accurate, the implicit question is: 'Where next?', which may be further general exploration, the end of your interview or a focus on one problem or aspect of a problem.

Three other skills for 'moving interviews forward' can be very useful when your interviewee has several problems or a problem with several elements. More precisely, they each offer a way of 'moving forward' if your interviewee wishes to.

The skills, adapted from Gilmore (1973), are called:

- Choice point
- Figure ground
- Contrast.

*Choice point* is a summary plus an explicit question along the lines of: 'Is there one of these you'd like to talk about first?'

*Figure ground* is when *you* suggest what to focus on first: 'Perhaps your main worry is ...?' Sometimes it's best to focus on your interviewee's main worry, other times on something more straightforward. Either way you offer your interviewee the choice.

A *contrast* is a summary followed by a hypothetical question. It can work very well: your interviewee becomes clearer and more energized. On the other hand, it can look like and be a premature and wrong solution and your interviewee can feel irritated by your superficial approach or demoralized. Much depends on the relationship between you, on your timing and your manner.

The following example illustrates these skills. Ola's partner has left him and their two children, aged 5 and 8. He's upset and frightened of the responsibility. His mother, who lives 100 miles away, has invited them all to stay with her, but Ola isn't sure. The children want to stay at home, near their school and friends. He hopes his partner will come back. He's also very worried about money.

A *summary* would be:

> Ola, you're very worried about what's best for your children and scared about what happens if your partner doesn't come back, but hoping she will. If she doesn't, money will be increasingly tight.

A *choice point:*

> Summary plus: Of all the things you've talked about – your relationship with your partner, maybe staying with your mother, looking after the children, money – which do you think we should look at first?

A *figure ground:*

> Summary plus: Perhaps the first thing for us to talk about is whether to stay with your mother or not?

A *contrast:*

> Summary plus: I wonder if it would be helpful for you to imagine what it would be like for your children at your mother's?

## Interpreting nonverbal communication

Useful information can be observed and conveyed nonverbally, especially as nonverbal communication (NVC) tends to operate outside or on the fringe of consciousness and is therefore more difficult to fake than words. It is the likely basis of many first impressions: 'There was something about her'; 'It was just a feeling'. It gives human communication great versatility but makes misinterpretations more likely. The influence of culture on NVCs adds considerably to this potential for error (Collett, 2004; Lago, 2006).

'Channels' of NVC can be categorized as follows:

1. The way we use space, including touch (technically known as proxemics).
2. Movements, gestures and expressions (kinesics).
3. More static aspects of the body and surroundings.
4. Aspects of speech other than words: tone, loudness, pauses, etc. (paralanguage).

### Use of space

How close people like to be physically to others varies; it matters who the other person is and what the situation is, but there are also consistent general preferences, and class, sex and race differences in these, for example, people from South America, Arab countries and Pakistan tend to stand closest, those from the UK, USA and Sweden farthest. This is not a trivial matter: it can lead to misunderstandings, with a kind of dance taking place, the pursuing person interpreting the other's behaviour as cold and unfriendly, the pursued person finding the other too 'pushy'.

Seating arrangements may also matter. It has been suggested, for example, that chairs placed across the corner of a desk are generally preferred to chairs across a desk or without a desk. Touch is a closely related NVC; again some marked cultural differences have been found. A pat on the arm may be a powerful way of making contact – especially if you do it 'naturally' – or it may be strongly resented as patronizing or intrusive. It may also be very unhelpful, for example, touching someone to stop them crying because *you* feel uncomfortable.

### Gestures etc.

There are many intriguing ideas about gestures (broadly defined); for example, are flared nostrils and tight lips signs of tension and fear? One of the most studied NVCs in this category is 'eye contact', which is used in part to help regulate conversations. In the UK the usual pattern is that one person talks and sometimes looks directly at the person who is listening, while the person listening looks at the person talking most of the time, until it is their turn to speak. Occasionally, two people's ways of indicating 'I want to speak' or 'It's your turn' take time to mesh or fail completely. Eye contact may also indicate interest or hostility, depending on cultural and other factors, and in some cultures *lack* of eye contact indicates interest.

### Static aspects of NVC
These include clothing, physique, even offices and buildings: what do your surroundings 'say' to your service users?

### Paralanguage
Novelists may convey paralanguage verbally, for example, ' "You're really amazing", she said, irritably.' This channel of NVC includes voice tone and volume, pauses, etc.

---

### Exercise

Notice such judgements in yourself and treat them as first impressions, that is, look for further evidence, for and against your judgement, as discussed earlier in this chapter.

---

The main problem in interpreting NVC accurately is its ambiguity. However, *changes* in a person's characteristic NVC are more likely to be significant, for example, their face 'lighting up' when talking about a particular person or topic. For general purposes, Scheflen's (1964) analogy is appropriate: 'a letter of the alphabet does not carry meaning until it is part of a word which is part of a sentence which is part of a discourse and a situation' (p. 324). NVCs are the letters, and sometimes a bit more; interpretations should, therefore, be cautious.

However, other responses can also be made. Consider someone who is swinging her foot (F). You can note F and just bear it in mind or say 'I notice you're swinging your foot' or 'You're angry' (said tentatively but still a strong interpretation) or 'I think F suggests perhaps that you're angry?' (probably more appropriately gentle). Alternatively, and again without interpreting: 'Can you say what F means to you?', or (if you've done appropriate training), 'Try stopping F and putting your foot on the ground. What happens?'

## Giving information

An important part of the skill of giving information is checking or putting aside your assumptions about people's knowledge, their ability to understand or remember the information, or their reaction to it. On the one hand, powerful emotions, selective memory, wishful thinking and information overload can make giving information futile. On the other hand, information can dramatically reduce distress and increase understanding.

Ways of giving complicated information so that it is more likely to be remembered and acted on include: use simple words and short sentences; categorize explicitly ('There are three aspects ...'); be specific; avoid jargon; consider repeating, checking understanding and providing written back-up material (Nichols, 1993). Another strategy is to give your client a list of possible questions about the information to help them clarify what they don't understand or would like to know (if anything). Be ready too to offer 'emotional care', that is, expecting people to feel anxious when threatened, angry when frustrated, sad about loss, and so on, and if they do, calmly and perhaps empathically accepting it (Nichols, 1993).

## Some communication difficulties and strategies

In this section some difficulties facing social workers and other helping professionals when trying to communicate are briefly reviewed. Much depends on personality and circumstances and there are different ways of responding well to someone who is angry, for example. Many of the strategies use skills reviewed in the rest of this chapter. 'General purpose' strategies are to paraphrase, to summarize, to use immediacy and to renegotiate the contract. Some other sources of advice and suggestions are Feltham and Dryden (2006), Bayne et al. (2008), Yalom (1989, 2001), Ross (2011) and Feltham and Horton (2012).

In alphabetical order, the difficulties and strategies are:

### Aggressive

Take preventive measures. If they haven't worked, try using the person's name. Paraphrase. Overall, show you are trying calmly to understand and want to help. Use assertive skills (see next section), for example, 'I'd like you to stop shouting' or 'I'd like to discuss the problem with you'. An aggressive person may be frightened. In any case threats are not likely to be useful: telling someone off sometimes heightens aggression. See also Flooded, below. Most of the contributors to Jones (2004) have experience of HMP Grendon, which specializes in people convicted of violent crimes. Iain Bourne's (2013) book is about training to face danger in the helping professions. He is a paramedic tutor in the London Ambulance Service.

## Bad news, giving

### Exercise

Social workers often give bad news to service users. What strengths do you bring to this skill? What do you find most difficult about it? What are the effects on you and what do you do to cope with them?

Several of the skills reviewed in this chapter and in Chapter 4 are sometimes relevant to giving bad news, particularly parts of 'giving information' (cold though that sounds), listening and the suggestions in this section on Crisis, Crying and Flooding.

### Beginning an interview

See skill of 'negotiating a contract'. Give interviewee a chance to compose themselves, to get used to the room and you.

### Complaints

Complaints can be seen as an opportunity to develop trust and goodwill, and from a PR point of view are very useful too. The person complaining may be playing a manipulative 'game' but is more likely to be upset and struggling. Assertive skills, listening and gathering information, and giving information (for example, about your organization's complaints procedure) may all be relevant. If the complaint is against you, and is going to be pursued, inform your manager/professional body/union/insurers quickly and make sure relevant notes etc. are up to date and in good order.

### Crisis

'Crisis' means an immediately threatening and highly stressful situation which requires **action**. The person in crisis is likely to feel overwhelmed, out of control, angry, fearful and despairing. The goal is to restore, as far as possible, their normal level of functioning (Parry, 1990; Egan, 2010).

## Crying

See Upset, Flooded.

## Emotionally blocked

Indications of emotional blocking – when someone is unaware of an emotion – are abrupt changes of topic and tension. Kennedy-Moore and Watson (1999) recommend saying very gently that the other person seems tense and wondering if it indicates anything (but not pushing for emotional expression) or – if you are trained to do so – using exaggeration or literal description (Bayne et al., 2008). However, interviewers and counsellors sometimes don't notice emotions which are being clearly expressed. They then use such techniques unnecessarily and perhaps unhelpfully.

## Ending an interview

Say 'In the last few minutes I'd like to ...' or, nearer to the end, 'Is there anything else you want to say to me?' Try a summary, or ask your interviewee or client to summarize. It is a good idea if possible to have some time to spare between interviews, both to prepare for the next one and because some people leave important information until near the end. A contract helps. Try to end positively (not the same as false optimism): often there will have been some progress in understanding, or some agreed action. If verbal signals fail, try nonverbal: sit more upright and, as a last resort, stand up.

## Flooded

'Flooded expression', for example, when someone cries and cries, or is taken over by any emotion for a long time, seems to be unhelpful (Kennedy-Moore and Watson, 1999). This is because it makes thinking and new perspectives impossible. In the model of counselling discussed in Appendix I, p. 210, emotions are clarified with the right words for the person feeling them (stage 1) and they can then – with sensitive timing as defined by your interviewee – be interpreted (stage

2), for example, 'I've felt guilty and ashamed about this for years – but really it's not my fault'. Flooding gets in the way of this natural process of 'getting things in perspective'.

Irvin Yalom takes the same approach to emotions (in psychotherapy, and by implication to some social work interviews). He wrote that: 'you encourage acts of emotional expression but you always follow with reflection upon the emotions expressed' (2001, p. 164). Earlier in the same book, he expressed this idea more formally: 'effective therapy consists of an alternating sequence: *evocation and experiencing* of affect followed by *analysis and integration* of affect. How long one waits until one initiates an analysis of the affective event is a function of clinical experience' (2001, p.71, italics in original). Techniques to suggest for possible control of flooding include deep breathing and distraction. When your interviewee or client is calmer, you might then discuss with them ways they can avoid or control flooding again, and other ways they might express their feelings.

## Keeping records

General issues which need to be considered include why records are kept and who has access to them (Bond, 2009). Writing a report – for yourself or others – can help clarify thinking. The stages of the counselling model provide an obvious structure. Part of the value of a structure is that it suggests relevant aspects of people or problems which may have been missed or insufficiently emphasized in the interview. It also encourages questions about the process of interviewing, for example, 'What stage are we at?', 'Where is it going?', 'What skills did I use?' and 'What other skills might I have used?' This possibility is more systematically illustrated in the two checklists (Table 5.1 and Appendix II). See also Note-taking below.

## Note-taking

Note-taking need not interfere with the pace and flow of the interview, and can become more important than listening. Against this, summaries help in remembering the relevant points, and notes can be made immediately after the interview. Compromises are possible, for example, not taking notes when your interviewee is talking personally. Obviously, note-taking should not intrude. Interviewees can take notes too, or write out/draw aspects of a problem. See also Keeping records.

## Nervous

Signs of being nervous – tension, restlessness, etc. – may indicate something else. Try to find out your interviewee's needs. Answer questions. Ask easy questions first (a good general principle too). Try to keep relaxed yourself, for example, by breathing slowly and deeply.

## Referral

Referral is often ethically responsible. However, while it can be a relief, it can also be disruptive and disappointing, especially for people who have been passed from one agency to another. Circumstances in which referral should be seriously considered include when you don't have the relevant experience or training, when there is a clash of personalities that persists and when you think another practitioner might offer a useful different view, for example: 'I wonder if it would be helpful for you to see X. She's ...'

## Questions which may be embarrassing

Introduce them: 'Some people find this an embarrassing question ...'

## Quiet, too

There are many reasons for being quiet. Resist the temptation to talk too much yourself. Try immediacy. Paper and pencil techniques can be more gentle. You can ask 'Would it help to sit and think about this for a while?'

## Talkative, too

Try summaries and a higher proportion of closed questions. Or remind your interviewee of the contract, particularly of time. Interrupt. Say 'Can we return to ...?'

## Upset

Try to keep calm yourself, though your being tearful or crying is *not* necessarily unprofessional. At the same time, it is disrespectful to expect everyone to be emotionally expressive (Kennedy-Moore and Watson, 1999), and sometimes avoiding emotion may be the best way of coping – at least in the short term.

## Assertive skills

Assertiveness can be defined in general terms as 'expressing and acting on your rights as a person, while respecting the rights of other people'. Rakos (1991) is the major review of research on assertiveness and since then there have been few studies (see Ames, 2008 and Box 5.3 for some exceptions) but widespread use of its ideas and skills.

---

### Box 5.3 Some recent research on assertiveness

Ames (2008) reviewed research suggesting that many members and leaders of organizations are seen as lacking the 'right touch' – as too assertive or not assertive enough. The research also suggests that being assertive – a balancing act between pushing hard enough for tasks to be achieved but not so hard that relationships are undermined – is an important factor in being effective, and difficult to do well. Moreover, it shows that many people lack awareness of how assertive or not they are. 'Multi-rater feedback systems' are one implication suggested, which echoes the emphasis on collecting client feedback discussed early in this chapter.

---

Assertive skills can improve conversations, meetings, interviews and counselling sessions dramatically. At one level they can show respect to service users and others. At another level, they can contribute to gathering better quality information and making fair and helpful decisions more often.However, two cautious notes are important. First, like interviewing, assertiveness is not just about techniques; it thrives on accurate self-awareness and adequate self-esteem. If you know what you like and dislike, for example, it is easier to say no assertively. Second, assertiveness theory typically emphasizes being direct, but some cultural groups value indirectness. 'Bicultural competence' (Rakos, 1991) is a useful notion here. It underlines the principle that using assertiveness skills in a prescriptive way is too simple, and it also respects cultural differences. For example, looking someone straight in the eye is impolite or worse in some cultures, but part of being assertive in others.

Bicultural competence treats assertiveness as a widening of the range of options: you can practise saying no, for example, both while looking someone in the eye and while looking away. Assertiveness, while a useful technique for coping with stress, also interacts with it. If someone is stressed, it is likely to impede their assertiveness (and their effectiveness generally of course).

There is another way in which assertiveness theory and skills can neglect the social and multicultural context. For example, suppose you are being harassed at work and you want to be more assertive by making a clear request to the person harassing you such as: 'You say that touching me on the shoulder doesn't mean anything, but it matters to me. I would like you to stop doing it'. You can be very pleased with the results of making this request, which is fine as far as it goes. However, it leaves the norms of the organization intact. One response to this issue is to say that, after considering costs and benefits, you have the option to take it further. Another response is that all techniques and theories have their own field of application and limits, that assertiveness operates at the individual level and other methods are more useful at the level of organizations or cultures. However, actually implementing other methods at these levels may call for assertive skills.

Assertiveness theory and skills can be applied with varying degrees of formality, ranging from a thorough, systematic analysis of situations and 'skills deficits' in a standard behavioural approach to a discussion of possible ways of feeling and behaving differently in a more 'humanistic' one. Rakos (1991) calls the more formal approach assertiveness *therapy* and the less formal approach assertiveness *training*. In either therapy or training, role play with coaching can be helpful, and some consideration of likely costs and benefits is very desirable before trying out the new skill in a real situation. 'Coaching' may sound as if there is one right way to be assertive. On the contrary, good coaching values individuality, authenticity and spontaneity, not a mechanical, polished but lifeless performance.

In the rest of this section, the basic elements of several assertive skills and their refinements are outlined and the key question of how to decide when to be assertive is considered, drawing mainly on Anne Dickson's approach. Dickson (1982, 2012) also discusses arguments for and against using each skill; for example, we some-times don't ask for what we'd like (make a request) because we:

- put others first: 'It's not that important.'
- are afraid of rejection

- don't want to impose. One or both of you might be embarrassed.
- expect the other person, especially if they care for you, to know without being asked: 'I shouldn't have to ask.'
- don't want to feel obliged to the other person.

On the other hand, there are consequences of not making requests:

- Frustration. Small irritations may build up until you 'explode' or you may express your frustration indirectly, for example, by nagging, sulking, complaining to others, being a 'martyr'.
- You may lose touch with what you do want.

The general choice everyone makes is whether the results of not asking for something are worse or better for them than those of asking and being refused. Being clear about your rights and the right of other people can be very helpful in making such choices. Table 5.2 lists a fairly representative set of assertive rights in its left-hand column. The format, taken from Bond (1986), makes explicit the 'respect for others' element in being assertive.

**Table 5.2** Assertive rights

| | | | |
|---|---|---|---|
| 1. | I have the right to be treated with respect. | *and* | Others have the right to be treated with respect. |
| 2. | I have the right to express my thoughts, opinions and values. | *and* | Others have the right to express their thoughts, opinions and values. |
| 3. | I have the right to express my feelings. | *and* | Others have the right to express their feelings. |
| 4. | I have the right to say 'No' without feeling guilty. | *and* | Others have the right to say 'No' without feeling guilty. |
| 5. | I have the right to be successful. | *and* | Others have the right to be successful. |
| 6. | I have the right to make mistakes. | *and* | Others have the right to make mistakes |
| 7. | I have the right to change my mind. | *and* | Others have the right to change their minds. |
| 8. | I have the right to say that I don't understand. | *and* | Others have the right to saythat they don't understand. |

| 9. | I have the right to ask for what I want. | *and* | Others have the right to ask for what they want. |
|---|---|---|---|
| 10. | I have the right to decide for myself whether or not I am responsible for another person's problem. | *and* | Others have the right to decide for themselves whether or not they are responsible for another person's problem. |
| 11. | I have the right to choose not to assert myself. | *and* | Others have the right to choose not to assert themselves. |

### Exercise

Consider the right-hand column of Table 5.2 first. How easy or difficult do you find each to accept as a right for other people? Then compare your reactions to the left-hand column. Are there any rights in either column that you want to cross out? Any to add? It can be helpful, when you are upset or angry in a way that seems out of proportion, to take each right in turn and see if you are accepting it or not.

## Making requests

The skill of making requests contrasts with paraphrasing: it is putting yourself to the fore rather than trying to see from another's point of view. In everyday life the two skills are complementary. Rogers (1975), at the level of personal qualities, argued for more empathy in relationships generally, but in everyday life for genuineness above all: stating wants, intentions and feelings (when 'appropriate' and in an assertive way).

The basic elements of making a request are:

1. Choose person and request carefully. Consider the possible costs and benefits, your rights and the other person's rights.
2. Write out the request; make sure it is brief, specific (concrete), and does not sabotage itself by implying either that they must agree or that you expect them to say no. Try to assume that you don't know their answer. The request can be either for someone to do something, for example, go for a drink, or to stop doing something, for example, playing music too loudly

for you. Dickson (2012) gives numerous excellent examples of this and the other assertive skills.

3. Rehearse (real or imaginary), with feedback from yourself and, ideally, from expert observers. Rehearsal and coaching might also take into account possible reactions to a range of replies, setting aside a time for constructive analysis of the outcome, and deciding when and where to make the request. Contingency plans would appeal to some people. Overall, the idea is to use assertiveness theory and methods flexibly and creatively and in a way that suits you.

4. Review the refinements in the next paragraph and consider their relevance to this request.

5. Rehearse again. Observe in particular *how* you ask. Slight adjustments to the way you stand, hold your shoulders, or expression, will make you look, and probably feel, more assertive.

6. Select time and place to actually make the request.

7. Try it.

8. Consider the outcome, using the principles of giving feedback outlined in this chapter (p. 111).

### Refinements

When asking someone to stop doing something, or to do something they do not want to do, *calm repetition* can be a key element. The request tends to become easier to say as you repeat it, and to be said more definitely, as long as it is what you genuinely want. Repetition is also a way (perhaps combined with paraphrasing) of responding to protests and irrelevant logic. Essentially, the idea is to say 'Yes I realize you are disappointed, but I would like … ', and so on. Second, you may like to suggest consequences (perhaps best held in reserve), or to combine your request with a compliment, itself an assertive skill and therefore with risks and benefits to be taken into account.

The other main skills, in brief, are:

### Saying no

Basic:

- brief;
- speak clearly and confidently;
- (watch for inappropriate smiles and apologies).

Refinements:

- notice your first reaction (to take it into account, not necessarily to act on it);
- if unsure, ask for time and/or further details;
- calm repetition may be useful (cf. Dickson's image of a swaying tree);
- offer an alternative?
- empathy?
- put in context?

## Giving compliments

Basic skill:

- specific (about the effect on you and/or what it is you like).

Refinements:

- not when making a request!

## Receiving compliments

Basic skill:

- thank the person straightforwardly;
- enjoy the compliment (if it pleases you).

Refinements:

- consider basic skill *plus* asking for detail;
- consider basic skill *plus* saying what you think;
- avoid complimenting them back too quickly.

## Giving criticism

Basic skill:

- specific about what it is the other person is doing, and about what you would like them to do that would be different (cf. the skill of making requests);
- specific about effects on you;
- one thing at a time;
- avoid labels like 'selfish' and 'lazy'.

Refinements:

- listen to the other person's reaction (you may have misinterpreted their behaviour, they may have misunderstood your constructive intent);
- specific about the consequences (a) if the other person changes, and/or (b) if they do not;
- put in context.

### Receiving criticism

The main perspective is that, even from someone you have little or no time for, criticism may contain useful information. Also using the skill well breaks a normal pattern of interaction and illustrates the assertive right that making mistakes is normal and human.

Basic skill:

- consider thanking them and agreeing with all or part of the comments;
- consider saying what you will do differently next time (if appropriate), or that you'll think about how to improve whatever was wrong.

Refinements:

If you disagree with all or part of the criticism, consider one or more of:

- thanking them;
- asking for examples or detail;
- saying 'I don't agree';
- paraphrasing.

### Exercise

How assertive do you think you are? Try listing occasions on which you, for example, wanted to say no but didn't, wanted to ask for something but didn't, wanted to compliment someone but didn't and so on. Taking into account the principle that no one is assertive all the time, what are the implications for improving your assertive skills?

## Preference theory, communication problems and strategies

Preference theory (as discussed in Chapter 4) suggests the conflicts which are most likely between people with different preferences (Table 5.3) and some strategies for trying to improve or resolve them (Table 5.4). The tables need qualifying:

1. Conflicts occur between people with the same preferences too.
2. Some conflicts are nothing to do with the preferences.
3. Opposites can be a powerful attraction – the other person is developed in ways we would like to be.

Examples of the main reactions and prejudices against people with different preferences from our own are that Introverts (Is) may feel overwhelmed, hurried, or invaded by Extraverts (Es), and Es may see Is as dull and slow; Sensing types (Ss) may be seen as boring by those with a preference for Intuition (Ns), and Ns as unreal by Ss; Thinking types (Ts) as obsessed with reasons and unsympathetic by Feeling types (Fs), and Fs as lacking any logic and too soft by Ts; Judging types (Js) as pushy and rigid by Perceiving types (Ps), and Ps as aimless and disorganized by Js.

These potential problems follow straightforwardly from the theory. Let's take a more specific example: a social worker who prefers ESFJ and a service user who prefers ISTJ. The social worker sees the service user as distant and impersonal and feels rebuffed and silly. If he applies preference theory, he will first accept that the service user (whether actually having a preference for Thinking or just behaving like it at the time) does not want to be friendly at this time. He therefore changes his own manner accordingly. In a sense, he switches to the other person's 'language'

**Table 5.3** Some communication problems between people with opposite preferences

| Between E and I | Need to talk v need to be alone. |
|---|---|
| Between S and N | Focus on details and realism v on general picture, links and speculation. |
| Between T and F | Being seen as unsympathetic and critical v being seen as illogical and too agreeable. |
| Between J and P | Controlling and planning v flexible and very open to change. |

**Table 5.4** Some strategies for managing and preventing communication problems between people with opposite preferences

| E with I | Allow time for privacy and to reflect. |
|---|---|
| I with E | Explain need for time alone, allow for the other person's need to talk in order to clarify. |
| S with N | Overall picture first, with relevant details later. |
| N with S | Say a particular idea is half-formed and/or include relevant detail. |
| T with F | Include effects on people, begin with points of agreement. |
| F with T | Include reasons and consequences, be brief. |
| J with P | Allow for some flexibility in plans, style of working, etc. and for the other's need not to be controlled. |
| P with J | Allow for some planning and structure and for the other person's need to control and decide. |

(in this case ST, as described in the next paragraph) while being ready to switch again if he thinks it appropriate. He then does not feel so rebuffed, even though people with a preference for Feeling tend to be more sensitive to perceived criticism and to need harmony more than those who prefer Thinking. Rather, he feels empathic and skilful and the service user feels more understood and more respectfully treated.

The four 'languages' suggested by Susan Brock in one approach to communication (see, for example, Allen and Brock, 2000) are ST, SF, NT and NF:

ST – brief and concise, emphasizes facts and logic.
SF – same practical emphasis as ST but warmer, friendlier, more personal.
NF – personal and general, interested in possibilities, with details (perhaps) to be worked out later.
NT – emphasis on reasons, logic and competence, calm and brief.

These four languages affect the content and tone of communications while E and I affect the pace, and JP the tendency to move towards closure (J) or to keep things open (P).

The theory also offers an explanation for strong mutual attraction of opposites, such as where Js are attracted to Ps' easy-going flexibility and Ps to Js' order: each person has what the other (relatively) lacks. They may then – especially if they don't know preference theory – attempt to change each other to be more like themselves. The theory predicts that these attempts will fail.

The best sources of detailed ideas and examples of preference theory applied to communication are Allen and Brock (2000), Tieger and Barron-Tieger (2001), VanSant (2003) and Zeisset (2006).

## Conclusions

You are likely to be already skilled in many aspects of listening, gathering information, giving information and being assertive, but probably with some scope for improvement. The approach taken in this chapter is for you to systematically analyse your current skills and to experiment with changes. Feedback from skilled observers can be particularly useful. Three sections of the chapter discuss possible ways of enriching your skills further. First, strategies for responding to what can be difficult aspects of interviewing, for example, when your interviewee is 'flooded' with emotion. Second, specific ways of taking individual differences in personality and communication style into account. Third, you may sometimes counsel an interviewee more than interview them, either in a 'pure' and explicit way or implicitly and more as a matter of degree. The model of counselling in the appendices is intended to clarify this distinction, with implications for your decisions about boundaries and referral.

### Putting it into practice 5

Some additional exercises on applying the ideas reviewed in this chapter are:

5a. R. D. Laing wrote 'It is not so easy for one person to give another a cup of tea' (1969, p. 106). What's your reaction? What did he mean? What are the implications for communication and interviewing? (Cf. the skill of immediacy, discussed in this chapter in the section on listening skills.)

5b. When you're listening well, what's happening? Is how you listen related to preference theory? What does your analysis suggest you do to improve your interviewing, bearing in mind the principles of small steps and developing your strengths most?

5c. Interview someone you know well about their personality, using preference theory to structure your interview and the skills for listening and gathering information to carry it out. Find someone as different from yourself in personality as you can.

5d. Collect feedback from, say, ten people using a brief form like the one described early in this chapter in the section on feedback. Do any themes emerge? (Beware of being too influenced by minority views.) What changes might be worth trying?

5e. What current limits to your counselling skills does a self-assessment using Appendix II (see p. 212) suggest? When would it be ethical for you to refer an interviewee? (Cf. the brief discussion of referral in the section on communication difficulties and strategies.)

## Further reading

Bayne, R. (2013) *The Counsellor's Guide to Personality: Understanding Preferences, Motives and Life Stories*, Basingstoke, Palgrave Macmillan.

This book, which equally might be addressed to social work practitioners, describes and discusses three leading contemporary theories of personality and shows how they can be used to increase self-awareness, improve relationships and help manage or resolve problems.

Dickson, A. (2012) *A Woman in Your Own Right: Assertiveness and You*, London, Quartet Books.

There is no doubt that this book is for men too! And the 30th anniversary edition is one of the best, and very practical, books on assertiveness. Anne Dickson discusses arguments for and against each assertive skill and each of the skills themselves in detail, with many excellent examples. Working in social work agencies and with service users who might be resistant to your intervention, managing to be assertive (and not inappropriately aggressive or passive) is invaluable. This also applies in management practices.

Ross, J. (2011) *Specialist Communication Skills for Social Workers: Focusing on Service Users' Needs*, Basingstoke, Palgrave Macmillan.

Ross takes respect as a major theme and the book is consequently particularly valuable for ideas about communicating with specific groups of service users, especially children, people who abuse substances such as drugs and alcohol and people with mental health problems.

## CHAPTER 6

# Groupwork skills for social work practice

**CHAPTER OVERVIEW**

In this chapter we explore:

- Definitions of the term 'group' and what understanding this means for understanding social aspects of human behaviour.
- Examples of the classic studies that have contributed to understanding group behaviour.
- The influence groups have upon individual members.
- Theoretical approaches to the development and structure of the group itself (group dynamics).
- Why and how social workers might set up a group.
- The skills necessary for conducting group sessions.

This chapter summarizes and explores key psychological theories of group (and organizational) dynamics (picking up on some of the issues identified in Chapter 3 about relationships within social work settings), developing a guide to groupwork skills which make use of such theory.

Individuals do not develop and negotiate their personalities, relationships and ways of coping with the world in isolation, as you will have already seen after reading Chapters 1and 2. From the moment of birth infants are faced with the need to form relationships with their parents, who will be the means of providing the warmth, comfort and food essential for survival. Shortly afterwards children's experience commonly includes more than one adult, and often other children. Subsequently they will progress to relationships in the nursery, the school and friends near their home, all of which will provide them with a means of establishing patterns of behaviour, gaining an identity and learning a variety of roles.

## Introduction

From the beginning of our lives we are faced with being members of a group, and as we grow older, the number of groups which are important to us and in which we are important, increases. Social workers need to recognize that their service users have a history of belonging to, and being influenced by, a variety of social behaviours. For instance, truanting behaviour in teenagers may be the result of peer group pressure. It may be easier for a child to miss school, and risk the consequences, than go against the other members of their peer group. The social worker must also understand the dynamics (i.e., interactions) in, for example, a family or a children's home, in order to intervene effectively. Further, there are behaviours that take place between members of different groups that are the result of social pressure, and the most common example is prejudice, where a dislike may start without any other rationale than that the other person is a member of a different group. An appreciation of group psychology not only helps with understanding and assessing a service user's situation, but also enables social workers to utilize group forces in a therapeutic way.

### Definition of the 'group'

A group can be defined in a number of ways, which relate to its function, the nature of its membership (why people join and whether membership is voluntary) and its goals and eventual purpose. The classic definition by Cartwright and Zander (1968) still holds good and describes the group as an aggregate of individuals standing in relations to each other. The kinds of relations exemplified will of course depend on or determine the kind of group, whether it is a family, or an audience, a committee, union or crowd. From this description it becomes clear that there are several kinds of group. It is worth noting this before moving on to consider what is important in the field of group dynamics. Groups can be divided into two categories:

*The primary group* is a group in which members come face to face, regardless of any other characteristics. These groups can be natural groups such as the family, or a group of friends, or they can be formal, like a school class, or a therapeutic group. It is the primary group which is central to this chapter.

*Secondary groups* are slightly more difficult to identify, but just as important because even though they do not necessarily come face to face, the potential members have characteristics in common. For instance, they may be single parent families, the parents of children who go to a particular school, or old people isolated in their homes. (See Twelvetrees, 1982/2008, for a discussion of secondary groups in the community.)

## The study of group behaviour

The first attempt at an analysis of group behaviour was made at the end of the last century by Le Bon (1917) whose book *The Crowd* illustrated his observation that individuals in a large group show behaviour that does not constitute the total of their behaviour as individuals. This means that there appears to be some feature of this large group which cannot be traced to individual members. He considered that some sort of 'collective mind' emerges and that in addition, forces of contagion and suggestibility are at work, and the group acts as if it is hypnotized. In the same year McDougall's book *The Group Mind* was published and in *Group Psychology and the Analysis of the Ego* (1922), Freud developed Le Bon's and McDougall's ideas in the context of psychodynamic theory, arguing that the binding force of the group derives from the emotional ties of the members, which are expressions of their libido. In other words the group members' energy is expressed through a very strong emotional connection to each other as with football supporters at a match or fans at a pop concert.

In the USA during the 1930s, social psychologists began to study group dynamics systematically. Kurt Lewin, one of the early researchers, became a very important name in this field. He established the Research Center for Group Dynamics at the Massachusetts Institute of Technology, and the National Training Laboratories in Bethel, Maine. In Britain, psychologists and some psychiatrists became interested in studying groups during the 1940s. The work of Bion, Maine, Jones and others at the Tavistock Institute led to innovations in group psychotherapy, and the study of organizations incorporating psychoanalytic theory. Other social scientists have made important studies of group behaviour, and it is useful here to distinguish briefly between the particular perspectives from which other disciplines have approached this subject. Sociologists have concentrated on studying natural groups such as the family, work groups, military prisons and hospitals, and are concerned with the function and meaning of the social institutions they study. So, for instance, they try to make useful statements about the functions of the family, or the meaning of the family in Western capitalist society. Anthropologists have generally employed the technique of participant observation and looked at the way groups live in particular societies. They are more concerned with how people establish their norms and value systems, and the different cultures that emerge. For instance, they might be able to show the significance of the event of childbirth in a society, and the consequent roles and rituals that emerge.

There are four main perspectives employed by psychologists:

1. They are interested in the way groups influence the behaviour, personality, social development and attitudes of the individuals within them, that is, the effects of the group on the individual member. This is particularly relevant in discussing group influences in vulnerable and disadvantaged groups.
2. They are interested in the characteristics of the groups themselves: how they form, change and develop norms, and how they are structured. This kind of study is the one most frequently referred to as the study of *group dynamics*. Matters of community relations, workplace relations, leadership and team development and multi-agency working may be thought of in this way.
3. Deriving from the study of group dynamics and the effect of group pressure on individuals, studies have emerged relating to the effectiveness of particular groups. These studies have been part of applied psychology, and are particularly relevant to education, training and therapy, although they also have applications to less palatable activities such as running prison camps, and torture.
4. There have also been investigations of intergroup cooperation and conflict, with obvious implications for political activity – alliances, warfare, dealing with terrorist activity, hijackers and sieges, and understanding the nature of prejudice. A range of different analyses of the 2011 summer riots in England have referred to studies of intergroup relations. These studies are also invaluable for understanding relationships in the context of multi-agency working.

## The individual in the group: social influence

Social influence is the phrase used by psychologists to describe the pressure for *similarity* which is active in all societies. This pressure affects and changes behaviour and attitudes in the direction of prevailing patterns in a particular culture or sub-culture. Although outstanding and unusual people are highly esteemed and a certain admiration is usually afforded to originality, on the whole society values those who share its collective culture and adhere to its rules (Cialdini and Goldstein, 2004; Ellemers et al., 2004).

There are three major forms of influence:

*Uniformity,* which is the similarity which rests on an individual's acceptance of the unspoken assumption that being like others is desirable.
*Conformity,* which is the similarity that develops when an individual gives in to social pressure to be like others.
*Obedience,* which is the similarity that rests on compliance with the demands of an authority figure.

Much social influence is at work within social work teams, which are discussed in Chapter 3. And most people are at the mercy of pressures which either cause or exacerbate their difficulties. The influence of the peer group on adolescents, which might cause them to deviate from the rules of wider society, particularly within the gang culture, is a common example of this. Similarly, a father who is out of work, and unable to fulfil the role that his family expect (to be like other fathers, as he sees them – the breadwinner, the authority figure, and so on) might see himself as inadequate, his relationships might deteriorate and his emotional health might reach a critical stage. All this as a result of his sense of what society expects and how he compares himself to his beliefs about other fathers.

Psychologists have investigated which factors are most important in influencing people towards uniformity, conformity and obedience. The significance of *social norms* in all three areas is evident. Social norms represent the expectations of all members of a society or group. They can be about what is acceptable behaviour in particular circumstances, or about attitudes group members may hold, or about what 'qualifications' members are expected to have achieved. In other words they are rules which represent values which group members consider important, and are thus incorporated into the culture of the society or group (Schultz et al., 2007).

Social norms may be internally or externally derived – in other words there may be pressure to behave in a particular way either because you believe that is the right thing to do for reasons that may stretch back to infancy and childhood (see Chaper 2) or because others want you to (external). Internal norms are the ones which are particularly relevant to behaviour during social interaction, and are consequently of most concern to psychologists. External norms are those which members bring to the group from their lives outside its influence. Social psychologists have made many studies of normative behaviour; some of these have taken place in a laboratory setting, and others in day-to-day living. For example, Garfinkel's classic (1967) study showed the importance of social norms for people's expectations about each others' behaviour. He hypothesized that there are many unseen rules which govern our behaviour, which we only discover when they are broken, leading to subsequent punishment. He told his students to test these hidden rules in their homes, by acting as 'paying guests' for a period of fifteen minutes. They were to be polite, respectful, and suitably distant towards their families, and only to speak when spoken to. The next day, the students' reports were filled with accounts of their parents' anxiety, astonishment, embarrassment and anger. They had been accused of selfishness and moodiness, and considering this experiment had only lasted for fifteen minutes, and did not constitute openly hostile behaviour, it is an illustration of just how powerful these norms actually are.

This set of normative expectations might also link to the behaviour of colleagues or service users. Another set of now classical social psychology experiments, carried out by Sherif in the 1960s, concerned the auto-kinetic effect. This is an optical illusion in which a stationary pinpoint of light viewed in an otherwise dark room appears to be moving. Sherif placed a large audience of participants in a darkened room and allowed them to make independent assessments about how far the light had moved. He then brought small groups of people together and asked them to repeat the task. The group's judgements *converged* on a central estimate of motion, and even when Sherif tested them later he found that group consensus persisted. Thus a social norm was established, and endured despite its lack of authentic foundation. All this suggests the human need to belong and the way in which we respond to pressure from others to be like them.

Studies of the pressure towards uniformity have indicated that the phenomenon of *modelling* is also important. This is copying the behaviour of an influential person, or model, such as a parent, group leader, or pop singer (see Chapters 1 and 2). Also, people often judge themselves by seeing how much they agree with other people. This is called social comparison, and contributes towards uniformity. Finally, uniformity is also brought about by the desire to avoid feeling odd or standing out from the crowd. Psychologists have called this objective self-awareness, but it is better described in daily use as self-consciousness.

Conformity may be understood in three ways: first, in terms of *compliance*, when people conform in their behaviour but do not necessarily alter their attitudes. Motives for compliance are often connected with survival, or status and security. An example would be a prisoner who changes his behaviour in order to conform to the rules of the institution (or even to the inmate sub-culture) but inwardly does not alter his original hostile feelings. Cohen and Taylor's (1972) study of long-term prisoners showed several examples of this, as did the work of Solomon Asch in a series of experiments in the 1950s. These involved a naïve participant having to say which of three comparison lines was equal in length to a standard line, when all four lines were simultaneously presented. When the individual tackled the task alone there was a high degree of accuracy. However, the naïve individuals were then placed in the midst of a group of the experimenter's confederates, who always chose the wrong line deliberately. Asch found that one-third of the time the naïve person agreed with the wrong answer in this situation.

This work demonstrated that individuals are greatly influenced by pressure towards conformity, even when they probably realize that the group consensus does not provide the correct solution. However, the results of this study have been criticized by other psychologists, who stress that the results should not be generalized: if there was always such pressure to outward compliance then new ideas would never be established, and individual innovations would never get accepted. It has also been found that committed *minorities* in groups can persuade other group members to their point of view, and compliance is thus related to more than majority pressure (Feldman, 2003).

Secondly, *identification* occurs when one person finds it important to be like another. This is referred to as classical identification. Sometimes it is important for someone to meet the *expectations* of another person. This is called reciprocal-role identification, and happens a great deal in marriages or between bosses and secretaries, or social workers and service users. Thirdly, a person might be happily influenced by another if she/he finds the behaviour and attitudes of that person consistent with his/her own values. This is called *internalization*. The influence of a religious leader or charismatic politician is a good example of this.Interest in obedience increased after the trials of the Nazi war criminals, who claimed that they had committed atrocities as a result of obeying orders, and felt that they should not be held individually responsible for their actions. Stanley Milgram performed a series of what are now famous studies to discover just how far people in general will go when ordered to do something. These are described in his book *Obedience to Authority* (1974). He set up a laboratory where naïve participants were told that they were assisting in an experiment to assess the effects of punishment on learning. The participant was told that the learner, to whom he was introduced, would be in the next room, wired up to a machine which would administer a shock every time the participant pressed a button. The person was shown a dial which would increase the shock from light to dangerous, and the experimenter told him that he should increase this each time a wrong answer was given. A battery was temporarily attached to a lead, and the individual was given a mild shock just to prove the machine worked. In fact this was the only shock to be administered, as the machine was a fake! Before running his experiments, Milgram sought the views of several psychologists and psychiatrists who said that it would be very unlikely that his participants would continue the experiment after the first couple of shocks.

During the experiment the participants asked the 'learner' certain questions, and when a wrong answer was given, the experimenter told the participant to press the shock button. After a few times the 'learner' started begging the person to stop, and the experimenter told the person to go on, despite the participant's protests. The 'learner' claimed that he had a weak heart, and when the final 'shock' was administered, the screaming stopped, and there was silence. The conditions were varied. Sometimes there was a window so that the participant could see the learner's reactions, at some times the experimenter appeared scruffy and inconsequential, at others well dressed and authoritative. Milgram thought that these factors might affect the degree of obedience. On average, about 62 per cent of participants obeyed the experimenter until told they might stop, and about one-third proceeded until the learner was silent. Some of the participants expressed great anguish both during the experiments and for some time afterwards, but this was not enough to stop them, and it seems that many people will do as they are told under particular circumstances even though they regret doing it.

Over the past twenty years there has been an important change imposing ethical controls on work in which participants are 'duped' in these ways. However this does not detract from the importance of the work described above and its significance for our own and others' behaviour.

## Group dynamics and structures

Social groups which exert influence over their members are not themselves uniform in nature, but are constantly changing as a result of the influence of individual members and external demands. Once a group has formed, a structural pattern begins to develop, and the role, interpersonal preference, communication, status and power structures emerge, along with patterns of normative behaviour. The developments and changes in these structures are referred to as group processes or group dynamics. The structure of a group may or may not be affected by formal organizations, but even if it is, informal group structures can be observed. So a team within the probation service has its formal structural relationships dictated by the Assistant Chief Probation Officer, so that the Senior Probation Officer is in charge of the office and makes the major decisions, but informally the Senior Probation Officer may frequently and deliberately enlist the skills of basic-grade colleagues in a variety of important tasks. Groups come together formally or informally in order to perform certain tasks, to be carried out as well as they are able. Groups in which all the members wish to participate, which agree on the tasks to be performed, and recognize the members who are most suitable for each role, are likely to be the most effective. All groups aim at close proximity to this state, but it can rarely be achieved without conflict, and it is this conflict which causes groups to develop and change their structure. A group which is concentrating upon personality or behavioural change in its members might be encouraging everyone to share their fears, anxieties and intimate details of their past lives. If some members do not reveal things in this way, others will feel frustrated and betrayed, and the group will not represent a 'safe' environment for change. The pressure aimed at the 'non-disclosing' members will be manifest in a struggle between the group and individual members about norms, criteria for membership, tasks and roles, and if all eventually agree and feel able to share their intimate feelings, then this is seen as a measure of effectiveness. The process by which the pressure is applied, the alliances which form and the changing patterns of communications, friendship and roles, are the dynamics of the group.

Ralph Linton (1949), one of the first social scientists to consider that a group was an entity, looked at group properties. He felt that these could be divided into structural (for example, patterns of relationship among members) and dynamic (for example, expressions of the changes in group relationships) properties; distinct from each other, but closely interwoven. Linton, and also Newcomb (1953), further analysed these properties in terms of status and role structure. The status structures were static, and referred to a collection of rights and duties attributed to the occupant of a particular position in a group. An individual is assigned to a status position and occupies it in relation to other statuses: someone who has been officially designated group leader because of their training in group psychotherapy has a right to occupy this status, because other people are members, whose status requires them to recognize the leader's status! The leader also has a duty to use the knowledge and skills which she has, and which have led to her achieving that status. The role structure represents the dynamic aspects of the status position, whereby the occupant of the role puts the rights and duties of her status into effect, and performs the tasks relating to the role of leader/psychotherapist, as in this example.

Linton stresses that status and role are quite inseparable, and that there can be no roles without statuses, and no statuses without roles. Newcomb employed the concept of position rather than status, with the role being seen as the behaviour of people who occupy positions. Every position which is recognized by the members of a group contributes in some way to the purposes of the group, and this contribution represents the group function.

## Types of group structure

The affect structure, or interpersonal preference structure, refers to the degree of attraction between group members, and is a powerful determinant of *group cohesiveness*. If attraction between group members is intense, then high value is placed on membership, and the group is said to be cohesive. This may be adversely affected by:

1. an increased number of members, which might mean priority has to be established in power and control of activities, with a greater number of people in subordinate positions;
2. the formation of sub-groups or cliques by people who are particularly attracted to each other. This means that an intergroup rivalry will occur within the main group, which will reduce cohesiveness and Figure 6.3 illustrates some examples of potential for rivalry and attempts to achieve power.

The affect structure can be diagramatically represented on a sociogram, a technique invented by Moreno (1934). The sociogram describes who likes whom, who is rejected by the group, who is the most popular, and where the cliques exist. Figure 6.1 an example of a sociogram, and illustrates friendship structures within a group.

Most groups are constrained by a communications structure which is imposed upon them. This might be that the area director cannot directly supervise the work of a basic-grade social worker, and so she has to do this via the team leader; or it might be that a

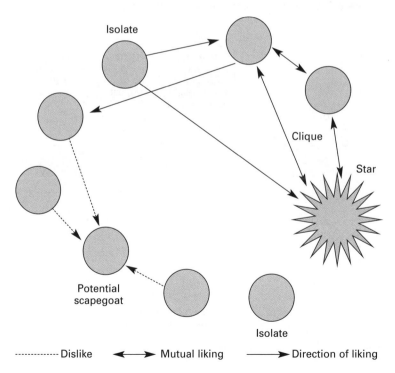

**Figure 6.1** A typical sociogram: friendship structures in a group

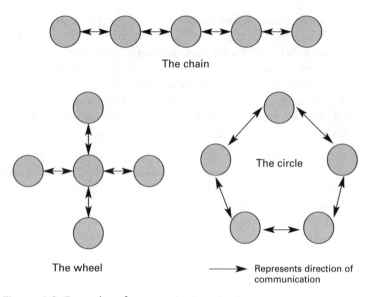

The chain

The wheel

The circle

⟶ Represents direction of communication

**Figure 6.2** Examples of communication structures

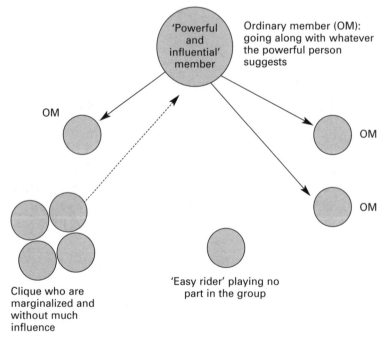

'Powerful and influential' member

Ordinary member (OM): going along with whatever the powerful person suggests

OM

OM

OM

Clique who are marginalized and without much influence

'Easy rider' playing no part in the group

**Figure 6.3** Power and communication structures

particular residential home has a policy that each worker's and resident's views and opinions have to be considered publicly before decisions are taken. Psychologists have studied whether different communications structures hinder the development of group processes or assist in the performance of group tasks. It is apparent that communication structures fulfil different functions more efficiently. The important variable is often the degree of centralization in a communication network structure (see Figure 6.2). The wheel is the most centralized pattern, and the circle the least centralized. The wheel facilitates simple decision-making, but is bad for the morale of peripheral group members. For more complex tasks the circle pattern often proves superior. This may be because of more active participation by all members, which itself increases morale, or because in the wheel the centralized person may well be overlooked.

The *power structure* in a group relates to the roles and status positions of its members. There is also an additional component which is related to the influence a member exerts over the others during social interaction. Social power has been defined as 'the potential influence of some influencing agent O, over some person, P. Influence is defined as a change in cognition, attitude, behaviour or emotion of P which can be attributed to O' (French and Raven, 1959). There are different types of powers which can be based on the ability of a group member to reward, coerce, provide expert knowledge, provide information or have other members wishing to be like him/her, or having a legitimate reason for power. Different power is important at different times during the life of a group, and although the sources of power are not independent (one person may have influence through more than one source of power) it is likely that power shifts between members. More recent work has focused in detail upon malevolent use and abuse of power (Kipnis, 2001) which sometimes occurs as part of the informal structure whereby information is 'leaked' or misused to stir conflict (see Kolb and Bartunek, 1992). In Chapter 8 these points are developed further in relation to 'leadership'.

As described earlier, the *role structure* represents the dynamic aspects of the status positions. Certain groups have formal roles, such as mother, father, son, daughter, teacher, therapist, and so on, but all have informal role structures in addition. The most important of these are 'leader', 'follower', 'scapegoat', 'lieutenant' (second in command and support to the leader). Again, there are various ways in which these informal roles are occupied. For instance the leader may be permanent, short-term, a task leader, or an emotional leader. The reason why certain individuals occupy particular roles varies according to the other aspects of structure, group task and personality.

## Groupwork

The first part of this chapter has focused attention upon the information available to explain aspects of social behaviour, and reflects upon the importance of a *social existence*. It is important for groupwork leaders to be aware that group members are influenced by the social constraints which have been described, as well as by their own personality and individual histories. Superimposed upon the interaction of the individual group members are developments in the group structure and group dynamics: the group itself can be understood independently of the effect its members have upon each other. The leader has to make sense of this aspect of group life in order to be useful to members seeking help and support.

Groupwork in many ways represents a break with the traditional social work relationship between professional worker and service user. It has grown in popularity in Britain since the 1960s, partly as a response to criticisms of traditional methods, and partly as a result of emerging as an established force in social work in the USA by 1960. The term 'groupwork' demands a more detailed definition and explanation, especially since within its broad framework there are a variety of models for practice deriving from a diverse body of theory, but at this stage groupwork may be described as 'social work in which one or more social workers is involved in professional practice with a group of probably more than four service users at the same time'. The aims and objectives and the shared characteristics of the members, and the tasks they perform, may vary greatly.

Despite an increase in popularity and a general acceptance of its validity as a method of social work, it is still true to say that groupwork in Britain remains a peripheral activity in most agencies. Many social work training courses only give it a brief acknowledgement (although this is not universally true), and it is generally seen as a method of 'prevention' rather than a serious way of dealing with social deprivation. Many agencies expect those of their staff with groupwork skills and commitment to develop groupwork activities as 'spare time extras', which reinforces this belief, even among social workers themselves. Residential and day-care institutions tend to value group activities more highly, due to the nature of their work (see Chapter 3). However, rarely is the work of these institutions seen to have as high a status as fieldwork. We hope this chapter will make a contribution towards persuading the reader of the potential of groupwork *generally* within social work practice.

A social worker should be aware of group influences upon individual service users, and also of changes in the structure of the formal (for example, therapeutic) and informal (for example, people in his office) groups with which he is involved. It is important for the social worker to realize that no member either starts or finishes her particular group experience solely as a member of one particular group. Even service users in long-term residential care and prisoners experience diverse effects and reactions to their circumstances, which reflect the influence of other groups to which they have belonged, currently identify with, and aspire to join in the future. Thus all people are influenced by the groups they have contact with, and either choose membership or drop out. In order to function at all, formal groups have to generate norms, even if they are constructed around simple issues such as the length of time group members have to remain together at each meeting. The more effective a group is to become, the more committed its members must be, and this in turn results in a more highly developed and complex set of group norms.

So, in order to sustain its membership, a group must reflect the needs of its members. The social worker setting up a group with highly specific aims and goals might find difficulty in directing the group towards these if the members themselves do not recognize them as their own. Groupwork goals should be flexible, and bear relationship to goals set by members, including the group leader. In order to do this successfully, the social worker has to maintain a grasp of:

- group dynamics (including defence mechanisms)
- shifting power relations
- communication patterns
- the skills needed to set up a group
- the skills needed to run a group
- running group meetings so that members are able to explore their own needs and the extent to which that group might meet them.

Groupwork is a generic term. There is no one theoretical or methodological approach which is all-embracing, and the only common feature is that a social worker will be involved in setting up, and probably running, the group: she may or may not be concerned with emotional or environmental change for the group members, and equally may or may not participate in group meetings. The intention of this section is to examine the groupwork skills appropriate to social work, and therefore the focus will be on social work intervention, rather than on group psychotherapy.

A frequently quoted and reasonably adequate definition of groupwork is offered by Konopka (1963). She suggested that 'Social groupwork is a method of social work which helps individuals to enhance their social functioning through purposeful group experiences, and to cope more effectively with their personal, group, or community problems'. This definition stresses the wide-ranging scope of the method, in that community problems can be dealt with as well as personal and group ones, but an emphasis remains upon the inadequacies of the group members, in that they need to 'cope more effectively' and have particular 'problems' in their lives. Groupwork may also be concerned with non-problem-centred groups such as 'support' and 'consciousness-raising' groups. These provide a chance to explore wider implications of an individual's position in society, and highlight certain features of particular lifestyles which can be destructive or inhibit growth and change. So for instance, a social workers' support group provides opportunities to explore the position of social workers in a bureaucratic system, the way their service users are treated as a result, and to gain help from, and give help to, their colleagues.

## The scope of groupwork

There are many types of activity which can be included within the term 'groupwork'. These may be divided into several related categories:

1. The method employed by the workers, especially in terms of leadership style.
2. The theoretical basis upon which the group is formed and conducted.
3. The goals of the group according to the worker.
4. The consumers of groupwork, and what they wish to achieve as members.

5. The format of group events – whether they occur regularly, or sporadically; are part of institutional life; whether membership fluctuates; the life-span of the group; and the nature of group activity (is it is primarily a 'talking' or practical group?)

Based on these components, several models of groupwork have emerged:

- Social groupwork
- Therapeutic groupwork or group therapy
- Community work
- Self-help and support groups

Within these models there is still opportunity to develop particular approaches. The models are probably distinguished by their focus on a particular section of the potential service user population: social groupwork is frequently offered to service users who need to develop their social skills and experiences, such as isolated mothers, or teenagers who are having problems at home or at school; group therapy to people suffering from emotional or psychiatric problems who have identified their needs (or had them identified) as having to change some aspects of their behaviour or emotional reactions; community work usually focuses upon people who identify the root of their problem in terms of environmental deprivation or social injustice, and this model operates in order to help them clarify the issues and work together to effect social change. Consciousness-raising became more popular in the late 1960s and 1970s, with the acknowledgement that social oppression had greatly restricted the political, social and emotional life of certain social groups. The most obvious of these are members of ethnic minorities, women, people with disabilities, children, the working class, pensioners and other sections of society which have learned to recognize the external constraints on their lives and make efforts to understand and change them.

The self-help or support group model is perhaps the widest-ranging in terms of who might benefit. Many self-help groups have emerged, initially under social work leadership. Any group of people with mutual needs or problems may benefit from regular contact with others tackling similar problems. An example of this might be people wishing to set up a playgroup for their own community, a group of ex-alcoholics in Alcoholics Anonymous, or a group of social workers discussing professional concerns.

## Embarking upon groupwork

Typically social work agencies put little pressure on their staff to undertake any groupwork, and it may well appear that they discourage it by giving work with individuals overriding priority. There are several explanations for this. Probably statutory responsibilities to individuals and families take precedence over working with groups. Also most social workers and social work managers lack training in groupwork, so perhaps avoid the possibility of getting out of their comfort zones. There are similarities in the aims and skills of all types of social work, but working with groups of service users can expose the social worker to a potentially threatening situation where she/he will be in the minority, and thus less 'powerful' than in other social work activities.

Additionally for several reasons groups are often best conducted by two social workers, and those groupworkers will be exposing their professional skills to scrutiny which rarely occurs firsthand outside the groupwork role. Although social workers report on their interactions with service users, and seek support from their senior staff, their interpersonal skills are rarely in question. Agencies evaluate social work according to the effectiveness of administration and action in connection with their peoples' lives. Less emphasis is placed upon personal contact and interaction with service users once social workers get beyond their training, and even then, social worker/service user contact is generally assessed by way of 'process recordings' or verbal accounts rather than personal observation by supervisors. Similarly, social workers rarely know the details of their colleagues' relationships with their service users, which provides difficulties for assessments of service users' needs in a team with respect to offering groupwork. However, there are several reasons why groupwork might be very acceptable to both service users and staff of statutory and voluntary agencies.

## Advantages of groupwork

1. Most people's lives involve situations where they are members of large and small groups. Their experiences result directly from their social position, and therefore it is often useful to confront their problems in a group setting. These are not necessarily emotional problems, but may involve difficulties in a variety of interpersonal settings, such as dealing with bureaucracies, people in authority, their own families, etc.

2. All members of the group have certain resources which may well provide help and support for other members.
3. Groups can be made up of people with similar problems and experiences who can provide reassurance, insight and support to each other, in the way professional workers cannot.
4. For people who wish to change some part of their behaviour or personality, a group experience is much more likely to be effective than the traditional one-to-one approach.
5. The social worker is potentially less powerful in the group situation where the other members are always in a majority. Thus his behaviour and decisions are always open to challenge.
6. Certain social worker/service user relationships are traditionally unfruitful. For instance where the prescribed statutory involvement requires control by the social worker over the service user, which is usually impossible. Problems may well be exacerbated by the imposed presence of an authority figure, but the service user may be able to confront and deal with them if they can be shared with others in a similar position.
7. There is a likelihood that once groupwork is established in an agency, it will be economical in terms of social work time. Certainly some people will always require some individual contact, either in relation to statutory tasks, or simply because they need to relate to a professional worker, but these contacts could be kept to a minimum.
8. Groupworkers have more chance to gain feedback on their professional ability both from service users and from their co-worker.

## Disadvantages of groupwork

1. If members of a group are really going to tackle important issues, they will not have the same guarantee of confidentiality as a one-to-one relationship with a social worker.
2. A great deal of time and effort is involved in setting up and running a group, and often colleagues in an agency may not be particularly supportive.
3. It is necessary to have access to certain physical resources: accommodation, equipment, catering facilities, transport, care facilities for pre-school children.
4. Sometimes, social workers find problems in running groups and may not be able to deal with certain 'explosive' situations

which arise, which may be more intense because of the group context.

5. Group membership and selection for membership inevitably results in 'labelling' of individuals as 'depressed mothers', 'school refusers', and so on. There may be a stigma attached to group membership because of this, as selection for membership depends upon individuals having some sort of identifiable 'problem'.

6. Individual members might find that they are not getting as much from the group sessions as they would from a one-to-one session, possibly because one or two other members constantly compete for attention, or they discover that they do not share the same experiences or difficulties as most of the other members of the group.

7. Particular individuals might experience rejection by the group which reflects their real-life difficulties. The degree to which this may or may not be helpful depends on the commitment of the member and the skill of the groupworkers.

### Deciding whether groupwork is appropriate

The decision to start a groupwork project is based upon three separate, but not mutually exclusive factors:

1. The social workers concerned should be committed to groupwork as a form of intervention. This is not to suggest that they are not also committed to other forms of social work, but that they must be convinced of the validity of groupwork itself.

2. There must be some means of identifying and acknowledging the needs of potential group members.

3. Certain basic physical resources must be available.

Most people's experience of social work does not include groupwork, and so prospective group members should be made fully aware of exactly what is being offered.

### Setting up the group

Groupwork needs careful preparation. Decisions have to be made which involve apparently endless permutations, the result being that a form of compromise has to be reached by the groupworkers as to:

- who the group members will be.
- the type of group they are going to run ('practical' or 'talking').
- the length and time of day for each session. Enough time must be available for 'ice-breaking' at each session, despite pressures that the members and workers will probably face concerning their commitments. One and a half to two hours is generally considered suitable. It is also important to take account of the daily routines of potential members, so that a group is not organized mid-afternoon for mothers who have to collect children from school, or an afternoon group for people who are at work.
- the frequency of the sessions and the duration of the life of the group. Many people may not favour a long-term commitment, but will be happy to meet as frequently as twice a week. For instance, a group for school children during the summer vacation may meet intensively for a relatively short period, enabling them to get to know each other quickly, and so gain the most from the experience. A community group wishing to confront specific problems in an area may wish to meet once a fortnight, as they may be dealing with separate tasks between meetings. It is often a good idea to set a limited number of sessions with the option for the group to review this in the light of experience and achievement at the end of that period.

### Aims of the group

The considerations which arise during the planning stages of a group's life must also be taken into account when planning the group's aims. It is important for the groupworkers to be clear about what they plan to achieve and how. These aims may be flexible, and should certainly be reviewed, preferably after each session. This does not mean, for example, that a group for school refusers or bereaved people must constantly focus on the central topic; indeed it may well be that not going to school or the loss is not particularly important for the future lives of the group members. It does mean that a group must set realistic aims which reflect the workers' intentions and abilities, and the members' needs. Being realistic would mean that a group for people attending a day centre for mental health service users would not aim to get the members back into full-time employment in three months. It might however aim at enabling the members to take an active part in planning their daily routines, to learn to talk about themselves and their difficulties with each other, and listen to the problems of other members, and it is likely that the group experience would enable them to achieve these aims.

## Selecting the group members

Referrals for groupwork may come from a variety of sources which clearly depend upon the agency and type of group. Groups which depend on a system of referral are usually those run by statutory agencies, or those which cater for the needs of a specific section of the population. Some will have methods of self-selection, as in the case of a community-based group, or there may be a method of group selection as in some therapeutic communities. Some groups are non-selective, and these would include 'drop-in' centres, playgroups, and luncheon clubs. They do, however, tend to attract people who identify in some way with the people who regularly attend. Apart from the referral and selection of members, it is necessary to establish whether a group is to be 'open' or 'closed': whether or not new members should be able to join, and others drop out at any stage. The decision about this rests with the group leaders, and should be clarified before potential members are recruited.

## Groupwork in action

The processes and dynamics of each group depend on the leadership and the members, but as we have seen earlier in this chapter, there are also certain developmental sequences which are common to all groups, regardless of the characteristics of members. These relate to group composition and size, group cohesiveness, and conflicts which surround the stated and unstated aims. They reflect the establishment of rules and norms, the degree of commitment and attraction of the members, and the way in which the group processes are handled by the group workers. The leader should be aware of the group processes, that is, the development of the group itself as distinct from the behaviour of the individuals comprising it. Several groupwork writers have described the stages of group development resulting from changes in the structure which occur in response to the group needs at a particular time. Tuckman (1965) has summarized the sequence of events in group development as *forming, storming, norming* and *performing,* and subsequent writers have suggested a final stage of *mourning*. Groupworkers have a specific part to play at each stage of development, and recognizing and understanding the stages will enable them to do this.

### Forming

Initially group members will come together knowing very little about each other, and why they are there. They will probably have accepted the leader's explanation that they can share similar problems and experiences with others, but there will be all sorts of doubts and anxieties in their minds about who speaks to whom, when to speak, whether or not to launch into discussion of their problems immediately, or whether they want to disclose anything at all to this bunch of strangers they are now faced with! At this stage the groupworkers play an important part in the interaction. They decide the style of introductions, which set the tone of the first and subsequent meetings. For instance, the leaders might start by telling the group their names, a bit about their work, why they set up the group and what they are hoping it will achieve. They could then ask the members to do something similar.

In practically oriented groups the workers may assign specific tasks to members, such as setting out chairs, making coffee, buying the provisions or checking the equipment, in order to establish individuals with a role. If the group is one in which members already know each other, as in a hospital or day centre, it is particularly important to stress the aims, functions and boundaries of the group, as distinct from the other activities which members might share. Groups in residential and day-care settings frequently do operate successfully, and most people are able to distinguish between their different roles in the group, and in other activities in the same setting.

### Storming

Once the members have established who they are and why they are there, it often appears important for some people, or the group as a whole, to rebel against the leaders, or to question the aims and usefulness of the group. It is also frequently true that they will not achieve their aims, or that their problems are insoluble. It is very much a reaction against the initial excitement and optimism on joining a group and meeting others with similar hopes and fears, and then realizing that there is more to effective group membership than just sharing these. The group leader has to avoid feeling the same hopelessness, and possibly has to exert more control over individuals than she/he might at some later stage. This is a difficult balance to maintain because too much or too little control could prevent the group from actually becoming a cohesive, effective force in its own right. It is important that the leader questions these attacks and hopeless feelings posed by the members, but does *not* attack the individuals who raise the doubts. It is likely that one or several members will say that they do not feel that sitting in a room for two hours a week will help with their particular difficulties.

Group leaders at all stages, but particularly this one, should respond as much as possible by *opening up* the issues rather than providing a definitive answer. This can be done in a number of ways. For instance, in response to a personal attack on the leader by a member it might be appropriate to offer straightforward explanation or denial, but it is likely to be more useful to ask whether other members have seen the leader in the same way, and if the group replies that they have, then the leader might carry on to ask what the group feels she/he could do to make it feel more comfortable. If not the group might focus on why the deviant member feels as he does. Although many people may remain silent during confrontation, if the leader opens up the discussion, other people are frequently able to contribute, and either support or refute the attack. Subsequent discussion may prove fruitful for all involved, enabling the group to resolve certain basic conflicts.

Similarly, if a member is 'going off at a tangent', or doing all the talking (often addressing themselves to the leaders rather than to the rest of the group), it is important to try and allow other members to control the discussion if possible. The leader could ask 'What do other people think?', or if this fails, something along the lines of 'It would seem as if Christine has a lot on her mind just now. I wonder if other people have had similar experiences ...' or 'whether other people can suggest to her how to deal with ...' If someone senses the group's lack of direction and is allowed to take over, other members may well feel that the group has no place for them, and their suspicions and anxieties will be confirmed. With appropriate 'facilitation' at this early stage, members should be able to deal with over-enthusiastic orators at a later stage of the group's development, preventing the need for too much leadership control over participation.

### Norming
During the 'storming' stage, individuals are trying to establish their roles, and work out their values in relation to the rest of the group

members. As members become more committed to the group and each other, they establish norms and as a consequence identify with the group and place a degree of emotional investment in its future development. This should not imply harmony – in fact establishing rules and norms by definition implies the existence of transgression. So at this stage there will be people who react against certain accepted norms in one way or another. They may be pushed into the role of 'scapegoat' by the group, which disapproves of their lack of conformity. They may be pressured into compliance, or they may emerge as new leaders, so altering basic group norms. The group leaders should now be less overtly involved in controlling the direction of the group, and perhaps be providing more in terms of comment and feedback on what they see happening. This is partly in order to allow them to 'check' with the rest of the members as to whether their own perceptions are correct. The leaders will make comments such as 'I feel the group is angry about something, I'm not sure what it is, but perhaps other people sense it also?' or 'I feel the group is concentrating upon things that people are saying rather than the way in which people are feeling, which appears to be quite different because ...' Other members will either agree or challenge the comments, and express the feelings they were unable to talk about. They might not be able to do this if the leader had made statements about the group mood such as 'The group is very angry because Colin arrived late.'

### Performing

This is the stage at which the group has managed to develop through its normative processes and changes in role structure, and concentrates upon the major task it has to perform in relation to its individual members, and its own development. Much of this also occurs during the 'norming' stage, and the distinction is often temporal rather than structural.

### Mourning

All groups have to end, and some have a natural life, for example, during the school holidays or during a stay in hospital, and some have deliberately imposed time limits. All endings engender feelings in individuals, and it is important that the group leaders should be aware of this and give opportunities for people to deal with them effectively. There will be a sense of loss and rejection on the part of members when they realize the life of the group is near its end. This may precipitate reactions of withdrawal, or attempts to arrange to see members individually, or informally outside the formal group. The leader should encourage the members to discuss their feelings about ending the group, and allow them to summarize the group development as they see it. They may wish to continue formally, and the leaders may well find it possible and useful to do so, but this will require a return to the planning stage, to decide exactly what the aims and objectives for extending the group might be. Leaders might feel guilty at ending a group, particularly if it was successful, but clearly this is not a reason to prolong its life.

### Recording and evaluating groupwork

As with other areas of social work, recording provokes a variety of responses in workers and service users, many of which are unfavourable. Most service users understandably object to details of intimate discussion being written and filed away. Even so, recording is particularly useful for groupworkers assessing a group's development, and in addition, provides the agency with evidence that a valid form of social work is actually taking place! The groupworkers may be helped to assess their own involvement in the group process when they write up and account for happenings during group sessions, and they should certainly be able to assess individual members' progress. The recording may possibly be made available to the whole group for discussion and referred to as a group 'diary'.

## Conclusions

Groups underlie human societies, including the family, community and organizations such as schools, factories and offices. The dynamics and processes that impact upon the characteristics and behaviours within groups and between groups appear to be endemic regardless of the personalities of the individuals within them. That is not to say that we all conform all the time – we might appear to do so but our attitudes may remain individualistic. We may be influenced by a group we belong to which might actually change our view of the world. We might find that we obey a leader in ways that surprise us and seem to be at odds with who we think we actually are. Over the life-span we are formed by our social experiences and by groups we are involved with. Groupwork has proven to be an influential means of offering support and the way to change for a variety of service users over many years and is returning to popularity (Preston-Shoot, 2007).

---

### Putting it into practice 6

6a. *Describe your seminar group or work-related team of colleagues* in terms of cohesiveness and power structure. What evidence would you use to construct your theory of this group's structure?

6b. *Observation of group discussion.* Make notes about either a seminar group or a team meeting (although it is ethical to let members of the group know you are doing this) and identify the ways in which decisions are made. Who makes a proposal for a solution to a problem? At what stage in the meeting is a proposal made? Are there counter proposals? What factors lead to a proposal being adopted? Are they about the force with which the proposal is made, who makes it, who supports it and so on?

6c. *How has being a member of this seminar group or team influenced you?* Have any group norms affected the way you think about things or your practice? Have you experienced any changes (positive or negative) in your self-image as a consequence of group membership? How do you know that it is the group that has influenced these things?

---

## Further reading

Bettelheim, B. (1979) *The Informed Heart: Autonomy in a Mass Age*, New York, Avon.

Bion, W.R. (1961) *Experiences in Groups*, London, Tavistock.

These books both take a broadly psychoanalytic perspective and both emerge from the post-World War II focus on groups and how they influence human behaviour and mental health for better or worse and most importantly how the group has a 'life of its own'. Bettelheim's book is an account of his observations of his own and others' experiences in a Nazi concentration camp. Inmates here were experiencing extreme dehumanizing conditions and their behaviours and emotions were often unpredictable and frightening. Bion's work, based on studies of therapeutic groups with ex-prisoners of war, also shows the power of the unconscious group mind and the ways in which groups defend themselves against processes and experiences that might be difficult or distasteful.

Both of these books bear an important relationship to those described below to accompany Chapter 7 (see p. 189).

Preston-Shoot, M. (2007) *Effective Groupwork*, Basingstoke, Palgrave Macmillan.

This book provides a clear and readable guide for setting up and running groups for service users with up-to-date evidence.

# PART III

# Theory in Practice

In the final two chapters of this book we examine ways in which some established approaches to practice with service users and leading and managing in organizations are re-emerging to become part of the contemporary social work practice and social work leadership repertoire of knowledge and skills. We are proposing here a model of *reflective and relational practice* that draws from work by Gillian Ruch, using psychoanalytic ideas; Jan Fook, who is concerned with the process of reflection in practice as a method of self-development; work on mentalization, a version of practical empathy based on the work of Peter Fonagy and colleagues at the Anna Freud Centre at University College London; and emotional intelligence, recently revised as an important device for social workers by David Howe. Taking these ideas further we show how they also mesh with the systemic thinking approach based upon the Tavistock Model of open systems theory, first proposed several decades ago.

Throughout the book we have tried to offer you a variety of approaches you might employ in different circumstances to develop your thinking, knowledge and practice. We recognize, too, that you might want to rethink a number of issues that you did not want to have to think about when you were new to practice. Experience, promotion and increased professional expertise and responsibility make us re-examine both what we need to know and (perhaps) our attitudes to things we used to take for granted.

In Chapter 7 we focus on describing and defining reflective and relational practice and ways and which this approach might enhance everyday working with others. In Chapter 8 we explore further the contribution this type of thinking will make towards effective leadership and management.

# Reflective and relational practice

## CHAPTER OVERVIEW

In this chapter we develop a model of practice that offers social work practitioners in statutory and voluntary organizations, at all levels of seniority, opportunities to think and reflect on their:

- practice with service users
- work with colleagues as supervisors and managers
- work with colleagues whom they supervise and manage
- organization
- service users' lives in the family or institution.

This model, which we call reflective-relational practice (see also Nicolson, 2014 for a more detailed discussion) differs from the ones proposed in Chapters 4 and 5, which are based on counselling practices that translate into social work. The one described in this chapter is an alternative (albeit complementary) perspective, based upon a *systemic* and *psychoanalytic* understanding of organizational consultancy and mentoring that is transferable between 'campus' and social work practice. It is valuable for social work students on both the academic and practice placement components of their training, and later when they are working and engaging with continuing professional development (CPD) throughout their careers.

There are other useful models too that complement the counselling and the systemic/psychoanalytic perspectives. One in particular is of the work of Jan Fook and Fiona Gardner (Fook and Gardner, 2010) on reflective practice. It emerged from their own practice with retrospective development of theory (Fook, 2002) differing from models we discuss below which emerged *from* psychoanalysis and open systems theory *into* practice. However the applications of the models share common features which we outline later in the chapter.

## Introduction: what is reflective and relational practice?

The word 'reflective' means contemplation, meditation or thinking. Reflective practice is about thinking at different levels and from different positions about the way you (and your colleagues) work. It is particularly concerned with thinking about relationships (Ruch, 2005) and, as Ruch argues, reflective practice in social work overlaps and develops within the traditions of relationship-based practice which in turn links with the psychoanalytic and more recently narrative traditions in social work (Ruch, 2004; Salzberger-Wittenberger, 1976; Schofield, 1998).

Reflective practice as an *idea* has become increasingly popular over the past decade but may still be rare *in practice* because of lack of time and because supervision, which could support it, frequently consists of 'box-ticking' rather than developmental work.

Recent reports, which have sought to 'mend' broken social work practices and agencies, particularly in child protection, have identified poor communication and lack of accountability in organizations (Laming, 2003; Munro, 2011) as critical factors in the undermining of social work quality. However, increasingly, in health and social care there has been an emphasis on following protocols rather than *thinking* (Ilott et al., 2006). A contemporary example was the privately run Winterbourne View Hospital for vulnerable people with learning disabilities. Following secret filming by a BBC TV crew for the programme *Panorama*, violent and humiliating abuse by staff to patients was witnessed and arrests were made. However it turned out that the Care Quality Commission, which regulates social care, had already been approached by a whistle-blower whose claims were overlooked because all the 'quality boxes' had been ticked. In the NHS there have been many similar aberrations including widespread negligence at Staffordshire NHS Foundation Trust where many older adults had died and suffered because senior managers and quality monitors had turned a blind eye to the detail of everyday care. It is only through reflective engagement in practice with service users and with staff that practitioners and managers can ensure practice is effective and high-quality, as we saw in Chapter 3, where ritual social defences against anxiety that are employed by organizations (Lokman et al., 2011; Menzies Lyth, 1988) were discussed. Box-ticking and other quality controls are part of such a defence system and as Fook and Gardner (2010) identify, managerialism and paperwork comprise a recognizable response from organizations towards uncertainty and risk.

Reflective and relational practice put additional emphasis on the role of relationships and the organization as a system for consideration (Nicolson, 2014). This approach brings the work of Peter Fonagy (2000) on *mentalizing techniques,* Goleman (2006) and Howe (2008) on *emotional intelligence,* the latter focusing on the emotionally intelligent social worker, into the mix. Mentalization involves the practitioner or manager considering what the other person is *feeling* at any one time, somewhat akin to empathy, while emotional intelligence is about holding the other person in mind, while you are working with them, as well as considering work you are planning in relation to the other person when they are not present. This may involve bringing intuition into play when evidence is not available.

## Systemic thinking

Systemic thinking as an approach to understanding organizations was introduced in Chapter 3. Here we suggest how thinking systemically enables meaningful reflection upon the service users and their family lives, organizations and your own roles within them (Campbell et al., 1994).

### Open systems theory and boundary management

Systemic thinking is a framework, or tool, for observing the way organizations behave (Schein, 1985; Lewin, 1947; Campbell et al., 1994) which evolved from General Systems Theory (von Bertalanffy, 1956; Miller and Rice, 1967) and focuses upon concepts related to organizational structure, particularly:

- 'system'
- 'task'
- 'role'
- 'authority'
- 'boundary'.

### System

An organization that *evolves* like an organism and adapts to its environment necessarily has *porous boundaries* so that it can 'take in' and 'put out' beyond itself. This kind of organism, an *open system,* is one that changes, develops and grows and is therefore healthy.

A *closed system* may feel more secure in that it may not have to accede to unwanted influence or demands, but without taking in and providing for the world outside it will atrophy as with any other closed (minded) system (Morgan, 2006). Examples of both open and closed systems might be a social work team that develops through influence from other teams, accepting new members and new ideas and allowing old ways of working (and some people) to go. The alternative is one that closes down as far as possible, preventing new people, practices and ideas from being incorporated into their culture (Flaskas, 2007). I was told by one group of practice managers that the assessment team in one area of their borough would never answer their phone or come to meetings, claiming they were busy and had never been to meetings in the past. Instead they would simply pass on the bare bones of information about service users who had been assessed with no opportunity for discussion and hearing the input of others. The other teams found this frustrating and potentially risky. It is worth noting that the assessment team ended up being broken up and dispersed later as a result of austerity measures and an attempt to ensure best practice across the organization.

Similarly a family might close up the boundary between outside and inside worlds, perhaps trying to keep themselves 'safe' from outside interference, but this is likely to lead them to failure because while avoiding scrutiny and disturbance from the outside, as they might see it, they don't gain support or advice or other resources that might help them.

### Task

The task refers to the work the organization and its staff are contracted to undertake. The system has a *primary task*, the main goal for the organization. This is also the task that people in the organization *believe* they are carrying out. While this might be a useful starting point for reflecting on the organization, it is also a simplistic umbrella to cover the multiple tasks that any organization offering social services to children, families, the mentally ill or other vulnerable adults has to provide (Zagier Roberts, 1994). There is also a concept of an 'anti-task'. This occurs when the anxieties are so high that defensive activities to alleviate the anxiety are employed. One department I visited was engaged in a group grievance against the senior managers, supported by the union. This task occupied much of their time and energy but prevented them from the acute anxiety about the primary task of assessment of children and families at risk in a context where their own employment and promotions were at risk (Jaques, 1960).

## Role

This means the activities that are contained within a particular job description. Essentially a social worker's role is defined by the primary task of the organization, that is, the statutory protection of service user groups. In taking part in this task, the social worker has a particular part to play, which is to work with a client group, with particular service users on their case load, to take their turn at assessment duty and to keep records (as well as other defined activities). It is not within the social work role to, for example, meet with senior staff from other agencies to develop policy, unless they have been given a special role to do this work. Understanding the boundaries of your own role is helpful in making sense of where you work ends and enables you to say 'no'.

## Authority

It is also important to reflect on the authority in the system (Obholzer and Roberts, 1994). Authority refers to the right to take an ultimate decision, which is binding on others. Formal authority resides within certain roles but there is also the potential for informal authority based on knowledge and personality (Halton, 2007). In a reflective group I ran, the first few meetings were all about the way the middle managers were abused by the senior staff. I kept asking the question 'where does the authority lie?' and later 'what would it take for you to take up your own authority?' The group felt very oppressed and depressed but eventually, thinking and reflecting on the system, they realized that it was not a group of individuals who were (it seemed) persecuting them specifically but that the lines of authority were being used to pass down unacceptable messages to bypass discussion and dissent. Perhaps, they considered, they didn't have to take every 'order' without challenge or criticism (Barge and Fairhurst, 2008). They had their own authority that could be used once they understood where its boundaries lay although they still worked within a hierarchy which was accountable to local authority administrations and to government.

## Boundary

'Boundary' is the term used in open-systems theory to describe the interface between different parts of the organization and the organization and the outside world (Hunter, 2005). In the case of social work this is the physical boundary to the, for example, social services building, the interview rooms, the website, the reception desk, the telephones, e-mail and so on and also between the different roles such as assessment/family support/manager, and so on. Most leaders in organizations have the knowledge and abilities by definition to manage and negotiate those boundaries. For example, the senior managers relate to government/local authorites/Department of Health in ways that junior social workers do not, but the senior staff are charged with having to manage the boundaries using knowledge and influence across the boundaries – inside with the staff and service users and outside with government and courts. Moreover, the porosity or opacity of the boundaries between the different organizations that have come together is central to functioning of at most levels.

## Reflecting on the 'organization in the mind'

Those of us working in organizations have a sense of what the organization is like – 'you don't have to be mad to work here' is a phrase frequently found on coffee mugs or posters on office walls. And how often does one hear (or say) 'you can't expect to get the message across in this place' (or something similar)? What does this type of discourse signify? While both types of message are negative (and not everyone feels that about their place of work, of course), there is an assumption the view is shared by colleagues. There is a sense of a mental place that we all understand about what happens in the organization.

The concept of the 'organization in the mind' was a model developed originally in the early 1990s by organizational and group relations consultants working at the Grubb Institute, the Tavistock Centre and the Tavistock Institute of Human Relations, to refer to what an individual perceives mentally about how organizations, relations in the organizations and the structures are connected. 'It is a model internal to oneself ... which gives rise to images, emotions, values and responses in me, which may consequently be influencing my own management and leadership, positively or adversely' (Hutton et al., 1997, p. 114, quoted in Armstrong, 2005, p. 4).

In other words, when we talk about our colleagues, guess what the senior management are doing/going to do and have fantasies about how well we fit, or don't fit, into the structure or system, we do so in the context of the organization we 'hold' in our mind which may or may not relate to that which other members of the organization hold (Pols, 2005).

The 'organization in mind' thus involves:

- an 'image' of the organizational structure and relationships within that structure;
- a sense of your own role and place within it;
- an emotional component;
- an awareness at a conscious and/or unconscious level of important information below the surface.

Organizations are experienced cognitively and emotionally by their members when they think about how their organizations work and are structured (see Lewin, 1947; Armstrong, 2005; Morgan, 2006). As Stokes (1994) explains it, everyone carries a sense of the organization in their mind but members from different parts of the same organizations may have 'different pictures and these may be in contradiction to one another. Although often partly unconscious, these pictures nevertheless inform and influence the behaviour and feelings of members' (p. 121). It is therefore important to note that your colleagues and managers may not understand the organization in the way that you do. In a reflective group I ran with a mental health team, one member kept saying that his managers were good and he had nothing to share with the others. Try as I could, though, it was difficult to distinguish between his and the others' experiences in objective terms; he held on to his sense of the organization but so did the others who said they had problems.

Hutton (2000) talks about it as 'a conscious or pre-conscious construct focused around emotional experiences of tasks, roles, purposes, rituals, accountability, competence, failure, success' (p. 2). Morgan suggests that an organization may serve as a 'psychic prison' in that the

> patterns and meanings that shape corporate culture and sub-culture may also have unconscious significance. The common values that bind an organization often have their origin in shared concerns that lurk below the surface of conscious awareness. For example, in organizations that project a team image, various kinds of splitting mechanisms are often in operation, idealizing the qualities of team members while projecting fears, anger, envy, and other bad impulses on to persons and objects that are not part of the team. (Morgan, 2006, p. 226)

This is not simply a matter of guesswork. It is an intellectual/ cognitive and *emotional* sense of an organization. Indeed to take this slightly further, as Gabriel and Schwartz (Gabriel, 2004, p.1) propose, 'what goes on at the surface of an organization is not all that there is, and ... understanding organizations often means comprehending matters that lie beneath the surface'.

Although not necessarily (in fact mostly not) made explicit, even the most clear-thinking senior members of organizations hold an image of the organization in mind, expressing their fantasy/belief/perception of the organization based on conscious and unconscious knowledge (Halton, 2007; James and Arroba, 2005).

## Structure in the mind

Laughlin and Sher (2010) have taken up a version of this concept which they name the 'structure in the mind' in their analysis of developing leadership in social care. They reassert, in their model, that not only do the local stakeholders (staff and service users) have a sense of the organization in the mind when considering, for instance, a particular local authority, but the range of stakeholders includes government bodies and service commissioners (in the round). They propose an inter-relationship between perceptions of communications from services (for example, 'that you [management] don't listen and/or understand') and perceived communications from 'Head Office' (or government or other bodies that control resources and practices) which include, for example, 'just do it', 'we know better' and 'be rational' (p. 9).

What is significant here, in the context of social work leadership, is that the organization and/or structure *in the mind* is where the leader and followers 'meet' emotionally as, similarly, do the various levels of leadership and governance bodies. It is a kind of 'virtual' space. Stating this in a slightly different way, this approach to the 'organization in the mind' takes the *personal* (conscious, preconscious and unconscious) level of thinking and links it to the *system* in which that person works (systemic thinking). As any organization comprises systems (with boundaries, inputs and outputs), groups and individuals, it follows that a person's experience of an organization and *experience of themselves* in relation to others who are in the same organization make up the culture, climate and everyday dynamics of any organizational context.

## Psychoanalytic thinking: reflecting on work with service users

There is a psychodynamic part of the systemic thinking analysis which links with the conscious and unconscious emotional consequences of the systemic properties and the impact of social and personal factors on the functioning of the organization (James and Huffington, 2004; Laughlin and Sher, 2010). There are many levels at which interaction is taking place and it is very hard to take them all in immediately. You need time to digest and think about what overt (conscious) and covert or latent (unconscious) messages were being conveyed. One level at which unconscious messages are conveyed is through 'countertransference', and this process can be used to make sense of what a service user, manager or supervisee you are working with might not be conveying to you in a conscious form. In other words, by reflecting in a careful and engaged way on residual and possibly half-formed impressions you might have experienced you might gain 'data' about what is going on in a family or organizational system.

## Countertransference

Countertransference occurs when you have the sensation of feeling something for or about another person that on a conscious level makes you feel 'out of place.' You realize that something is going on between you but it is difficult to put your finger on it. This may be something of a conundrum at first sight but it happens frequently in everyday life as well as in therapy and social work practice.

For example, you meet someone socially and while you are talking about an apparently innocuous subject, even something as bland as the weather, you have the feeling that you are talking out of turn, or being silly, or are too tall, too fat or in control. This happens at work too, of course, and often with your manager or one of your staff. How often have you had the experience of finding someone 'creepy' but can't explain why or feel that you can't trust your manager even though there is nothing obvious to fault her meetings with you? I worked with someone I had a great deal of respect for but who made me feel absolutely exhausted within five minutes of meeting him. It felt strange because he wasn't boring or self-obsessed (in fact the opposite). I came to understand over a couple of weeks that he was projecting his own sense of exhaustion on to me, in part because I had a valency to receive this projection as I (like him) always felt I could and should be doing more. He was away from work for some time with a stress-related condition and gradually learned that he did not have to be the one to do everything!

Winnicott (1949) and Heimann (1950), as well as Klein (1959/1975) understood this feeling of countertransference to be a key emotional response (in their case) of the *analyst to the patient*. However, countertransference is equally significant for making sense of an emotional response that a social worker has to a service user or team of colleagues. Heimann saw the value of the analyst's awareness of countertransference as about helping the patient to sustain (and thus work with) his feelings, allowing the analyst to check whether the mood and behaviour were understood (see Hinshelwood, 1991). This is also important in reflective practice with service users, although unlike working as an analyst, you may prefer to make a note of what you are experiencing to think about and discuss in supervision rather than feed back the feelings to the service user.But what exactly goes on in a countertransference experience? Bion (1961) has described countertransference as an experience of strong feelings, *which can be believed as justified by the objective situation*. In other words, when you do reflect on how you feel and reflect on what went on to bring these feelings about, you gain important information. Sometimes this is vital. You may realize you felt uneasy because the person you were meeting was uneasy about what they were telling you but you could not 'see' this at the time of the meeting. To explain the concepts underlying this in more depth, it is now necessary to outline Klein's theories of 'position' and 'projective identification'.

## Position

Klein held a different view from Freud's about the development of human psychology. Rather than following sequential stages of development (see Chapter 1), Klein thought that there was constant movement back and forth between mental positions, which she saw as a constellation of attitudes and mechanisms (Segal, 1993; Hinshelwood, 1991) that worked together and acted on preoccupations. She described the *paranoid-schizoid position* and the *depressive position* as being different ways of dealing with anxiety. Throughout life the paranoid-schizoid position may be used under stress.

## The paranoid-schizoid position

The paranoid-schizoid position (Klein, 1959; Segal, 1993) from the start of life is a reaction to frightening phantasies of annihilation in which life itself is under threat, and to cope with it, the infant separates the good from the bad. Thus the breast, which fulfils the infant's needs (food, comfort), is experienced separately from the one that is not available and denies the infant food and comfort thus placing her in danger of annihilation. This was recognized by Klein as the process of 'splitting' to defend the ego from (the phantasy) danger. Of course there *are* good and bad external objects but (more likely) some people only behave badly towards others *sometimes*. Therefore splitting is ultimately a distortion of reality. So as Spillius (2007) summarizes, for Klein unconscious phantasy accompanies gratification as well as frustration, and both hate and love are innate and not particularly dependent on the external world.

An infant has innate unconscious knowledge (although hazy) of the physicality of her parents (and thus later of herself). As the infant feels the mother's body to be the source of all good and bad things the infant/child attacks the mother's body (in phantasy) out of frustration and in order to get possession of her mother's riches. These sadistic attacks arouse anxiety in the infant, which can be a spur to development, although also inducing a feeling in the infant that her own body is dangerous (Spillius, 2007). Thus if you 'attack' someone they become dangerous objects. If anxiety about attacking the mother's body becomes excessive it leads to neurosis (or even psychosis in extreme cases).

For Klein, the first three months of infancy allows a 'normal' paranoid-schizoid position characterized by persecutory anxiety about good and bad or dangerous objects. The baby splits these objects in phantasy as 'totally' good and bad. Without this splitting the baby may not grow up to be able to understand that there *are* good and bad objects (people and situations) to which they will have to relate. Thus splitting is a developmental benefit if the infant receives good enough care.

In adulthood, however, a person may still split the good from the bad in ways that do not enhance development and are potentially harmful to the person themselves and the other people they relate to – this may well be a problem in the workplace. So, for example, the individual might see colleagues or service users as all bad or all good and behave in ways that 'demonize' or 'idealize' others, which will have a detrimental impact on their judgement that could play out across the system.

## Projective identification

One way in which we deal with emotional discomfort or intolerable feelings is by projective identification, which takes place while in the paranoid-schizoid position. Projective identification is a process by which an individual actively gets rid of their own intolerable feelings by *pushing them into another person.*

While it can be a powerful way of communicating feelings, it can also be a destructive attack unconsciously intended to destroy the comfort of the other by evoking the unbearable feelings a person has in the other.

Briefly the process involves deep splitting on the part of someone who needs to get rid of their hated parts although it has been suggested that Klein (and thus others) considered that it might be that good parts are also projected into a love object, which is equally unrealistic. Thus a manager or member of staff might be perceived by an influential person as 'doing no wrong', which can be a particularly destructive process in an organization, taking it away from its primary task and grip on reality.

## The depressive position

Klein considered that in the depressive position we move away from the extreme belief that objects are either all good or all bad towards a more realistic mix of emotions. Thus the concept of 'mixed' feelings towards objects arises, such as anger and remorse. The success of this step depends entirely upon the process of internalizing a good loving object producing an internal state of well-being. Thus anxieties and fears are *for* the object rather than *of* the object and relationships allow for greater separateness (see, for example, Hinshelwood, 1991).

## Supervision: the container and contained

The relationship between a supervisor and supervisee is one of great trust. If the relationship is to work the supervisee must have complete faith that the supervisor will be honest and also keep her confidence and advise her on appropriate actions. Similarly the supervisor must feel able to be honest with the supervisee about her work without fear of being undermined or even accused of bullying. This relationship is crucial if the organization is to function and develop and support its staff. The alternative is burnout, sickness, low morale, high turnover and the increased risk of system failure to protect a vulnerable child or adult.

The work of Wilfred Bion (a psychoanalyst who himself was analysed by Melanie Klein) provides important insights into group and organizational behaviours (as discussed in Chapters 3 and 6). As part of his clinical work he developed the key concepts of the container/contained to describe initially the role of the mother and the infant and the psychoanalyst and patient. This model is particularly valuable in the supervisory relationship.

Bion proposed that there is a fundamental emotional connection between the mother and her baby, which is mirrored in other therapeutic relationships. The mother caring for her baby experiences what Bion calls 'maternal reverie'. That means that she can sense, and then hold on to, the baby's frustrations and anxieties and later feed them back to the baby in a form that is manageable. Thus the mother gives the baby a sense that the terrors that appear to lurk in the imagination about the outside world are not quite as they seem. They can be observed, understood and managed. Of course this is a particular template of inter-subjectivity which does not apply to all and there may of course be negative containment that causes great emotional and psychotic distress in individuals during childhood and later life (Grotstein, 2007).

In similar vein the psychoanalyst relates to their patient by creating a safe place in which the analyst holds the patient's fears until they can be managed. Mothers and analysts do not necessarily find this an easy or comfortable experience themselves. They may worry for the person they are caring for, feel perhaps that they themselves may not have the strength to contain the anxieties about particular circumstances. A mother living in a crisis-torn world where there is not enough food or she is in danger may act as the container but without support and without the belief that she can turn the baby's fear into something benign. In the 1997 film *Life is Beautiful*, a Jewish-Italian father and son are taken to a Nazi concentration camp and the father persuades his son right up until the camp is liberated that they are taking part in a game. The young son believes this story even to the last when his father gets him to hide in a box (from which he is eventually liberated) while the father himself dies at the hands of the Nazi guards.

In supervision the senior practitioner will have had experience of much of what the social worker is having to face in their work and should be able to act as a container for frustrations and anxieties. and the social worker benefits from the experience of having the anxieties contained. This process in social work relies on the abilities of both supervisor (or manager) and supervisee to think and reflect on their practice and how it might be done differently and to value what is being done well. There is of course an apparent expectation that social workers hold all the anxieties for junior staff, senior managers and service users. This is emotionally and physically dangerous, but the ability to hold some anxieties for yourself and others that can be 'processed' and represented as less terrifying, or at least until they are tolerable, is valuable.There are of course, particularly in austere times, occasions where the supervisor may not be able to contain anxieties, as when jobs are threatened or mistakes have been made and social workers are scapegoats of the public and the media. However, even then the container/contained relationship and reflection enable more measured responses within and outside of the organization.

## 'Turning a blind eye'

Psychoanalytic practice has been particularly mindful of what we know and don't know and what we see but don't see. This is critical when working with service users who wish to keep a close watch to prevent their family or personal boundary being crossed by professional social workers.

'Turning a blind eye' means literally not 'seeing' evidence of behaviour, processes or events taking place in front of our eyes. By implication this suggests that the blind eye is turned towards unpalatable information and thus likely to raise questions of morality and/or corruption in relationships and organizations or worries that we are not being given the full story by service users in cases of potential abuse. Not every individual or group who turns a blind eye is necessarily immoral or corrupt. Indeed frequently we 'choose' to ignore impending dangers to our *own* safety from threatening individuals or regimes, as for example in violent interpersonal relationships (Nicolson, 2010b) or mass extermination of an ethnic or social group (Laquer, 1982).

There are different levels at which we *fail* or *chose not* to see or recognize this information. The complexity of the processes in which individuals engage with and *construct* their reality is articulated by Steiner (1985) who asserts:

In recent years it has become evident that our contact with reality is not an all or none affair ... [and there is a situation] in which we seem to have access to reality but choose to ignore it because it proves convenient to do so. I refer to this mechanism as turning a blind eye because I think this conveys the right degree of ambiguity as to how conscious or unconscious the knowledge is. (p. 161)

In this extract from Steiner's paper he makes clear that to 'see' or 'not to see' (consciously or unconsciously) represents *an action* by the individual(s) involved.One intriguing example, not immediately related to social work although a graphic illustration of 'not seeing', was the case of Eddie Chapman, a British double agent during World War II, who worked both for the British Secret Service and its German counterpart, the Abwehr (MacIntyre, 2007). Most of the Abwehr were anti-Nazi, as were many upper-class Germans, including Chapman's German handler Stephan von Gröning. Von Gröning's status benefitted from Chapman's (apparent) skills as a spy even though Chapman's 'exploits' against the British (including faked sabotage) were fabrications. However, 'Chapman [also] needed von Gröning to believe him, and von Gröning needed Chapman to succeed, forging a strange, unspoken complicity' (p.226). The fear for the spymaster was to have an inactive agent. 'If von Gröning suspected he was being lied to, that the entire tale of sabotage, heroism and escape was a monstrous fabrication, he said nothing and the heavy-lidded eyes chose not to see' (p. 227).

This intriguing relationship must have had both conscious and unconscious elements to it. What flies against 'logic' is that the man with the (apparent) power (von Gröning) was prepared to place his desire for Chapman's success above the 'truth' that the 'intelligence' he was gaining was, in fact, a fiction. Was von Gröning thus a traitor? Perhaps the (unspoken) anti-Nazi ethos of the Abwehr unconsciously engaged him (and of course Chapman) in a destructive phantasy towards Hitler? Perhaps the issue was simply that von Gröning had initially believed and trusted Chapman, boasted of his agent's exploits so that the 'truth' that he had been betrayed (and had been totally unaware of that betrayal) was so intolerable and shameful that he colluded unconsciously with Chapman in a joint phantasy cover-up. The outcome, at the time, was that von Gröning kept his sense of self/pride intact and Chapman kept his cover.

It could be argued that in some cases it is (unconsciously) in the interests of social workers and their managers to believe a service user's story even when closer scrutiny would make the lie glaringly obvious.

The cases of Jasmine Beckford and Maria Colwell, for example, where social workers were criticized for not seeing what was going on despite the fact that abuses were being reported to them by neighbours. Remember also how social workers and doctors only saw the chocolate covering Peter Connelly's face but not the cuts, burns and bruises beneath it and the doctor who examined him just before he died only saw a bad-tempered toddler and not a baby with a broken back.

## Conclusions

Reflective and relational practice with the intention of looking critically at yourself, your relationships and your organization gradually enables you to look bravely at truths that you might previously have preferred not to know so that you come to understand that effective practice is about *seeing, feeling and thinking* rather than turning a blind eye to danger. Psychoanalytic and systemic thinking had been off the social work training and practice agenda for at least two decades until the publication of the Munro report (Munro, 2011) on child protection and the development of the 'Hackney Model' of integrated systemic practice (Goodman and Trowler, 2012). A similar approach also has a valuable contribution to make to best practice with vulnerable adults and within mental health services. Gillian Ruch (2005) makes a plea for rethinking the role of emotion in child and family social work.

As an alternative but complementary model to the one identified in Chapters 4 and 5, which translates counselling skills into social work practice, this chapter introduced a model which linked systemic thinking and psychoanalysis. In the following chapter focusing on leadership, some of these themes will be developed further.

### Putting it into practice 7

7a. In reflective practice it is useful to explore some of the images of the organization you 'hold in mind' particularly the impact the images might have on i) working collaboratively and ii) service delivery.

Specific examples of these images are:

- images (and fantasies) held about 'management' which highlight the construction of 'authority' in the system and its impact on practice;
- images (and fantasies) held about the 'others' (e.g. colleagues in the same organization but on a different site or a different unit) which brings boundary management into play;
- how these images (and fantasies) facilitate and hinder practice with service users.

It is also useful to think and reflect similarly on your encounters with service users.

7b. Put yourself in the 'mind' of another person in your organization (a member of your team, an administrator, someone at a different level of the organization from yourself. Then describe what you see – particularly how you and your team might be seen and how junior and senior staff are viewed from this fantasy perspective.

## Further reading

Reading here would include the reading for Chapter 3.

Fook, J., and Gardner, F. (2010) *Practising Critical Reflection: A Resource Handbook*, Maidenhead, McGraw-Hill/Open University Press.

It is important to consider the work of Jan Fook and her colleagues on Critical Reflection. The book includes not only a clear model of their approach with examples throughout but also access to a website with greater detail.

Huffington, C., Armstrong, D., Halton, W., Hoyle, L., and Pooley, J. (2007) (eds), *Working Below the Surface: The Emotional Life of Contemporary Organizatons*, London, Karnac.

This edited volume sets out key examples of theory and practice about what lies behind the defensive facades of organizational life and is particularly useful for examining authority, systems, change management and leadership.

## CHAPTER 8

# Leadership and management in social work organizations

**CHAPTER OVERVIEW**

In this chapter we show that:

- Leadership in social work practice occurs at all levels.
- Leadership is formally and informally transmitted across the organization in different ways according to the task.
- Good leadership can be transformational.
- Poor leadership can be disastrous.
- Effective followership is vital if leadership is to work.
- Leaders might feel powerless as well as powerful and conversely a follower may feel more powerful than a leader

In this chapter we examine the increasingly important concept of 'leadership', focusing on it as a *process* rather than the characteristics of a *person* (Fairhurst, 2009). We also make the case for *reflective-relational leadership* that takes account of emotional and social intelligence and reflective practice (Comte, 2005; Nicolson, 2014).

Social workers take the lead, or follow, with each of their cases. Their managers lead their particular team. Throughout the hierarchical structure of all social work agencies leadership/followership takes place according to the role a person occupies (team manager) or according to the particular project they are involved in (for example, a serious case review). When you are the principal worker on a project or a case you lead, if you are involved with someone else's project or case you follow.

## Introduction: what do we know about leadership?

Leadership is an idea, practice and process with popular currency in contemporary life. Sporting, political, organizational and professional leadership have all come into question. Leadership appears to be at the heart of whether an organization succeeds or fails. From Gordon Brown, the ex-prime minister, through to the late Muammar Gaddafi, the contentious Libyan leader, the quality of politicians' leadership has been constantly analysed and their failings and successes attributed to their leadership abilities. The deaths at the Mid Staffordshire Hospital Foundation Trust (http://www.midstaffspublicinquiry.com/news/2013/02/publication-inquiry-final-report) and the corruption leading to failure at Enron are examples of failed and corrupt leadership. There is little doubt now that leadership across the social work profession is under pressure and under scrutiny (Laming, 2003; Munro, 2011).

Why has leadership become such a key issue, and what is currently known about leaders and leadership? The ongoing attempt to identify the characteristics necessary for effective leadership has been described as an 'obsession' studied more extensively than almost any other characteristic of human behaviour (Higgs, 2002; Tourish, 2008). Alimo-Metcalfe and Alban-Metcalfe (2009) in their comprehensive review of the literature, show that formal studies of leadership date back (at least) to the beginning of the twentieth century. They propose, that despite changes in the way leadership has been studied and the underlying epistemological stance taken by the researchers, 'in all cases, the emphasis has been on identifying those factors that make certain individuals particularly effective in influencing the behaviour of other individuals or groups and in making things happen that would not otherwise occur or preventing undesired outcomes' (p. 2). As 'many have pointed out, that in spite of the plethora of studies, we still seem to know little about the defining characteristics of effective leadership' (Higgs, 2002, p. 3). Even so this does not appear to have quelled the appetite for pursuing an ideal of leadership, impelled by the changing demands of organizations, echoed across public sector institutions such as the NHS, including mental health services and CAMHS (Child and Adolescent Mental Health Service), as well as wider children's services and services for vulnerable adults (Collier and Esteban, 2000).

## What does it take to lead effectively?

What factors might actually contribute to understanding how certain characteristics might be more or less relevant or effective in particular organizations (Fairhurst, 2009; Liden and Antonakis, 2009; Uhl-Bien, 2006)? One important set of findings suggest that leadership does have an effect on organizational performance – for good and for ill (Currie et al., 2009; Schilling, 2009). But in addition, or conversely, the context, culture, climate and/or structure of an organization each has an impact on the performance of the people who lead in it (Carroll et al., 2008; Goodwin, 2000; Michie and West, 2004). Bullying that is taken for granted by management impacts upon the culture of an organization. If the leadership is aggressive and there is a culture of blame, this process of relating to each other transmits across the team or organization to the 'followers'.

Focusing on the relationship(s) between 'leadership' and 'followership' and context has revitalized contemporary research, particularly through the development of qualitative research, discursive and social constructionist epistemologies (Keith Grint, 2005; Uhl-Bien, 2006), although it is unclear at this stage how far a connection might be developed between this research and its applications, for example in social work services (Fambrough and Hart, 2008).

## Theory and leadership

Leadership research and theory is prolific, with the consequence that numerous, frequently overlapping, models of leadership are available to agencies attempting to analyse or train leaders and indeed managers, as until relatively recently little distinction had been made between these two categories. Over the past fifty years leadership theories have shifted through different points of focus from the 'trait' (or 'great man') approach in the 1940s, through the 'behavioural' perspectives in the 1950s, whereby some styles of behaviour were seen as being more or less influential on potential followers. Then since the 1960s and 1970s the focus has been upon 'situational' leadership, based mostly upon Fiedler's 'contingency' theory which proposed that different leadership styles were needed for different situations (see Alimo-Metcalfe and Alban-Metcalfe, 2009; Weston, 2008, for further details). During the 1970s and 1980s leadership research, albeit prolific, had reached an all time low in terms of its perceived contribution to theory and added value to knowledge for practice, so that as Cummings (1981, p. 366, quoted in a review by Bryman, 2004) asserted, 'As we all know, the study and more particularly the results produced by the study of leadership has been a major disappointment for many of us working within organizational behaviour'.

Bryman unpicked the implications of the phrase 'as we all know' used by Cummings, noting that it was 'simultaneously sweeping and damning' (2004, p. 730). Bryman also picks out Miner's (1975) suggestion for temporarily abandoning the concept because of its limited utility in helping us understand organizational behaviour.

Why had leadership research reached this nadir during those decades? Why has there been a more recent upsurge of interest in leadership again almost to the point of saturation?

Bryman in his review suggests that the renewed confidence and interest in the study of leadership has come from improved measurement and analytic techniques; greater use of meta-analysis so that more systematic reviews could be compiled; the emphasis on *transformational leadership* and *charismatic leadership* which have provided a fulcrum for the area of research; more and better cross-cultural studies; and greater diversity in the types of leadership and organizational contexts that have been studied.

A factor that may also have contributed to the idea that leadership research continues to be fruitful is that a greater diversity of methodological approaches have been added and Bryman's review specifically focused on the value added by qualitative research.

Towards the end of the 1980s and beyond, thinking about the meaning(s) of leadership came to take greater precedence than in the previous two decades, possibly because of a perceived dearth of leadership *per se*.

These deliberations cast light on:

- the *interactions between leaders and followers* and organizational cultures (Avolio et al., 2004; Lewis, 2000; Schilling, 2009);
- the *management of emotion* (George, 2000; Lewis, 2005; Pescosolido, 2002);
- the *processes* of leadership (Collinson, 2005; Dopson and Waddington, 1996; Vangen and Huxham, 2003).

Even so, or perhaps because of the use of qualitative approaches and related conceptualization, Alvesson and Sveningsson (2003) were able to entitle a paper arising out of their study of leadership in a research and development company: 'The great disappearing act: difficulties in doing "leadership".' By this they meant that during their study they were able to identify how the existence of the label 'leadership' led to an assumption that the concept had an empirical reality. However the results of their work indicated that leadership might be better explained as a *process or series of processes of interaction*. This conclusion raises questions about mainstream thinking on leadership which presumes observable and possibly measurable characteristics (Alvesson and Sveningsson, 2003, p. 361; see also Ford, 2010).

Of late there has been reconsideration and development of ideas about leadership in context taking account of the relevance of some earlier studies of organizations (for example, Lewin, 1947) and open systems theories (Laughlin and Sher, 2010) and new epistemological positions (Ford, 2010).

## Emotional dimensions

Models of leadership and organization theory have evolved over time and leadership and organizational structures and cultures are intrinsically linked in the literature. Leadership, if it is to motivate, innovate and move organizations to change, has to have an *emotional dimension* and, thus, effective leaders have a clear *emotional agenda* (as well as a strategic and structural one) which is particularly acute in social services working to serve people's social care needs (Ashforth and Humphrey, 1995; Bolton, 2000; Pye, 2005).

Exploring organizations and leadership at the level of 'emotion' has become contested territory, as recognition that organizations and their leaders need to take account of emotional engagement (Alimo-Metcalfe and Alban-Metcalfe, 2009; Vince and Broussine, 1996) at all levels of the workplace, has emerged. Prior to the 1980s, organizational literature had been dominated by a cognitive orientation (George, 2000) which favoured the rational, 'masculine' and scientific explanations of organizations and their leaders. This notion therefore ignored the (so-called) irrational and 'feminine' characteristics of emotion, which were deemed detrimental to productivity and success. At that time emotions were regarded as the culprits that distort an individual's perceptual and cognitive faculties and therefore should be kept under control (Alvesson and

Sveningsson, 2003; Clarke et al., 2007; Dasborough, 2006; de Raeve, 2002; Ford, 2006).

As social and occupational psychologists began to study the effects of positive and negative moods on decision-making, job satisfaction, choice of work-based activities and organizational climate, however (Isen and Means, 1983; Rafaeli and Sutton, 1987, 1989), 'emotion' as part of organizational life gained impetus once again. This resurgence coincided with leadership theorists studying how moods and emotions could affect the quality of leadership (George, 2000).

It is possible to trace a rough trajectory from the 'hard-nosed' scientific management, with the organization perceived as a 'machine' in the early twentieth century, through towards a more humanistic, emotional and sometimes even spiritual way of thinking about contemporary leadership and organizational metaphors towards the twenty-first century, all of which are potentially transformational, not simply to the individuals concerned, but to the organizational dynamics.

Hochschild's (1983) *The Managed Heart* has been credited with being one of the earliest examples of research into emotions and organizational settings (Ashkanasy et al., 2002). She looked particularly at the airline industry and how airline cabin crew managed their emotions for dealing with difficult passengers and to promote a particular airline image. She termed this emotional management *'emotional labour'* (Hochschild, 1983).

Since this publication, the study of emotions in organizations has increased (Ashkanasy et al., 2002), with academics concentrating on key concepts such as emotional labour, emotional intelligence, mood analysis and Affective Events Theory (AET), and most recently a return to psychodynamic understanding of organizations and groups (Ford, 2010; Schwarz, 1990). Since the 1990s a plethora of literature has emphasized the role of emotional concerns in private sector organizations such as the airline industry (Hochschild, 1983; Taylor and Tyler, 2000; Tyler and Abbott, 1998), the service sector (Crang, 1994), merchant banking (McDowell and Court, 1994; Pugh, 2001), the law (Harris, 2002) and image consultancy (Bryson and Wellington, 2003; Wellington and Bryson, 2001).

However, emotionality in the public sector was mostly neglected until the 2000s when a surge of literature began to be published analysing the NHS (Allan and Smith, 2005; Bolton, 2000; G. Cummings et al., 2005; Hunter, 2005; Lewis, 2005; McCreight,

2005; McQueen, 2004; Michie and Gooty, 2005; Michie and West, 2004; Smith, 1992) and the fire service (D. Archer, 1999; Scott and Myers, 2005; Ward and Winstanley, 2006; Yarnal et al. 2004).

## Emotionally and socially intelligent leadership

The 'discovery' of emotional intelligence (EI), despite ongoing valid critiques (see below), marked a turning point in contemporary organizational theories and approaches to leadership because of the tradition that emotions represent a threat to rationality – a view that has been widespread particularly in North America and North-western Europe (Fambrough and Hart, 2008; Weston, 2008).

Mayer and Salovey (1995), who conceived the idea of emotional intelligence, defined it as the ability to manage and understand one's own and other people's emotions in a consistent way so as to reflectively promote emotional and intellectual growth. Goleman (1998) who popularized the concept, identified emotional intelligence as a set of competencies, redefined and restated by George (2000) as follows:

- The expression and appraisal of emotion.
- Enhancing cognitive process and decision-making.
- Emotional knowledge.
- Managing emotions.

These characteristics appear to have much in common with the rhetoric of transformational qualities of leadership, although in many ways EI has become a management 'tool' rather than a critical model. To this end (apparently) Goleman (Goleman, 2000; Goleman et al., 2001) focused on 'styles' and 'performance' which seem far away from the 'heady' descriptions below of qualities of emotionally intelligent leadership, which refer to feelings, empathy and creativity.

### The expression and appraisal of emotion

An emotionally intelligent person will be able to understand their own and others' feelings and be able to empathize, which may enable them to be manipulative for better or for worse.

## Enhancing cognitive processes and decision-making

Having emotional intelligence allows a person to use emotion to be creative, solve problems, make decisions and flexible plans for themselves and on behalf of a group. An emotionally intelligent leader will be able to judge their mood and make decisions accordingly. If the person is in a negative mood this may mean choosing to wait until such negative episodes have passed in order to make a comprehensive decision.

## Emotional knowledge

Emotionally intelligent people understand how other people may be affected by their negative moods and therefore may take care not to spread bad feeling around the group.

## Managing emotions

Many leaders are able to manage their followers' emotions as well as their own, but as indicated below, developing the qualities required to manage emotions effectively is highly complex and more about processes than style or performance (Fambrough and Hart, 2008; Hughes, 2005). As Fambrough and Hart argue, 'emotional intelligence' has passed into common use among organizational leaders with little recognition of the way it has been identified as problematic.

## What might be attractive about emotional intelligence to leaders in social work organizations?

The idea of emotional intelligence captured the imagination of some active in training NHS staff, for example, as a means to improve staff relationships and enable clinicians to empathize with their patients (Amendolair, 2003; Luker and McHugh, 2002). McQueen (2004), reflecting on the 1960s when health care workers were encouraged to hide their emotions from their patients for the sake of maintaining a professional role, suggests that in recent decades this view of nursing has changed and health care workers frequently display emotions to illustrate their commitment to patient care (Williams, 2000). McQueen suggests that emotionally intelligent nurses are important for building strong patient–nurse relationships (Conger and Kanungo, 1988 and Lewis, 2005).

Nurses with high emotional intelligence are able to build rapport quickly with their patients through communication and interactive skills (Schutte et al., 2001). There is returning pressure that social workers too might engage in a more emotionally intelligent approach, taking the unconscious into their work (Cornish, 2011; Gillian Ruch, 2005).

McQueen also states that 'emotional labour calls upon and engages' emotional intelligence (2004, p. 103). In order for patients to feel cared for, nurses have to constantly *perform* positive emotions and behaviours such as warmth, friendliness and consideration. However, when confronted with a 'difficult' patient nurses may experience negative emotions such as frustration, irritation or anger. The nurses must be emotionally intelligent enough to identify their emotions and then perform emotional labour to submerge the negative emotions in favour of more positive emotions (Bolton, 2003).

While EI *per se* needs to be understood more critically (Fambrough and Hart, 2008), the introduction of emotional management and engagement by leaders (and others) needs further scrutiny despite the best efforts of some management gurus. Emotion is a fact of personal, interpersonal and organizational life, particularly in the context of social work services (Howe, 2008; Morrison, 2007; Zeidner et al., 2004).

## Social intelligence

In 2006, taking account of advances in neurological psychology, Goleman (2006) proposed that because humans are *designed* for social connection, rapport and supportive emotional interactions enhance performance of managers and leaders. He listed these qualities under the umbrella of 'social intelligence' (SI) and identified four dimensions:

- *Synchronization* – whereby matching moods lead to a sense of rapport;
- *Attunement* – listening fully;
- *Social cognition* – understanding how people interact;
- *Social facility* – finding it easy to interact with others.

While some people have little difficulty meeting these criteria and mastering their social intelligence, others (such as Narcissists, Machiavellian and Psychopathic types), Goleman argues, do not have the capacity for social intelligence, and thus he proposes a means of *selecting* effective leaders by testing these qualities. This model, albeit individualistic, has something to offer through extending the theoretical underpinnings of 'people skills' and emphasizing the importance of taking followers and colleagues seriously in decision-making.

Following EI and SI in bringing management/organizational theories together with developments in psychology, particularly cognitive neuroscience and evolutionary psychology, is the reconsideration of the role of intuition in understanding leadership and organizational behaviours (Sadler-Smith, 2008). Sadler-Smith brings the idea of the 'gut feeling' into the foreground to explore the influence of this sense upon decision-making particularly under pressure (for example, in assessment of risk in children's services).

It seems that while there is a continuing trend towards an evidence-based understanding of leadership, there is also an emergence of features of human life that are difficult to explain and measure, although all the proponents cited above stick to the view that these characteristics are scientifically explicable and measureable despite challenges from both positivist and critical social constructionist positions (Ashforth and Humphrey, 1995; Conte, 2005).

## Who is responsible – the social worker or the boss?

The high-profile example of Sharon Shoesmith, Director of Haringey Children's Services, who was sacked in 2008 following the Ofsted Report on the death of the baby Peter Connelly, is illustrative of how leadership/followership works or fails to work. The Report's verdict on the Children's Services in Haringey was 'damning'. The review team identified a string of 'serious concerns' about the local authority's child protection services, which they condemned as 'inadequate'. A series of reviews identified missed opportunities when officials could have saved the little boy's life if they had acted properly on the warning signs in front of them. In 2011 the Court of Appeal stated that Shoesmith had been unfairly dismissed, had been made into a 'public sacrifice' and had not been given the opportunity to defend herself. For further information see the website: http://news.sky.com/skynews/Home/UK-News/Baby-P-Sharon-Shoesmith-Haringey-Council-Boss-When-Peter-Connelly-Died-Appeals-Over-Sacking/Article/200910115400994.

The story of Shoesmith's (apparently failed) leadership was preceded by the outcome of the inquiry into the death of Victoria Climbie, also involving Haringey Children's Services. The Laming inquiry into her death established that responsibility for child protection rested with the leader of the (consequently restructured) service. He suggested that if a manager did their job by asking pertinent questions or looking in a case file then such tragedies could be avoided. Laming highlighted 'widespread organizational malaise' as the principal reason that Victoria Climbie had not been protected (Laming, 2003, para 1.17). He stressed this point again – that the safety and well-being of children cannot depend on the abilities or 'inclinations' of individual members of staff but it is the organizations which must accept accountability. But 'who' are the organization? What is the responsibility of the senior management team running the service and what is the responsibility of the social work practitioner and their manager?

Eileen Munro's (2011) review of child protection services emphasized, as with the Laming inquiry, that failures in child protection are systemic but particularly that there has been an overemphasis on reducing risk through bureaucracy that has over-loaded the system, thus leaving the most vulnerable children and families without the support they need.

These reports both make it clear that social workers need to be better trained, more vigilant and less inclined to believe stories they are told (here it would perhaps be useful to take another look at the section on 'turning a blind eye' in Chapter 7). The reports also make it clear that the organizations themselves have much to improve both in reducing bureaucracy and improving communication.

## Distributed leadership

Distributed leadership has been a useful model in social work organizations but brings into question where the buck stops when a child at risk or vulnerable adult dies. Distributed leadership occurs when, at various levels, leadership behaviour, identity, role and responsibility are formally distributed to more than one individual or group of individuals. This model of practice has been at the forefront of much social scientific leadership research over the past ten years (Buchanan et al., 2007; Day et al., 2004; Gronn, 2002; Mehra et al., 2006). The implication of this interest in distributed leadership is that organizations have changed and previous models – including the charismatic, 'hero' leader and the 'command-and-control' organizational structures – are dysfunctional in a context where organizational change is rapid and diversification of strategic leadership and management essential (Butterfield et al., 2005; Dent, 2005; Goodwin, 2000). In a competitive, diverse and divergent environment, leadership needs to be distributed in order to enhance democratic governance, thus enhancing legitimacy and increasing survival chances (Currie et al., 2009). This is at odds with the Haringey/Shoesmith/Balls debacle and raises important questions for social workers. Social workers are professionally trained practitioners although they (mostly) operate in an over-managed, command-and-control system where they frequently feel disempowered.

Distributed leadership also implies that organizations where it is practised have (relatively) flat hierarchies with diverse service needs and expertise across all sectors of the organization (Huffington et al., 2007).

With this shift in focus of many leadership practices and leadership studies the definition of such leadership has been proposed as 'a status ascribed to one individual, an aggregate of separate individuals, sets of small numbers of individuals acting in concert or larger plural-member organizational units' (Gronn, 2002, p. 428). Gronn suggests also that when leadership is distributed it may be that the duration of that influence is limited, perhaps (structurally) to a single project and therefore (psychologically) distributed leadership might mean having to 'give up' leadership as well as take it up (Huffington et al., 2007). Furthermore, according to Gronn (2002), the most common understanding of distributed leadership, witnessed by the growing number of references to it in the research and policy literature, is that it applies to numerous people across an organization taking some degree of a leadership role or responsibility.

More importantly, Gronn identified distributed leadership as *concerted action*, meaning that there are many roles comprising a 'leadership complex' with at least three potential forms:

- *Collaborative modes of engagement* which arise spontaneously in the workplace. This suggests that leadership practice is 'stretched over' the context of the organization and not a function of those in managerial roles. However, if the team leader, business manager and other colleagues share ideas for change or particular activities they *may* 'pool their expertise and regularize their conduct to solve a problem after which they may disband' (Gronn, 2002, p. 430). This may be a particular case or change management project for instance.

- The *intuitive understanding* that develops as part of a close working relationship among colleagues. These relationships tend to happen over time when organization members come to rely on each other and develop a close working relationship, to solve problems or bring about change and others might be involved in a 'framework of understanding'. This brings with it some problems related to power, influence and the impact on followers if they feel (or are) out of the loop.
- The variety of *structural relations* and institutionalized arrangements which constitute attempts to regularize distributed action. Thus, for example, if there were dissatisfaction with existing arrangements for particular practices, a team of 'equals' might emerge to find ways to improve or change the problematic practices. You will recall the discussion of power relationships and power-communication structures from Chapter 6.

Gronn argues the importance of examination of these different forms of concerted action to understand where influence (and thus leadership and power) might lie in any organizational context. Emotionally, however, these different models of distributed leadership suggest the impact of these structures and practices at a deeper level (Gabriel, 2004) particularly around authority (Halton, 2007; Hirschhorn, 1997) competition (Morgan, 2006) rivalry and envy (K. T. James and Arroba, 2005; Stein, 2005).

Emotional engagement, while available to human consciousness, also takes place at an unconscious level (Gabriel, 2004; Hugh, 1986; Lyons-Ruth, 1999; Morgan, 2006; Willmott, 1986), and anxiety or stress is particularly salient when having to take potentially life-saving decisions (James and Huffington, 2004; Menzies, 1970).

## Transformational leadership and followership

Transformational leadership is leadership that achieves transformational change in an organization through helping the 'followers' to learn and develop. Through transformational leadership members of the organization have had their frame of reference challenged and successful leadership occurs when thinking and feelings are accordingly transformed (Hafford-Letchfield et al., 2008).The ideas that have formerly characterized transformational leadership models, such as 'charisma', 'influence', 'inspiration','thoughtfulness' and 'consideration', have intellectual roots beyond contemporary management theory and training. They are more closely related to group and organizational theories with late nineteenth- and early twentieth-century origins (De Board, 1978; Gabriel, 2004), from which much contemporary organizational theory has emerged.

To reiterate from the more detailed discussion about understanding groups from Chapter 6, the first significant attempt to analyse group behaviour was made at the start of the twentieth century by Le Bon (1917/1920), whose book *The Crowd* illustrated his observation that individuals in a large group can demonstrate a 'collective mind' which emerges when people are bound together in some way. McDougall's book *The Group Mind* (1922/2009) and Sigmund Freud's *Group Psychology and the Analysis of the Ego* (1921/1922) also focused on what would subsequently come to be recognized as unconscious group processes. Freud developed Le Bon's and McDougall's ideas in the context of psychodynamic theory, arguing that the binding force of the group derives from the *emotional* ties of the members, which are expressions of their libido or drive.

Studies of (and human 'experiments' about) group psychology, taking some of this perspective on board, flourished after World War II, conducted and further developed by psychiatrists in the newly formed NHS. In Britain the work of Wilfred Bion, Tom Main, Maxwell Jones and others led to innovations in both group psychotherapy and the study of organizations. Bion's work on group relations and dynamics which contributed to the development of the Group Relations Training Programme (GRTP) at the Tavistock Institute in 1957 evolved into the Leicester Conferences with other organizations using this model across the world (Miller, 1993). Contemporary knowledge and understanding continues to reflect back upon this early work.

What was learnt during this period about group dynamics and group relations represents an important dimension in the understanding of contemporary organizations and the relationship between leaders and followers which we saw in Chapters 3 and 6 in our discussion of teams and group dynamics. It is important to note how the intellectual journey from work on emotional labour to social intelligence and intuition has so far largely neglected to explore the extent to which unconscious processes remain part of the emotional context of human social interaction (Allan and Smith, 2005, p. 21).

In social work (as in medicine and nursing) it is inevitable that negative events, such as a child death or a vulnerable adult's suicide, will take place. When death does occur social workers may display emotions (consciously and unconsciously), such as anger, depression, anxiety and fear (Allan and Smith, 2005; Obholzer and Roberts, 1994; Allan 2001; Smith et al., 2003). Obholzer asserts that '[he] believes that many of the organizations' difficulties that occur in hospital settings arise from a neglect of the unconscious psychological impact of death and near-death on patients and staff' (1994, p.171). He explains that hospitals are sites where anxieties about social taboos such as death are *contained,* that is that staff and the organization overall takes away the anxiety and the responsibility for care from the relatives. Patients and staff are socialized to believe that hospitals are institutions where illness is treated and that medical knowledge and practice is infallible. When death does occur, medical staff and the patient's relatives may feel *duped* by the institution they believed would save their loved one. Similarly when social work practices fail, individuals, particularly in cases where babies and young children are tortured, abused and die of their injuries and neglect, are 'sacrificed' (as discussed above in the case of Sharon Shoesmith) to allay public distress and guilt. Shoesmith herself maintains that the death of Peter Connelly will remain with her for the rest of her life.

At the turn of the nineteenth to the twentieth centuries psycho-analytic ideas were seen to have something new and important to say, not only about the psychology of the individual and the role of the individual unconscious, but about *unconscious processes when people converge in groups and crowds,* as shown above. From psychoanalytic theory we take up ideas again today specifically about the relationships which exist between followers and leaders, made explicit in the paradigm shift from transactional to transfor-mational leadership. Working together and accepting or resisting influence comes not only with an observable set of behaviours and measurable emotions, but with unconscious and 'secret' ones including dependency, envy, power, anger, authority and emotional contagion, which may be either conscious or unconscious but have important consequences for behaviours (Burke et al., 2006; Simpson and French, 2005; Stein, 2005; Whiteley, 1997).

In a landmark study of leadership in the NHS (Nicolson et al., 2011), for example, we saw how two senior managers found themselves unable to influence despite their senior roles, legitimacy and operational power. As Gabriel (2004) has argued elsewhere, 'emotions are no simple side-effects of mental life' as 'emotion lies at the heart of human motivation' (p.215). In another study of children's services managers (followers) (Nicolson, 2010a) it seemed that this group of middle managers saw the senior managers as all-powerful and difficult to trust and difficult to challenge.

## Conclusions: towards reflective-relational leadership

Reflective-relational leadership is potentially transformational, resting its main case on being leadership with an emotionally and socially intelligent approach. Holding a systemic, psychoanalytic and reflective stance towards practice, including leadership and organizational consultancy, brings together the best of social work practices from the last 30 years. Even though social workers have frequently acted and seen themselves as service users' advocates, they have always lived with the danger of missing vital evidence about their own and others' behaviours. There has been a history of social workers and their managers failing to see 'what is going on' and as a consequence families, vulnerable individuals and social workers themselves have suffered in various ways. Anxiety-driven, risk-averse, box-ticking leadership and management has demonstrably failed and the only alternative is for organizations and their professional staff to face their systemic weaknesses and manage (rather than defend themselves from) anxieties (Cornish, 2011; Munro, 2011). While there has been something of a restatement of the value of psychoanalytic theory in social work (Bower, 2005), critical and radical perspectives also need to be taken into account with a focus on depth and providing an appropriate place for emotion (Houston, 2001; Ritchie and Woodward, 2009). As Featherstone and colleagues suggest in their rejoinder to Munro (Featherstone et al., 2011), thinking systemically in order to counter the excessive managerial culture is unlikely to mitigate the corrosive effects of rising social inequalities.

'Reflective-relational leadership' offers a model to takes different approaches to social work practice seriously.

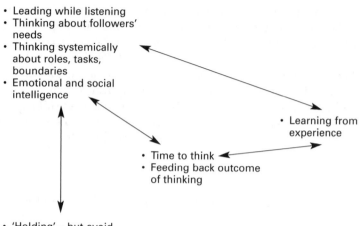

- Leading while listening
- Thinking about followers' needs
- Thinking systemically about roles, tasks, boundaries
- Emotional and social intelligence

- Learning from experience

- Time to think
- Feeding back outcome of thinking

- 'Holding' – but avoid strain on yourself as leader
- Reframing anxieties and taking care of self and others
- Managing staff and organizational anxieties

**Figure 8.1** Reflective-relational leadership

## Putting it into practice 8

8a. What impact might the intervention of the (then) Children's Secretary Ed Balls have had upon middle managers and social work practitioners, when he publicly removed Sharon Shoesmith from office in Haringey Children's Services?

8b. Think of an example of transformational leadership from your organization or your social work course. What made it transformational? Did it rely upon just one individual?

8c. Imagine sharing leadership across your organization and think of ways it might be more effective than top-down/ command-and-control leadership and in what way it might not be effective. What are the risks of distributing leadership in this way?

## Further reading

There are now numerous new and classic books on the market about leadership and management and there is increasing interest in their relevance to social work practice. Hafford-Letchfield and colleagues' 2008 book, *Leadership and Management in Social Care* (London, Sage) focuses on social work practice. It is clearly set out and relevant to all of you who aspire or practise as leaders and managers and also those of you who want to make sense of the management structures you are working within.

Keith Grint's very short introduction is just what it says and overviews key theories of leadership providing a helpful means of getting to grips with this vast area of research and theory (Grint (2010) *Leadership: A Very Short Introduction*, Oxford, Oxford University Press). It is easy to understand and quick to read – both great advantages.

# Concluding remarks

This book is our attempt to show some important ways in which psychological knowledge, research and practice might contribute to social work theory and practice. Our plan has been to bring the student and practitioner to a rapid awareness of what psychology can offer, introducing different perspectives from research as well as recognizing psychology as underpinning aspects of practice and professional development.

Social workers and their managers are faced every day with complex and challenging tasks, holding responsibilities to ensure the safety and well-being of vulnerable children, families and lone adults. The responsibilities that come with this role are daunting and it is no surprise that social workers and their managers sometimes fail. It is also no surprise that it is these intermittent failures that skew public attention from the majority of social work practice that succeeds.

This being the case, we have demonstrated ways in which social workers might look after and manage themselves and each other in positive, developmental ways. We identified how psychology may be applied theoretically to understand groups of service users and communities; how social workers relate to each other and their organizations, and how organizations may be helped to change into more reflective and relational ones.

The well-being of the social worker her/himself has also been at the heart of this book and we have brought together thinking about self-care, particularly working with strengths. Social work is a challenging and sometimes relentless set of tasks in what are often felt to be unforgiving organizations. Social work, though, is a vital profession – one which makes an important contribution to challenging oppression, social exclusion and structural inequalities. The burden of these challenges may feel and in reality be massive. Social workers, their managers and the systems they work in share responsibility for ensuring that the social worker is cared for and enabled to care for those they are charged to protect.

We thus offered a variety of practical guides to working with others individually and in groups drawing attention to the role of personality type and how recognition of difference provides a framework for mutual understanding. We focused on different approaches (counselling and psychoanalytic) to working with others while suggesting how theory underpins all effective, evidence-based social work practice and leadership.

# A note on counselling

This appendix discusses an integrative model of counselling or 'problem management'. Some problems cannot be solved in any complete sense, but all problems can be 'managed' (Egan, 2010). As with the skills, the idea is for you to try out those parts of the model which make sense to you and 'fit' you, and to do this gradually and systematically, that is, practice with analysis/feedback as discussed early in Chapter 5. The model will either clarify part of what you do already, and perhaps crystallize it, or suggest new aspects of counselling to integrate into your own style.

The three-stage model of counselling outlined in Table A1.1 is broadly consistent with other widely used approaches, for example, Feltham and Dryden (2006), Egan (2010) and Hill (2009). Many of the interviewing skills discussed in Chapter 5 are counselling skills too, but with different emphases, for example, fewer questions and more paraphrasing.

In Stage 1, the counsellor uses listening skills to help the client clarify, and to begin to form a trusting relationship. Stage 1 is sufficient for some clients: change of attitude, or a decision about what to do, emerges naturally, without further help.

**Table A1.1** A three-stage model of integrative counselling

| |
|---|
| **Stage 1: Support** |
| The counsellor respects and empathizes with the client and is genuine. The client explores their thoughts and feelings about one or more problems. |
| **Stage 2 (if necessary): Challenge or new perspectives** |
| The counsellor suggests, or helps the client suggest, new ways of looking at a problem. The client explores their reactions to this new perspective. |
| **Stage 3 (if necessary): Action** |
| The counsellor and the client decide what if anything to do about a problem. |

Stage 2 is, if necessary, offering new perspectives to the client. The client may then see his or her problem differently, 'reframe' it, feel differently about it. Stages 1 and 2 are sufficient for some clients. Stage 3 is, if necessary, helping the client decide what to do, and to evaluate the results. Good goals are specific and realistic. Listening and new perspective skills can be used throughout and taking small steps is a useful principle.

The notion of small steps is related to another issue: how much change is possible? Some problems can be solved while others are best understood as normal human variation. Recognizing limits to change can liberate a person to put energy into other things: 'I'm never going to be an X but I can manage X and concentrate on what I can do well, my strengths and potential strengths' (as discussed in Chapter 4).

The three-stage model is a guide, not a mechanical procedure. Thus, some clients present one problem clearly, others many confused problems at once. Some need only Stage 1 (or, more rarely, only a later stage), or Stage 1 for one problem, but all three stages for another, and so on. It is flexible for style of counselling too. Each counsellor can give the model their own emphasis and flavour but, in general terms, the main value of the model remains: it *slows down* the way we normally respond to problems, with the aim of being more effective and saving time overall. It is thus impeccably logical – indeed obvious – but not what we usually do. Instead, we tend to think about actions before exploring a problem sufficiently or to feel stuck and hopeless.

The model also provides a map and a framework. The map allows the counsellor to locate a particular point in the session or the purpose of a particular intervention, with implications for what to do next, and the framework can organize counselling techniques from other approaches, turning a haphazard eclecticism into a more systematic one.

Appendix II is a checklist for analysing a counselling session. The guidelines for using the checklist for analysing interviews (Table 5.1) also apply here.

# A checklist for analysing your counselling sessions

## Preparation

*Did I:*

Plan the interview? (But responding to your client's aims is a strong priority.)
Prepare the seating etc?
Clear my mind?
Negotiate or renegotiate a contract (if appropriate)?

## Stage 1

*Did I:*

Attend?
Paraphrase emotions?
Paraphrase content?
Summarize?
Use any of the other techniques for 'moving interviews forward' (if appropriate)?
Control the process (as opposed to the content)?

## Stage 2 (if appropriate)

*Did I:*

Earn the right (through being sufficiently empathic) to suggest a new perspective?

## Stage 3 (if appropriate)

*Did I help my client:*

Set workable goals?
Examine the consequences of achieving the goals?

Choose which goals to pursue?
Generate a variety of strategies?
Evaluate the strategies?
Decide on action(s)?

## Overall:

How is my client?
Was I empathic?
Respectful (accepting)?
Genuine?
How was the balance between support and challenge?
Did I overuse any skills or neglect others?
What about pace?
Mannerisms?
Posture?
Which stage is each problem in?
What of value did this interview achieve?
Are there any changes to my approach to try next time?
What state am I in? Is there anything it would be helpful to do
e.g. relax, write in journal style, talk to someone?

# Gordon Lawrence's descriptions of the sixteen MBTI 'types' emphasizing motives and values

## ENTJ

Intuitive, innovative ORGANIZERS; analytical, systematic, confident; push to get action on new ideas and challenges. Having Extraverted THINKING as their strongest mental process, ENTJs are at their best when they can take charge and set things in logical order. They value:

Analysing abstract problems, complex situations
Foresight; pursuing a vision
Changing, organizing things to fit their vision
Putting theory into practice, ideas into action
Working to a plan and schedule
Initiating, then delegating
Efficiency; removing obstacles and confusion
Probing new possibilities
Holding self and others to high standards
Having things settled and closed
Tough-mindedness, directness, task-focused behaviour
Objective principles; fairness, justice
Assertive, direct action
Intellectual resourcefulness
Driving toward broad goals along a logical path
Designing structures and strategies
Seeking out logical flaws.

## ISFP

Observant, loyal HELPERS; reflective, realistic, empathic, patient with details. Shunning disagreements, they are gentle, reserved and modest. Having Introverted FEELING as their strongest mental process, they are at their best when responding to the needs of others. They value:

Personal loyalty; a close, loyal friend
Finding delight in the moment
Seeing what needs doing to improve the moment
Freedom from organizational constraints
Working individually
Peacemaking behind the scenes
Attentiveness to feelings
Harmonious, cooperative work settings
Spontaneous, hands-on exploration
Gentle, respectful interactions
Deeply held personal beliefs
Reserved, reflective behaviour
Practical, useful skills and know-how
Having their work life be fully consistent with deeply held values
Showing and receiving appreciation.

## ESTJ

Fact-minded practical ORGANIZERS; assertive, analytical, systematic; push to get things done, working smoothly and efficiently. Having Extraverted THINKING as their strongest mental process, they are at their best when they can take charge and set things in logical order. They value:

Results; doing, acting
Planned, organized work and play
Common-sense practicality
Consistency; standard procedures
Concrete, present-day usefulness
Deciding quickly and logically
Having things settled and closed
Rules, objective standards, fairness by the rules
Task-focused behaviour
Directness, tough-mindedness
Orderliness; no loose ends
Systematic structure; efficiency
Categorizing aspects of their life
Scheduling and monitoring
Protecting what works.

## INFP

Imaginative, independent HELPERS; reflective, inquisitive, empathic, loyal to ideals; more tuned to possibilities than practicalities. Having Introverted FEELING as their strongest mental process, they are at their best when their inner ideals find expression in their helping of people. They value:

Harmony in the inner life of ideas
Harmonious work settings; working individually
Seeing the big picture possibilities
Creativity; curiosity, exploring
Helping people find their potential
Giving ample time to reflect on decisions
Adaptability and openness
Compassion and caring; attention to feelings
Work that lets them express their idealism
Gentle, respectful interactions
An inner compass; being unique
Showing appreciation and being appreciated
Ideas, language and writing
A close, loyal friend
Perfecting what is important.

## ESFJ

Practical HARMONIZERS, workers with people; sociable, orderly, opinioned; conscientious, realistic and well tuned to the here and now. Having Extraverted FEELING as their strongest mental process, they are at their best when responsible for winning people's cooperation with personal caring and practical help. They value:

An active, sociable life, with many relationships
A concrete, present-day view of life
Making daily routines into gracious living
Staying closely tuned to people they care about so as to avoid interpersonal troubles
Talking out problems cooperatively, caringly
Approaching problems through rules, authority, standard procedures

Caring, compassion, and tactfulness
Helping organizations serve their members well
Responsiveness to others and to traditions
Being prepared, reliability in tangible, daily work
Loyalty and faithfulness
Practical skillfulness grounded in experience
Structured learning in a humane setting
Appreciation.

## INTP

Inquisitive ANALYSERS; reflective, independent, curious; more interested in organizing ideas than situations or people. Having Introverted THINKING as their strongest mental process, they are at their best when following their intellectual curiosity, analysing complexities to find the underlying logical principles.

They value:

A reserved outer life; an inner life of logical inquiry
Pursuing interests in depth, with concentration
Work and play that is intriguing, not routine
Being free of emotional issues when working
Working on problems that respond to detached intuitive analysis and theorizing
Approaching problems by reframing the obvious
Complex intellectual mysteries
Being absorbed in abstract, mental work
Freedom from organizational constraints
Independence and nonconformance
Intellectual quickness, ingenuity, invention
Competence in the world of ideas
Spontaneous learning by following curiosity and inspirations.

## ENFJ

Imaginative HARMONIZERS, workers with people; expressive, orderly, opinioned, conscientious; curious about new ideas and possibilities. Having Extraverted FEELING as their strongest mental process, they are at their best when responsible for winning people's cooperation with caring insight into their needs. They value:

Having a wide circle of relationships
Having a positive, enthusiastic view of life
Seeing subtleties in people and interactions
Understanding others' needs and concerns
An active, energizing social life
Seeing possibilities in people
Thorough follow-through on important projects
Working on several projects at once
Caring and imaginative problem solving
Maintaining relationships to make things work
Shaping organizations to better serve members
Sociability and responsiveness
Structured learning in a humane setting
Caring, compassion, and tactfulness
Appreciation as the natural means of encouraging improvements.

## ISTP

Practical ANALYSERS; value exactness; more interested in organizing data than situations or people; reflective, cool and curious observers of life. Having Introverted THINKING as their strongest mental process, they are at their best when analysing experience to find the logical order and underlying properties of things. They value:

A reserved outer life
Having a concrete, present-day view of life
Clear, exact facts (a large storehouse of them)
Looking for efficient, least-effort solutions based on experience
Knowing how mechanical things work
Pursuing interests in depth, such as hobbies
Collecting things of interest
Working on problems that respond to detached, sequential analysis and adaptability
Freedom from organizational constraints
Independence and self-management
Spontaneous hands-on learning experience

Having useful technical expertise
Critical analysis as a means to improving things.

## ESTP

REALISTIC ADAPTERS in the world of material things; good-natured, easy-going; oriented to practical, firsthand experience; highly observant of details of things. Having Extraverted SENS-ING as their strongest mental process, they are at their best when free to act on impulses, or responding to concrete problems that need solving. They value:

A life of outward, playful action in the moment
Being a troubleshooter
Finding ways to use the existing system
Clear, concrete, exact facts
Knowing the way mechanical things work
Being direct, to the point
Learning through spontaneous, hands-on action
Practical action, more than words
Plunging into new adventures
Responding to practical needs as they arise
Seeing the expedient thing and acting on it
Pursuing immediately useful skills
Finding fun in their work and sparking others to have fun
Looking for efficient, least-effort solutions
Being caught up in enthusiasms.

## INFJ

People-oriented INNOVATORS of ideas; serious, quietly forceful and persevering; concerned with work that will help the world and inspire others. Having Introverted INTUITION as their strongest mental process, they are at their best when caught up in inspiration, envisioning and creating ways to empower self and others to lead more meaningful lives. They value:

A reserved outer life; spontaneous inner lifePlanning ways to help people improve
Seeing complexities, hidden meanings

Understanding others' needs and concerns
Imaginative ways of saying things
Planful, independent, academic learning
Reading, writing, imagining; academic theories
Being restrained in outward actions; planful
Aligning their work with their ideals
Pursuing and clarifying their ideals
Taking the long view
Bringing out the best in others through appreciation
Finding harmonious solutions to problems
Being inspired and inspiring others.

## ESFP

REALISTIC ADAPTERS in human relationships; friendly and easy with people, highly observant of their feelings and needs; oriented to practical, firsthand experience. Extraverted SENSING being their strongest mental process, they are at their best when free to act on impulses, responding to needs of the here and now. They value:

An energetic, sociable life, full of friends and fun
Performing, entertaining, sharing
Immediately useful skills; practical know-how
Learning through spontaneous, hands-on action
Trust and generosity; openness
Patterning themselves after those they admire
Concrete, practical knowledge; resourcefulness
Caring, kindness, support, appreciation
Freedom from irrelevant rules
Handling immediate, practical problems and crises
Seeing tangible realities; least-effort solutions
Showing and receiving appreciation
Making the most of the moment; adaptability
Being caught up in enthusiasms
Easing and brightening work and play.

## INTJ

Logical, critical, decisive INNOVATORS of ideas; serious, intent, very independent, concerned with organization; determined, often stubborn. With Introverted INTUITION as their strongest mental process, they are at their best when inspiration turns insights into ideas and plans for improving human knowledge and systems. They value:

A restrained, organized outer life; a spontaneous, intuitive inner life
Conceptual skills, theorizing
Planful, independent, academic learning
Scepticism; critical analysis; objective principles
Originality, independence of mind
Intellectual quickness, ingenuity
Non-emotional tough-mindedness
Freedom from interference in projects
Working to a plan and schedule
Seeing complexities, hidden meanings
Improving things by finding flaws
Probing new possibilities; taking the long view
Pursuing a vision; foresight; conceptualizing
Getting insights to reframe problems.

## ENTP

Inventive, analytical PLANNERS OF CHANGE; enthusiastic and independent; pursue inspiration with impulsive energy; seek to understand and inspire. Extraverted INTUITION being their strongest mental process, they are at their best when caught up in the enthusiasm of a new project and promoting its benefits. They value:

Conceiving of new things and initiating change
The surge of inspirations; the pull of emerging possibilities
Analysing complexities
Following their insights, wherever they lead
Finding meanings behind the facts
Autonomy, elbow room; openness
Ingenuity, originality, a fresh perspective
Mental models and concepts that explain life
Fair treatment
Flexibility, adaptability
Learning through action, variety and discovery
Exploring theories and meanings behind events

Improvising, looking for novel ways
Work made light by inspiration.

## ISFJ

Sympathetic MANAGERS OF FACTS AND DETAILS, concerned with people's welfare; stable, conservative, dependable, painstaking, systematic. Having Introverted SENSING as their strongest mental process, they are at their best when using their sensible intelligence and practical skills to help others in tangible ways. They value:

Preserving; enjoying the things of proven value
Steady, sequential work yielding reliable results
A controlled, orderly outer life
Patient, persistent attention to basic needs
Following a sensible path, based on experience
A rich memory for concrete facts
Loyalty, strong relationships
Consistency, familiarity, the tried and true
Firsthand experience of what is important
Compassion, kindness, caring
Working to a plan and schedule
Learning through planned, sequential teaching
Set routines, common-sense options
Rules, authority, set procedures
Hard work, perseverance.

## ENFP

Warmly enthusiastic PLANNERS OF CHANGE; imaginative, individualistic; pursue inspiration with impulsive energy; seek to understand and inspire others. With Extraverted INTUITION as their strongest mental process, they are at their best when caught up in the enthusiasm of a project, sparking others to see its benefits. They value:

The surge of inspirations; the pull of emerging possibilities
A life of variety, people, warm relationships
Following their insights wherever they lead
Finding meanings behind the facts

Creativity, originality, a fresh perspective
An optimistic, positive, enthusiastic view of life
Flexibility and openness
Exploring, devising and trying out new things
Open-ended opportunities and options
Freedom from the requirement of being practical
Learning through action, variety, and discovery
A belief that any obstacles can be overcome
A focus on people's potential
Brainstorming to solve problems
Work made light and playful by inspiration.

## ISTJ

Analytical MANAGERS OF FACTS AND DETAILS; dependable, conservative, systematic, painstaking, decisive, stable. Having Introverted SENSING as their strongest mental process, they are at their best when charged with organizing and maintaining data and material important to others and to themselves. They value:

Steady, systematic work that yields reliable results
A controlled outer life grounded in the present
Following a sensible path, based on experience
Concrete, exact, immediately useful facts, skills
Consistency, familiarity, the tried and true
A concrete, present-day view of life
Working to a plan and schedule
Preserving and enjoying things of proven value
Proven systems, common-sense options
Freedom from emotionality in deciding things
Learning through planned, sequential teaching
Scepticism; wanting to read the fine print first
A focus on hard work, perseverance
Quiet, logical, detached problem solving
Serious and focused work and play.

**Acknowledgement:** Adapted from *Descriptions of the 16 Types* by Gordon D. Lawrence © 1995 Center for Applications of Psychological Type, Inc (not to be reproduced without written permission).

# References

Ainsworth, M.S. (1964) 'Patterns of attachment behaviour shown by the infant in interaction with his mother', *Merril-Palmer Quarterly*, 10, pp. 51–8.

Ainsworth, M.S. (1996) 'Attachments and other affectional bonds across the life cycle', in C.M. Parkes, J. Steveson-Hinde and P. Marris (eds) *Attachment Across the Life Cycle*, London, Routledge.

Alimo-Metcalfe, B., and Alban-Metcalfe, J. (2009) 'Engaging leadership part one: competences are like Brighton Pier', *International Journal of Leadership in Public Care,* 5(1), 10–18.

Allan, H. T. (2001) 'Nursing the clinic and managing emotions in a fertility unit: findings from an ethnographic study', *Nursing Inquiry,* 8, 51–60.

Allan, H. T., and Smith, P. (2005) 'The introduction of modern matrons and the relevance of emotional labour to understanding their roles: developing personal authority in clincal leadership', *International Journal for Quality in Health Care*, 1(1).

Allen, J. and Brock, S. A. (2000) *Health Care Communication and Personality Type,* London, Routledge.

Allport, G. W. (1961) *Pattern and Growth in Personality,* London, Holt, Rinehart & Winston.

Alvesson, M., and Sveningsson, S. (2003) 'Managers doing leadership: the Eetra-ordinarization of the mundane', *Human Relations,* 56(12), 1435–59.

Amendolair, D. (2003) 'Emotional intelligence essential for developing nurse leaders', *Nurse Leader,* November/December, 25–27.

Ames, D.R. (2008) 'In search of the right touch. Interpersonal assertiveness in organizational life', *Current Directions in Psychological Science*, 17, pp. 381–5.

Anderson, J. (2000) *Learning and Memory: An Integrated Approach,* Chichester. Wiley, 2nd edn.

Anderson, M. (ed.) (1982) *Sociology of the Family*, Harmondsworth, Penguin.

Andrews, M., Day Sclater, S., Squire, C., and Tamboukou, M. (2007) 'Narrative research', in C. Seale, G.Gobo, J. Gubrium and D. Silverman (eds), *Qualitative Research Practice,* London, Sage, pp. 97–112.

Archer, D. (1999) 'Exploring "bullying" culture in the para-military organization', *International Journal of Manpower*, 20(1–2), 94–105.

Archer, J. (1999) *The Nature of Grief: The Evolutional and Psychology of Reactions to Loss*, London, Routledge.

Armstrong, D. (2005) *Organisation in the Mind: Psychoanalysis, Group Relations and Organisational Consultancy*, London, Karnac.

Aron, E. (2010) *Psychotherapy and the Highly Sensitive Person: Improving Outcomes for that Minority of People who are the Majority of Clients*, London, Routledge.

Ashforth, B. E., and Humphrey, R. H. (1995) 'Emotion in the workplace: a reappraisal', *Human Relations*, 48(2), 97–125.

Ashkanasy, N. M., Hartel, C. E. J., and Daus, C. S. (2002) 'Diversity and emotion: the new frontiers in organizational behavior research', *Journal of Management*, 28(3), 307–38.

Ashley, O. S., Marsden, M. E., and Brady, T. M. (2003) 'Effectiveness of substance abuse treatment programming for women: a review', *American Journal of Drug and Alcohol Abuse*, 29(1), 19–53.

Ashworth, P.D. (1979) *Social Interaction and Consciousness*, Chichester, Wiley.

Avolio, B. J., Gardner, W. L., Walumbwa, F. O., Luthans, F., and May, D. R. (2004) 'Unlocking the mask: a look at the process by which authentic leaders impact follower attitudes and behaviors', *Leadership Quarterly*, 15(6), 801–23.

Ayre, P. (1998) 'Significant harm: making professional judgements', *Child Abuse Review*, 7(5), 330–42.

Baltes, P. B., Lindenberger, U., and Staudinger, U. M. (2007) *Life Span Theory in Developmental Psychology*, New York: John Wiley & Sons, Inc.

Bandura, A. (1977) *Social Learning Theory*, New York, General Learning Press.

Barge, J. K., and Fairhurst, G. T. (2008) 'Living leadership: a systemic constructionist approach', *Leadership*, 4(3), 227–51.

Barnes, M. (1999) 'Users as citizens: collective action and the local governance of welfare', *Social Policy and Administration* 33:1, pp. 73–90.

Baron, R. A. and Byrne, D. (2004) *Social Psychology*, London, Allyn & Bacon, 10th edn.

Baron, R. S. and Kerr, N. L. (2003) *Group Process, Group Decision and Group Action*, Buckingham, Open University Press.

Baron-Cohen, S. (2004) *The Essential Difference*, Harmondsworth, Penguin.

Barton, R. (1976) *Institutional Neurosis*, Bristol, J. Wright.

Bayne, R. (2004) *Psychological Types at Work: An MBTI Perspective*, London, Thomson.

Bayne, R. (2005) *Ideas and Evidence: Critical Reflections on MBTI Theory and Practice*, Gainesville, FL, CAPT.

Bayne, R. (2013) *The Counsellor's Guide to Personality: Understanding preferences, motives and life stories*, Basingstoke, Palgrave Macmillan.

Bayne, R. and Jinks, G. (2010) *How to Survive Counsellor Training: An A–Z Guide,* Basingstoke, Palgrave Macmillan.

Bayne, R., Jinks, G., Collard, P. and Horton, I. (2008) *The Counsellor's Handbook: A Practical A–Z Guide to Integrative Counselling and Psychotherapy,* 3rd end, Cheltenham, Nelson Thornes.

Beckett, C., and Taylor, H. (2010) *Human Growth and Development,* 2nd edn, London, Sage.

Belsky, J. (1997) 'Attachment, mating, and parenting', *Human Nature,* 8(4), 361–81.

Belsky, J. (1999) *The Psychology of Ageing: Theory, Research and Interventions,* Pacific Grove, CA, Brooks-Cole.

Belsky, J. (2001) 'Developmental risks (still) associated with early child care', *Journal of Child Psychology and Psychiatry,* 42, 845–59.

Bentall, R. (2006) 'Madness explained: why we must reject the Kraepelinian paradigm and replace it with a complaint-orientated approach to understanding mental illness', *Medical Hypotheses,* 66(2), 220–33.

Berger, P. (1966) 'Identity as a problem of knowledge', *Archives européennes de sociologie,* 7, 105–115.

Berger, P. and Kellner, H. (1964/1982) 'Marriage and the construction of reality', in M. Anderson (ed.) *Sociology of the Family,* Harmondsworth: Penguin.

Bettelheim, B. (1979) *The Informed Heart: Autonomy in a Mass Age,* New York, Avon.

Biddle, S.J.H. (2010) 'Physical activity', In D. French, K. Vedhara, A. A. Kaptein and J. Weinman (eds) *Health Psychology,* 2nd edn, Oxford, BPS Blackwell.

Bifulco, A. (2004) 'Maternal attachment style and depression associated with childbirth; preliminary results from European/US cross-cultural study', *British Journal of Psychiatry,* 184(suppl 46), s31–s37.

Bifulco, A., Jacobs, C., Bunn, A., Thomas, G., and Irving, K. (2008) 'The attachment interview (ASI) as an assessment of support capacity exploring its use for adoption-fostering assessment', *Adoption and Fostering,* 32, 33–45.

Bifulco, A., and Thomas, G. (2013) *Understanding Adult Attachment in Family Relationships: Research, Assessment and Intervention,* London, Routledge.

Bion, W. R. (1961) *Experiences in Groups, and Other Papers,* London, Tavistock Publications.

Bisson, J. I. (2007) 'Post-traumatic stress disorder', *Occupational Medicine,* 57(6), 399–403.,

Bjorklund, D. F., and Pellegrini, A. D. (2000) 'Child development and evolutionary psychology', *Child Development,* 71(6), 1687–708.

Bolton, G., Howlett, S., Lago, C. and Wright, J. K. (eds) (2004) *Writing Cures: An Introductory Handbook of Writing in Counselling and Therapy,* Hove, Brunner-Routledge.

Bolton, S.C. (2000) 'Emotion here, emotion there, emotional organisations everywhere', *Critical Perspectives in Accounting,* 11, 155–71.

Bolton, S. C. (2003) 'Who cares? Offering emotion work as a "gift" in the nursing labour process', *Journal of Advanced Nursing,* 32(3), 580–6.

Bonanno, G. A., Galea, S., Bucciarelli, A., and Vlahov, D. (2006) 'Psychological resilience after disaster: New York City in the aftermath of the September 11th terrorist attack', *Psychological Science,* 17(3), 181–6.

Bond, M. (1986) *Stress and Self-awareness: A Guide for Nurses,* Oxford, Heinemann.

Bond, T. (2009) *Standards and Ethics for Counselling in Action,* London, Sage, 3rd ed.

Boon, J., Davies, G.W. and Noon, E. (1993) 'Children in court', in R. Bayne and P. Nicolson (eds) *Counselling and Psychology for Health Professionals,* London, Chapman & Hall.

Borden, W. (2000) 'The relational paradigm in contemporary psychoanalysis: toward a psychodynamically informed social work perspective', *The Social Service Review,* 74(3), 352–79.

Boul, L. A. (2003) 'Men's health and middle age', *Sexualities, Evolution and Gender,* 5(1) 5–22.

Bourne, I. (2013) *Facing Danger in the Helping Professions,* Milton Keynes, OU Press.

Bower, M. (2005) *Psychoanalytic Theory for Social Work Practice,* London, Routledge.

Bowlby, J. (1951) *Maternal Care and Mental Health,* Geneva, World Health Organization; New York, Shocken Books.

Bowlby, J, (1969/1982) *Attachment and Loss, Volume 1,* New York, Basic Books.

Bowlby, J, (1980) *Attachment and Loss, Volume 3,* New York, Basic Books.

Bowlby, J. (1988) *A Secure Base: Parent–Child Attachment and Healthy Human Development,* London: Routledge.

British Psychological Society (1988) 'The future of the psychological sciences', paper prepared by the Scientific Affairs Board of the BPS, Leicester.

Brown, A. (1979) *Groupwork,* London, Heinemann.

Brue, S. (2008) *The 8 Colors of Fitness,* Delroy Beach, FL, Oakledge Press.

Bryman, A. (2004) 'Qualitative research on leadership: a critical but appreciative review', *Leadership Quarterly,* 15(6), 729–69.

Bryson, J. R., and Wellington, C. A. (2003). 'Image consultancy in the United Kingdom: recipe knowledge and recreational employment', *Service Industries Journal,* 23(1), 59–76.

Buchanan, D. A., Addicott, R., Fitzgerald, L., Ferlie, E., and Baeza, J. I. (2007) 'Nobody in charge: distributed change agency in healthcare', *Human Relations,* 60(7), 1065–90.

Bull, R. (2010) 'The investigative interviewing of children and other vulnerable witnesses: psychological research and working/professional practice', *Legal and Criminological Psychology*, 15, 5–23.

Burke, C. S., Stagl, K. C., Klein, C., Goodwin, G. F., Salas, E., and Halpin, S. A. (2006) 'What type of leadership behaviors are functional in teams? A meta-analysis', *Leadership Quarterly*, 17(3), 288–307.

Burr, J.A. and Nicolson, P. (2004) R*esearching Health Care Consumers: Critical Approaches*, Basingstoke, Palgrave Macmillan.

Busuttil, W. (2004) 'Presentations and management of post traumatic stress disorder and the elderly: a need for investigation', *International Journal of Geriatric Psychiatry*, 19(5), 429–39.

Butterfield, R., Edwards, C., and Woodall, J. (2005) 'The New Public Management and managerial roles: the case of the police sergeant', *British Journal of Management*, 16(4), 329–41.

Campbell, A. (2002) *A Mind of Her Own: The Evolutionary Psychology of Women*, Oxford, Oxford University Press.

Campbell, D., Caldicott, D. and Kinsella, K. (1994) 'Key concepts of systemic thinking', in D. Campbell et al. (eds), *Systemic Work with Organizations*, London, Karnac Books, pp. 9–27.

Cardonna, F. (1994) 'Facing an uncertain future', in A. Obholzer and V. Zagier Roberts (eds) *The Unconscious at Work: Individual and Organisational Stress in the Human Services*, London, Routledge.

Carr, S. (1997) *Type Clarification: Finding the Fit*, Oxford, Oxford University Press.

Carroll, B., Levy, L., and Richmond, D. (2008) 'Leadership as practice: challenging the competency paradigm', *Leadership*, 4(4), 363–79.

Cartwright, D. and Zander, A. (1968) (eds) *Group Dynamics: Research and Theory*, New York, Harper & Row.

Castelli, P., Goodman, G. S., and Ghetti, S. (2005) 'Effects of interview style and witness age on perceptions of children's credibility in sexual abuse cases', *Journal of Applied Social Psychology*, 35(2), 297–317.

Chesborough, S. (2009) 'Do social work students learn differently? MBTI implications for teaching strategies that address social work students' current learning styles', *Journal of Psychological Type*, 69, 23–41.

Cialdini, R. B., and Goldstein, N. J. (2004) 'Social influence: compliance and conformity', *Annual Review of Psychology*, 55(1), 591–621.

Clarke, C., Hope-Hailey, V., and Kelliher, C. (2007) 'Being real or really eeing someone else? Change, managers and emotion work', *European Management Journal*, 25(2), 92–103.

Clegg, F. (1988) 'Disasters: can psychologists help the survivors?', *The Psychologist*, vol. 1, 4, pp. 134–5.

Clulow, C. (1994) 'Balancing care and control: the supervisory relationship as a focus for promoting organisational health', in A. Obholzer and V. Zagier Roberts (eds) *The Unconscious at Work; Individual and Organisational Stress in the Human Services*, London, Routledge.

Cohen, S. and Taylor, L. (1972) *Psychological Survival,* Harmondsworth, Penguin.

Colic-Peisker, V., and Walker, I. (2003) 'Human capital, acculturation and social identity: Bosnian refugees in Australia', *Journal of Community and Applied Social Psychology,* 13(5), 337–60.

Collard, P. (2013) *Journey into Mindfulness. Gentle Ways to Let Go of Stress and Live in the Moment,* London, Gaia Books.

Collett, P. (2004) *The Book of Tells,* London, Bantam.

Collier, J., and Esteban, R. (2000) 'Systemic leadership: ethical and effective', *Leadership and Organization Development Journal,* 21(4), 207–15.

Collins S. (2008) 'Statutory social workers: stress, job satisfaction, coping, social support and individual differences', *British Journal of Social Work,* 38, 1173–93.

Collins S., Coffey M and Morris L. (2010) 'Social work students: stress, support and well-being', *British Journal of Social Work,* 40, 963–982.

Collinson, D. (2005) 'Dialectics of leadership', *Human Relations,* 58(11), 1419–1442.

Conte, J. M. (2005) 'A review and critique of emotional intelligence measures', *Journal of Organizational Behavior,* 26, 433–40.

Conger, J. A. and R.N. Kanungo (1988) 'The empowerment process: integrating theory and practice', *Academy of Management Review,* 13(3), 471–82.

Cooper, C. L., Dewe, P. J. and O'Driscoll, M. P. (2001) *Organizational Stress. A Review and Critique of Theory, Research and Applications,* London, Sage.

Cornish, S. (2011) 'Negative capability and social work: insights from Keats, Bion and business', *Journal of Social Work Practice,* 25(2), 135–48.

Crang, P. (1994) 'It's showtime: on the workplace geographies of display in a restaurant in southeast England', *Environment and Planning D – Society and Space,* 12(6), 675–704.

Craven, S., Brown, S., and Gilchrist, E. (2007) 'Current responses to sexual grooming: implication for prevention', *Howard Journal of Criminal Justice,* 46(1), 60–71.

Crossley, M. L. (2003) 'Formulating narrative psychology: the limitations of contemporary social constructionism', *Narrative Inquiry,* 13(2), 287–300.

Cummings, G., Hayduk, L., and Estabrooks, C. (2005) 'Mitigating the impact of hospital restructuring on nurses: the responsibility of emotionally intelligent leadership', *Nursing Research,* 54(1), 2–2.

Cummings, J. N. (2004) 'Work groups, structural diversity, and knowledge sharing in a global organization', *Management Science,* 50(3), 352–64.

Cummings, L. L. (1981) 'State of the art', *Decision Sciences,* 12(3), 365–77.

Currer, C. (2001) *Responding to Grief: Dying, Bereavement and Social Care,* Basingstoke, Palgrave Macmillan.

Currie, G., Lockett, A., and Suhomlinova, O. (2009) 'The institutionalization of distributed leadership: a'Catch-22' in English public services', *Human Relations,* 62(11), 1735–61.

Curtis Committee (1946) *Report of the Care of Children Committee,* London, HMSO.

Dasborough, M. T. (2006) 'Cognitive asymmetry in employee emotional reactions to leadership behaviors', *Leadership Quarterly,* 17(2), 163–78.

Davenport, R.B. and Pipes, D.S. (1990) *Introduction to Psychotherapy: Common Clinical Wisdom,* London, Prentice-Hall.

Davies, G. M. (1988) 'The use of video in child abuse trials', *The Psychologist: Bulletin of the British Psychological Society,* 1, pp. 20–2.

Day, A., and Howells, K. (2002) 'Psychological treatments for rehabilitating offenders: evidence-based practice comes of age', *Australian Psychologist,* 37(1), 39–47.

Day, D. V., Gronn, P., and Salas, E. (2004) 'Leadership capacity in teams', *Leadership Quarterly,* 15(6), 857–80.

De Board, R. (1978) *The Psychoanalysis of Organizations,* London, Tavistock.

D'Cruz, H., Gillingham, P., and Melendez, S. (2007) 'Reflexivity, its meanings and relevance for social work: a critical review of the literature' *British Journal of Social Work,* 37(1), 73–90.

de Raeve, L. (2002) 'The modification of emotional responses: aproblem for trust in nurse–patient relationships?', *Nursing Ethics,* 9(5), 465–71.

Dent, M. (2005). 'Post-New Public Management in public sector hospitals? The UK, Germany and Italy', *Policy and Politics,* 33(4), 623–36.

Dickens, J. (2011) 'Social work in England at a watershed,as always: from the Seebohm Report to the Social Work Task Force', *British Journal of Social Work,* 41(1), 22–39.

Dickson, A. (1982) *A Woman in Your Own Right. Assertiveness and You,* London, Quartet Books.

Dickson, A. (2012) *A Woman in Your Own Right. Assertiveness and You,* London, Quartet Books, revised 30th anniversary edition.

Diener, E. (2000) 'Subjective well-being: the science of happiness and a proposal for a national index', *American Psychologist,* 55(1), 34–43.

Dinnerstein, D. (1976) *The Rocking of the Cradle and the Ruling of the World,* New York, Harper & Row.

Dion K. K., Berschid E., and Hatfield E. (1972) 'What is beautiful is good', *Journal of Personality and Social Psychology,* 24, 285–90.

DiTiberio, J. K. and Hammer, A. L. (1993) *Introduction to Type in College,* Palo Alto, CA, Consulting Psychologists Press (CPP).

Dobson, S., Upadhyaya, S., and Stanley, B. (2002) 'Using an interdisciplinary approach to training to develop the quality of communication with adults with profound learning disabilities by care staff',

*International Journal of Language and Communication Disorders,* 37(1), 41–57.

Dominelli, L. (1996) 'Deprofessionalizing social work: anti-oppressive practice, competencies and postmodernism', *British Journal of Social Work,* 26(2), 153–75.

Dopson, S., and Waddington, I. (1996) 'Managing social change: aprocess-sociological approach to understanding organizational change within the national health service', *Sociology of Health and Illness,* 18(4), 525–50.

Douglas, J. W. B. and Bloomfield, J. M. (1958) *Children Under Five,* London, Allen & Unwin.

Douglas, T. (1978) *Basic Groupwork,* London, Tavistock.

Dovidio, J.F., Glick, P., and Rudman, L.A. (2005) (eds) *On the Nature of Prejudice: Fifty Years after Allport,* Oxford, Blackwell Publishing.

Dube, S. R., Anda, R. F., Felitti, V. J., Chapman, D. P., Williamson, D. F., and Giles, W. H. (2001) 'Childhood abuse, household dysfunction, and the risk of attempted suicide throughout the life span', *JAMA: The Journal of the American Medical Association,* 286(24), 3089–96.

Duncan, B. L., Miller, S. D., Wampold, B.E. and Hubble, M.A. (eds) (2010) *The Heart and Soul of Change. Delivering What Works in Therapy,* 2nd edn, Washington, DC, APA.

Eckerman, C.O. and Whatly, J. L. (1977) 'Toys and social interaction between infant peers', *Child Development,* 48, pp. 1645–56.

Egan, G. (2010) *The Skilled Helper,* 10th edn, Pacific Grove, CA, Brooks/Cole.

Ehlers, A, Mayou, R.A. and Bryant, B. (2003) 'Cognitive predictors of posttraumatic stress disorder in children: results of a prospective longitudinal study', *Behaviour Research and Therapy,* 41, 1–10.

Ellemers, N., De Gilder, D., and Haslam, S. A. (2004) 'Motivating individuals and groups at work: a social identity perspective on leadership and group performance', *Academy of Management Review,* 29(3), 459–478.

Epstein, S. (1979) 'The stability of behavior: I. On predicting most of the people much of the time', *Journal of Personality and Social Psychology* 37, 1097–126.

Erikson, E. (1950/1963) *Childhood and Society,* New York, Norton.

Erikson, E. (1959/1980) *Identity, Youth and Crisis,* New York, Norton.

Fairhurst, G. T. (2009) 'Considering context in discursive leadership research', *Human Relations,* 62(11), 1607–33.

Fambrough, M. J., and Hart, R. K. (2008) 'Emotions in leadership development: a critique of emotional intelligence', *Advances in Developing Human Resources* 10(5), 740–58.

Farber, B.A. and Doolin, E. M. (2011) 'Positive regard', *Psychotherapy,* 48, 58–64.

Featherstone, B., Broadhurst, K., and Holt, K. (2011) 'Thinking systemically, thinking politically: building strong partnerships with children and families in the context of rising inequality', *British Journal of Social Work*, 2.

Feldman, S. (2003) 'Enforcing social conformity: a theory of authoritarianism', *Political Psychology*, 24(1), 41–74.

Feltham, C. and Dryden, W. (2006) *Brief Counselling*, 2nd edn, Maidenhead, Open University Press.

Feltham, C. and Horton, I. (2012) *The Sage Handbook of Counselling and Psychotherapy*, 3rd edn, London, Sage.

Ferguson, H. (2001) 'Social work, individualization and life politics', *British Journal of Social Work*, 31(1), 41–55.

Ferlie, E., Ashburner, L and Pettigrew, A. (1996) *The New Public Management in Action*, Oxford, Oxford University Press.

Festinger, J. R. P. and Raven, B. H. (1959) *Social Pressures in Informal Groups: A Study of a Housing Community*, London, Harper & Row.

Fineman, S. (1993) *Emotion in Organisations*, London, Sage.

Fineman, S., Gabriel, Y., and Sims, D. (2010) *Organizing and Organizations*, 4th edn, London, Sage.

Flaskas, C. (2007) 'Systemic and psychoanalytic ideas: using knowleges in social work', *Journal of Social Work Practice*, 21(2), 131–47.

Fonagy, P. (2000) 'Attachment and borderline personality disorder', *Journal of the American Psychoanalytic Association*, 48(4), 1129–46.

Fook, J. (2002) 'Theorizing from practice', *Qualitative Social Work*, 1(1), 79–95.

Fook, J., and Gardner, F. (2010) *Practising Critical Reflection: A Resource Handbook*, Maidenhead, McGraw-Hill/Open University Press.

Ford, J. (2006) 'Discourses of leadership: gender, identity and contradiction in a UK public sector organization', *Leadership*, 2(1), 77–99.

Ford, J. (2010) 'Studying leadership critically: a psychosocial lens on leadership identities', *Leadership*, 6(1), 47–65.

Foster, A. (2001) 'The duty to care and the need to split', *Journal of Social Work Practice: Psychotherapeutic Approaches in Health, Welfare and the Community*, 15(1), 81–90.

Frattaroli, J. (2006) 'Experiential disclosure and its moderators: a meta-analysis', *Psychological Bulletin*, 132, 823–65.

French, J. R. P. and Raven, B. H. (1959) 'The bases of social power' in D. Cartwright, *Studies in Social Power*, Ann Arbor, MI, University of Michigan Press.

Freud, S. (1922) *Group Psychology and the Analysis of the Ego*, London, Hogarth.

Freud, S. (1949) *An Outline of Psychoanalysis*, New York, Norton.

Funder, D.C. (2013) *The Personality Puzzle*, 6th edn, London, W. W. Norton.

Gabriel, Y. (2004) *Organizations in Depth: The Psychoanalysis of Organizations*, London, Sage.

Gannon, L.R. (1992) 'Sexuality and the menopause', in P.Y.L. Choi and P. Nicolson (eds) F*emale Sexuality: Psychology, Biology and Social Context*, Brighton, Harvester.

Gannon, L.R. (1999) *Women and Ageing: Transcending the Myths*, London, Routledge.

Gannon, L. (2002) 'A critique of evolutionary psychology', *Psychology, Evolution and Gender*, 4(2), 173–218.

Garfinkel, M. (1967) *Studies in Ethnomethodology*, Englewood Cliffs, NJ, Prentice-Hall.

Gendlin, E. T. (1981) *Focusing*, 2nd edn, London: Bantam.

George, J. M. (2000) 'Emotions and leadership: the role of emotional intelligence', *Human Relations*, 53(8), 1027–55.

Gerber, I. Weiner, A., Battin, D.and Arkkin, A.(1975) 'Brief therapy to the aged and bereaved', in B. Shoenberg et al. (eds), *Bereavement: Its Psychosocial Aspects*, New York, Columbia University Press.

Gerdes K. E., Segal, E. A. and Lietz, C. A. (2010) 'Conceptualising and measuring empathy', *British Journal of Social Work*, 40, 2326–43.

Gibbs, D. (1999) 'Disabled People and the Research Community', paper presented to the ESRC Seminar Series 'Theorising Social Work Research: Who Owns the Research Process?' Belfast, 20.9.99. Available electronically at http://www.elsc.org.uk.socialcareresource/tswr/seminar2/gibbs.htm.

Gilmore, S.K. (1973) *The Counselor-in-Training*, London, Prentice-Hall.

Gilligan, C. (1982/93) *In a Different Voice: Psychological Theory and Women's Development*, Cambridge, Mass., Harvard University Press.

Glassop, L.I. (2002) 'The organisational benefits of teams', *Human Relations*, 55(2) 225–49.

Goffman, I. (1961). *Asylums: Essays on the Social Situation of Mental Patients and Other Inmates*, New York, Doubleday Anchor.

Goleman, D. (1998) 'The emotionally competent leader', *Healthcare Forum Journal*, 41(2), 36–8.

Goleman, D. (2000) 'Leadership that gets results', *Harvard Business Review*, 78(2), 78–90.

Goleman, D. (2006) *Social Intelligence: The new science of human relationships*, New York, Random House.

Goleman, D., Boyatzis, R., and McKee, A. (2001) 'Primal leadership: the hidden driver of great performance', *Harvard Business Review, Reprint RO111C*, 42–51.

Goodman, G. S. (2006) 'Children's eyewitness memory: a modern history and contemporary commentary', *Journal of Social Issues*, 62(4), 811–32.

Goodman, S., and Trowler, I. (eds) (2012) *Social Work Reclaimed: Innovative Frameworks for Child and Family Social Work Practice*, London, Jessica Kingsley.

Goodwin, N. (2000) 'Leadership and the UK health service', *Health Policy,* 51(1), 49–60.

Gott, M. (2005) *Sexuality, Sexual Health and Ageing,* Maidenhead, McGraw-Hill.

Gough, B. and McFadden, M. (2001) *Critical Social Psychology: An Introduction,* Basingstoke, Palgrave Macmillan.

Grint, K. (2005) 'Problems, problems, problems: the social construction of "leadership"', *Human Relations, 58*(11), 1467–94.

Grint, K. (2010) *Leadership: A Very Short Introduction,* Oxford, Oxford University Press.

Gronn, P. (2000) 'Distributed properties: a new architecture for leadership', *Educational Management and Administration,* 28(3), 317–38.

Gronn, P. (2002) 'Distributed leadership as a unit of analysis', *Leadership Quarterly,* 13(4), 423–51.

Grotstein, J. S. (2007) *A Beam of Intense Darkness: Wilfred Bion's Legacy to Psychoanalysis,* London, Karnac.

Hafford-Letchfield, T., Leonard, K., Begum, N., and Chick, N. F. (2008) *Leadership and Management in Social Care,* London, Sage.

Halton, W. (2007) 'By what authority? Psychoanalytic reflections on creativity and change in relation to organizational life',in C. Huffington, D. Armstrong, W. Halton, L. Hoyle and J. Pooley (eds), *Working Below the Surface: The Emotional Life of Contemporary Organizations,* London, Tavistock, pp. 107–24.

Harré, R. and Secord, P. F. (1972) *The Exploration of Social Behaviour,* Oxford, Blackwell.

Harris, L. C. (2002) 'The emotional labour of barristers: an exploration of emotional labour by status professionals', *Journal of Management Studies,* 39(4), 553–84.

Harris, T. and Bifulco, A. (1996) 'Loss of parent in childhood, attachment style and depression in adulthood', in C.M. Parkes, J. Steveson-Hinde and P. Marris (eds) *Attachment Across the Life Cycle,* London, Routledge.

Heffernan, K. (2006) 'Social work, new public management and the language of a service user', *British Journal of Social Work,* 36(1), 139–47.

Heimann, P. (1950) 'On countertransference', *International Journal of Psycho-analysis,* 31, 81–4.

Herzog, C. (1996) 'Research design in studies of ageing and cognition', in J.E. Birren and K.W. Schaie (eds) *A Handbook of the Psychology of Aging,* New York: Academic Press.

Hesse, E., and Main, M. (2000) 'Disorganized infant, child, and adult attachment: collapse in behavioral and attentional strategies', *Journal of the American Psychoanalytic Association,* 48(4), 1097–127.

Higgs, M. J. (2002) *Leadership: The Long Line, a view on how we can make sense of leadership in the 21st Century,* Henley, Henley Business School, University of Reading.

Hill, C.E. (2009) *Helping Skills: Facilitating Exploration, Insight and Action*, 3rd edn, Washington, DC, APA.

Hill, C.E. and Lent, R.W. (2006) 'A narrative and meta-analytic review of helping skills training: time to revive and dormant area of inquiry', *Psychotherapy*, 43, 154–72.

Hinshelwood, R. (1991) *A Dictionary of Kleinian Thought*, London, Free Associations.

Hirschhorn, L. (1997) *Reworking Authority: Leading and Following in the Post-modem Organization*, Cambridge, MA, MIT Press.

Hochschild, A. R. (1983) *The Managed Heart: Commercialization of Human Feeling*, Berkeley, London: University of California Press.

Holloway, E. (1995) *Clinical Supervision: A Systems Approach*, London: Sage.

Holmes, J. (2010) *Exploring in Security: Towards an Attachment-Informed Psychoanalytic Psychotherapy*, London Routledge.

Horne, J. (2006) *Sleepfaring: A Journey through the Science of Sleep*, Oxford, Oxford University Press.

Houston, S. (2001) 'Beyond social constructionism: critical realism and social work', *British Journal of Social Work*, 31(6), 845–61.

Howe, D. (2008) *The Emotionally Intelligent Social Worker*, Basingstoke, Palgrave Macmillan.

Hubble, M.A., Duncan, B.L. and Miller, S.D. (eds) (1999) *The Heart and Soul of Change: What Works in Therapy*, Washington, DC, APA Press.

Huffington, C., James, C., and Armstrong, D. (2007) 'What is the emotional cost of distributed leadership?', in C. Huffington, D. Armstrong, W. Halton, L. Hoyle and J. Pooley (eds), *Working Below the Surface: The Emotional Life of Contemporary Organizatons*, London, Karnac, pp. 67–84.

Hugh C, W. (1986) 'Unconscious sources of motivation in the theory of the subject: an Exploration and critique of Giddens' dualistic models of action and personality', *Journal for the Theory of Social Behaviour*, 16(1), 105–21.

Hughes, J. (2005) 'Bringing emotion to work: emotional intelligence, employee resistance and the reinvention of character', *Work Employment and Society*, 19(3), 603–25.

Hunter, B. (2005) 'Emotion work and boundary maintenance in hospital-based midwifery', *Midwifery*, 21(3), 253–66.

Hutton, J. (2000) *Working with the Concept of Organisation-in-the-Mind*, London: The Grubb Institute.

Hutton, J., Bazelgette, J., and Reed, B. (1997) 'Organisation-in-the-mind', in J. E. Neumann, K. Kellner and A. Dawson-Shepherd (eds) *Developing Organisational Consultancy*, London, Routledge.

Ilott, I., Rick, J. O., Patterson, M., Turgoose, C., and Lacey, A. (2006) 'What is protocol-based care? A concept analysis', *Journal of Nursing Management*, 14(7), 544–52.

Inciardi, J. A., Martin, S. S., and Butzin, C. A. (2004) 'Five-year outcomes of therapeutic community treatment of drug-involved offenders after release from prison', *Crime and Delinquency,* 50(1), 88–107.

Isen, A. M., and Means, B. (1983) 'The influence of positive affect on decision-making strategy' *Social Cognition,* 2(1), 18–31.

Israel, E., and Stover, C. (2009) 'Intimate partner violence: the role of the relationship between perpetrators and children who witness violence', *Journal of Interpersonal Violence,* 24(10), 1755–64.

Jainchill, N., Hawke, J., and Messina, M. (2005) 'Post-treatment outcomes among adjudicated adolescent males and females in modified therapeutic community treatment', *Substance Use and Misuse,* 40(7), 975–96.

James, K. T., and Arroba, T. (2005) 'Reading and carrying: a framework for learning about emotion and emotionality in organizational systems as a sore aspect of leadership development' *Management Learning,* 36(3), 299–316.

James, K., and Huffington, C. (2004) 'Containment of anxiety in organizational change: a case example of changing organizational boundaries', *Organizational and Social Dynamics: An International Journal of Psychoanalytic, Systemic and Group Relations Perspectives,* 4(2), 212–33.

Jaques, E. (1960) 'Disturbances in the capacity to work', *International Journal of Psycho-Analysis,* 41, 357–7.

Jones, D. (ed.) (2004) *Working with Dangerous People: The Psychotherapy of Violence,* London, Radcliffe Medical Press.

Jones, L., Hughes, M., and Unterstaller, U. (2001) 'Post-traumatic stress disorder (PTSD) in victims of domestic violence: a review of the research', *Trauma Violence Abuse,* 2(2), 99–119.

Keirsey, D. (1998) *Please Understand Me II,* Del Mar, CA, Prometheus Nemesis.

Kennedy-Moore, E. and Watson, J.C. (1999) *Expressing Emotion: Myths, Realities and Therapeutic Strategies,* London, Guilford Press.

Kerr, N. L., and Tindale, R. S. (2004) 'Group performance and decision making', *Annual Review of Psychology,* 55(1), 623–55.

Kipnis, D. (2001) 'Using power: Newtons's second law', in A.Y. Lee-chai and J.A. Bargh (eds) *The Use and Abuse of Power: Multiple Perspectives on the Causes of Corruption,* London, The Psychology Press.

Klein, M. (1959/1975) 'Our Adult world and its roots on infancy', in *The Writings of Melanie Klein: Envy and Gratitude and Other Works 1946–1963* (Vol. 3, pp. 247–63), London, Hogarth Press.

Kohlberg, L. (1969) 'Stage and sequence: the cognitive developmental approach to socialisation', in D. A. Goslin (ed.) *Handbook of Socialisation: Theory and Research,* Chicago, Rand McNally.

Kolb, D. M. E., and Bartunek, J. M. E. (1992) *Hidden Conflict in Organizations: Uncovering Behind-the-Scenes Disputes,* Thousand Oaks, CA, Sage Publications, Inc.

Konopka, G. (1963) *Social Groupwork: A Helping Process,* Englewood Cliffs, NJ: Prentice-Hall.

Kosslyn, S.M. and Rosenberg, R.S. (2004) *Psychology. The Brain, the Person, the World,* 2nd edn, London, Allyn & Bacon.

Lago, C. (2006) *Race, Culture and Counselling,* 2nd edn, Maidenhead, Open University Press.

Laing, R.D. (1969) *Self and Others,* Harmondsworth, Penguin.

Lambert, M.J. and Shimokawa, K. (2011) 'Collecting client feedback', *Psychotherapy,* 46, 72–79.

Laming, H. (2003) *The Victoria Climbié Inquiry,* London: HMSO.

Laquer, W. (1982) *The Terrible Secret: Suppression of the Truth About Hitler's 'Final Solution',* Harmondsworth, Penguin.

Laughlin, R., and Sher, M. (2010) 'Developing leadership in a social care enterprise: managing organizational and individual boundaries and anxiety', *Organizational and Social Dynamics,* 10(1), 1–21.

Lawrence, G. (1997) *Looking at Type and Learning Styles,* Gainsville, FL, CAPT.

Lawrence, G. (2009) *People Types and Tiger Stripes,* Gainsville, FL, CAPT. 4th edn.

Layard, R. (2006) 'Happiness and public policy: a challenge to the profession', *Economic Journal,* 116(510), C24–C33.

Lazarus, A.A. and Mayne, T.J. (1990) 'Relaxation: some limitations, side effects, and proposed solutions' *Psychotherapy,* 27, 261–6.

Le Bon, G. (1917/1920) *The Crowd: A Study of the Popular Mind,* New York, Transaction Books.

Leach, J. (2004) 'Why people "freeze" in an emergency: temporal and cognitive constraints on survival responses', *Aviation, Space and Environmental Medicine,* 75(6).

Leach, J. and Ansell, L. (2008) 'Impairment in attentional processing in a field survival environment', *Applied Cognitive Psychology,* 22(5), 643–65.

Leary, M.R., Tate, E.B., Adams, E.E., Allen, A.B. and Hancock, J. (2007) 'Self-compassion and reactions to unpleasant self-relevant events: the implications of treating oneself unkindly', *Journal of Personality and Social Psychology,* 92, 887–904.

Lehtonen, J. (2012) 'At the crossroads of psychoanalysis and neuroscience', *Scandinavian Psychoanalytic Review,* 35(1), 9–20.

Leon, G. D., Sacks, S., Staines, G., and McKendrick, K. (2000) 'Modified therapeutic community for homeless mentally ill chemical abusers: treatment outcomes', *American Journal of Drug and Alcohol Abuse,* 26(3), 461–80.

Lev-Wiesel, R., and Amir, M. (2003) 'Postraumatic growth among holocaust child survivors', *Journal of Loss and Trauma: International Perspectives on Stress and Coping,* 8(4), 229–37.

Lev-Wiesel, R., Amir, M., and Besser, A. (2004) 'Posttraumatic growth among female survivors of childhood sexual abuse in relation to the perpetrator identity', *Journal of Loss and Trauma: International Perspectives on Stress and Coping,* 10(1), 7–17.

Lewin, K. (1947) 'Frontiers in group dynamics: concept, method and reality in social science: social equilibria and social change', in D. Cartwright (ed.) *Field Theory in Social Science: Selected Theoretical Papers* (Vol. 1, pp. 188–237), New York, Harper & Brothers.

Lewis, K. M. (2000) 'When leaders display emotion: how followers respond to negative emotional expression of male and female leaders', *Journal of Organizational Behavior,* 21, 221–34.

Lewis, P. (2005) 'Suppression or expression: an exploration of emotion management in a special care baby unit', *Work Employment and Society,* 19(3), 565–81.

Liden, R. C., and Antonakis, J. (2009) 'Considering context in psychological leadership research', *Human Relations,*62(11), 1587–605.

Linder, R. (2000) *What Will I do with My Money? How Your Personality Affects Your Financial Behavior,* Chicago, IL: Northfield.

Linley, A. (2008) *Average to A+: Realising Strengths in Yourself and Others,* Coventry, CAPP Press.

Linley, A., Willars, J and Biswas-Diener, R. (2010) *The Strengths Book,* Coventry, CAPP Press.

Linton, R. (1949) *The Study of Man,* New York: Appleton-Century-Croft.

Lloyd, C., King, R., and Chenoweth, L. (2002) 'Social work, stress and burnout: a review', *Journal of Mental Health,* 11(3), 255–65.

Lokman, P., Gabriel, Y., and Nicolson, P. (2011) 'Hospital doctors' anxieties at work: patient care as intersubjective relationship and/or as system output', *International Journal of Organizational Analysis,* 19(1), 29–48.

Lord, C.G., Lepper, M.R. and Preston, E. (1984) 'Considering the opposite: a corrective strategy for social judgement', *Journal of Personality and Social Psychology,* 47, 1231–3.

Luker, K. A. and G.A. McHugh (2002) 'Nurse prescribing from the community nurse's perspective', *International Journal of Pharmaceutical Practice,* 10(4), 273–80.

Lumby, J. (2003) 'Distributed leadership in colleges: leading or misleading?', *Educational Management Administration Leadership,* 31(3), 283–93.

Lymbery, M. (2006) 'United we stand? Partnership working in health and social care and the role of social work in services for older people', *British Journal of Social Work,* 36(7), 1119–34.

Lyons-Ruth, K. (1999) 'The two-person unconscious: intersubjective dialogue, enactive relational representation, and the emergence of new forms of relational organization', *Psychoanalytic Inquiry: A Topical Journal for Mental Health Professionals,* 19(4), 576–617.

Lyubomirsky, S., Sousa, L. and Dickerhoof, R. (2006) 'The costs and benefits of writing, talking and thinking about life's triumphs and defeats', *Journal of Personality and Social Psychology,* 90, 692–708.

Macdonald, G., and Macdonald, K. (2010) 'Safeguarding: a case for intelligent risk management', *British Journal of Social Work,* 40(4), 1174–91.

MacIntyre, B. (2007) *Agent ZigZag,* London, Bloomsbury.

Marris, P. (1986) *Loss and Change*, London: Tavistock.

McCreight, B. S. (2005) 'Perinatal grief and emotional labour: a study of nurses' experiences in gynae wards', *International Journal of Nursing Studies,* 42(4), 439–48.

McDougall, W. (1922/2009) *The Group Mind*, Cambridge, Cambridge University Press.

McDowell, L., and Court, G. (1994) 'Performing work: bodily representations in merchant banks', *Environment and Planning D – Society and Space,* 12(6), 727–50.

McLeod, J. (2009) *An Introduction to Counselling,* Buckingham, Open University Press, 4th edn.

McQueen, A. C. H. (2004) 'Emotional intelligence in nursing work', *Journal of Advanced Nursing,* 47(1), 101–8.

Macan, T. (2009) 'The employment interview: a review of current studies and directions for future research', *Human Resource Management Review,* 19, 203–18.

Maguire, G.P., and Rutter, D.R. (1976) 'History-taking for medical students. 1. Deficiencies in performance', *Lancet,* September, 11, 556–8.

Main, M. (1995) 'Recent studies in attachment: overview with selected implications for clinical work', in S. Goldberg, R. Muir and J. Kerr (eds) *Handbook of Attachment,* Hillsdale, NJ, Analytic Press, pp. 407–74.

Maines, D. R. (1989) 'Review: [untitled]', *American Journal of Sociology,* 94(6), 1514–16.

Marris, P. (1996) 'The social construction of uncertainty', in C.M. Parkes, J. Steveson-Hinde and P. Marris (eds) *Attachment Across the Life Cycle,* London, Routledge.

Martin, D. (1962) *Adventure in Psychiatry,* London: Cassirer.

Mayer, J. D., and Salovey, P. (1995) 'Emotional intelligence and the construction and regulation of feelings', *Applied and Preventive Psychology,* 4(3), 197–208.

Mead, G. H. (1934/67) *Mind, Self, and Society*, Chicago: The University of Chicago Press.

Mehra, A., Smith, B., Dixon, A., and Robertson, B. (2006) 'Distributed leadership in teams: the network of leadership perceptions and team performance', *Leadership Quarterly,* 17(6), 232–45

Menzies, I.E.P. (1970) *A Functioning of Social Systems as a Defence against Anxiety,* London, Tavistock.

Menzies Lyth, I. (1988/1992) *Containing Anxiety in Institutions: Selected Essays*, London, Tavistock.

Michie, S., and Gooty, J. (2005) 'Values, emotions, and authenticity: will the real leader please stand up?', *Leadership Quarterly,* 16(3), 441–57.

Michie, S., and West, M. A. (2004) 'Managing people and performance: an evidence based framework applied to health service organizations', *International Journal of Management Reviews,* 5–6(2), 91–111.

Milgram, S. (1963) 'Behavioural study of obedience', *Journal of Abnormal and Social Psychology,* 67, 371–8.

Milgram, S. (1974) *Obedience to Authority,* New York, Harper & Row.

Miller, D. (1993) 'Some organizational consequences of CEO succession', *Academy of Management Journal,* 36(3), 644–59.

Miller, E. J. and Gwynne, G. V. (1972) *A Life Apart,* London, Tavistock.

Miller, E. J., and Rice, A. K. (1967) *Systems of Organisation: The Control of Task and Sentient Boundaries,* London, Tavistock.

Miner, J. B. (1975) 'The uncertain future of the leadership concept: Revisions and clarifications', *Journal of Applied Behavioral Science,* 18(3), 293–307.

Mitchell, J. (2000) *Mad Men and Medusas: Reclaiming Hysteria and the Effects if Sibling Relations on the Human Condition,* Harmondsworth, Penguin.

Moreno, J. L. (1934) *Who Shall Survive? A New Approach to the Problems of Human Interrelations.* Washington, DC, Nervous and Mental Diseases Publishing.

Morgan, G. (2006) *Images of Organisation,* London, Sage.

Morrison, T. (2007) 'Emotional intelligence, emotion and social work: context, characteristics, complications and contribution', *British Journal of Social Work,* 37(2), 245–63.

Munro, E. (1996) 'Avoidable and unavoidable mistakes in child protection work', *British Journal of Social Work,* 26(6), 793–808.

Munro, E. (2011) *Munro Review of Child Protection,* London: London School of Economics.

Myers, I.B. with Kirby, L.K. and Myers, K.D. (1998) *Introduction to Type,* 6th edn, Oxford, Oxford University Press.

Myers I.B. with Myers, P.B. (1980) *Gifts Differing,* Palo Alto, CA, Consulting Psychologists Press (CPP).

Myers, I.B., McCaulley, M.H., Quenk, N.L., and Hammer, A.L. (1998) *Manual: A Guide to the Development and Use of the Myers-Briggs Type Indicator,* 3rd edn, Palo Alto, CA, Consulting Psychologists Press (CPP).

Myers, K.D. and Kirby, L.K. (1994) *Introduction to Type Dynamics and Type Development,* Palo Alto, CA, Consulting Psychologists Press (CPP).

Neff, K.D. and Vonk, R. (2008) 'Self compassion versus global self-esteem: two different ways of relating to onself', *Journal of Personality,* 77, pp. 25–50.

Nettle, D. (2007) *Personality,* Oxford, Oxford University Press.

Newcomb, T.M. (1953) *Social Psychology: A Study of Social Interaction,* London, Routledge & Kegan Paul.

Nichols, K. A. (1993) *Psychological Care in Physical Illness,* 2nd edn, London, Chapman & Hall.

Nicolson, P. (1994) 'The Experience of Being Burgled', unpublished report for Frizzell Financial Services, Bournemouth, UK.

Nicolson, P. (2010a) *Psychology and Domestic Violence: A Critical Perspective*, London, Taylor & Francis.

Nicolson, P. (2010b) *Alice in Wonderland: Lost in (un)familiar places*, Tavistock and Portman NHS Foundation Trust/University of East London, London.

Nicolson, P. (2012) 'Oedipus at work: a family affair?', *Psychodynamic Practice*, 18(4) 427–40.

Nicolson, P. (2014) *A Critical Approach to Human Growth and Development: A Textbook for Social Work Students and Practitioners*, Basingstoke, Palgrave Macmillan.

Nicolson, P., Bayne, R., and Owen, J. (2006) *Applied Psychology for Social Workers*, Basingstoke, Palgrave Macmillan.

Nicolson, P., Fox, R., Gabriel, Y., Heffernan, K., Howorth, C., Ilan-Clarke, Y., et al. (2011) *Leadership and Better Patient Care: Managing in the NHS*, London, HMSO.

Norcross, J.C. and Wampold, B.E. (2011) 'Evidence-based therapy relationships: research conclusions and clinical practices', *Psychotherapy*, 46, 98–102.

Obholzer, A., and Roberts, V. Z. (1994) *The Unconscious at Work: individual and organizational stress in the human services*, London, Routledge.

Orbach, S. (1999) *The Impossibility of Sex*, Harmondsworth. Penguin.

Parkes, C.M. (1972) *Bereavement: Studies of Grief in Adult Life*, New York: International Universities Press.

Parry, G. (1990) *Coping with Crises*, London, Routledge.

Parton, N. (1996) 'Child protection, family support and social work: a critical appraisal of the Department of Health research studies in child protection', *Child and Family Social Work*, 1(1), 3–11.

Pelled, L. H. (1996) 'Demographic diversity, conflict, and work group outcomes: an Intervening process theory', *Organization Science*, 7(6), 615–31.

Pennebaker, J.W., Colder, M. and Sharp, L.K. (1990) 'Accelerating the coping process', *Journal of Personality and Social Psychology*, 58, 528–37.

Pescosolido, A. T. (2002) 'Emergent leaders as managers of group emotion', *Leadership Quarterly*, 13(5), 583–99.

Pfeiffer, E. (1977) 'Psychopathology and social pathology', in J.E. Birren and K.W. Schaie (eds) *Handbook of the Psychology of Aging*, New York, Academic Press.

Piaget, J. (1965) *The Moral Judgment of the Child*, New York, The Free Press.

Piaget, J. (1972) *The Psychology of the Child*, New York, Basic Books.

Piaget, J. (1990) *The Child's Conception of the World*, New York, Littlefield Adams.

Pols, J. (2005) 'Enacting appreciations: beyond the patient perspective', *Health Care Analysis*, 13(3), 203–21.

Preston-Shoot, M. (2007) *Effective Groupwork,* Basingstoke, Palgrave Macmillan.

Provost, J.A. (1993) *Applications of the Myers-Briggs Type Indicator in Counseling: A Casebook,* 2nd edn, Gainesville, FL, CAPT.

Pugh, S. D. (2001) 'Service with a smile: emotional contagion in the service encounter' *Academy of Management Journal,* 44(5), 1018–27.

Pye, A. (2005) 'Leadership and organizing: sensemaking in action', *Leadership,* 1(1), 31–49.

Quenk, N.L., Hammer, A.L. and Majors, M.S. (2001) *MBTI Step II Manual,* Palo Alto, CA, Consulting Psychologists Press.

Rafaeli, A., and Sutton, R. I. (1987) 'Expression of emotion as part of the work role', *Academy of Management Review,* 12(1), 23–37.

Rafaeli, A., and Sutton, R. I. (1989) 'The Expression of emotion in organizational life', *Research in Organizational Behavior,* 11, 1–42.

Rainer, T. (1978) *The New Diary,* New York, St Martin's Press.

Rakos, R. (1991) *Assertive Behaviour: Theory, Research and Training.* London: Routledge.

Reese, D. J. and Sontag, M.-A. (2001) 'Successful Interprofessional Collaboration on the Hospice Team', *Health and Social Work,* 26(3), 167–75.

Regehr, C., Stern, S., and Shlonsky, A. (2007) 'Operationalizing evidence-based practice: the development of an Institute for Evidence-Based Social Work', *Research on Social Work Practice,* 17(3), 408–16.

Reivich, K.J., Seligman, M.E.P., and McBridge, S. (2011) 'Master resilience training in the US army', *American Psychologist,* 66 (1), 22–34.

Reynierse, J. (2012) 'Toward an empirically sound and radically revised type theory', *Journal of Psychological Type,* 72, 1–25.

Rice, L.N. (1974) 'The evocative function of the therapist', in D.Wexler and L.N. Rice (eds) *Innovations in Client-centred Therapy,* New York, Wiley.

Riessman, C. K., and Quinney, L. (2005) 'Narrative in Social Work', *Qualitative Social Work,* 4(4), 391–412.

Ritchie, A., and Woodward, R. (2009) 'Changing lives: critical reflections on the social work change programme for Scotland', *Critical Social Policy,* 29(3), 510–32.

Roberts, B. (2000) *Biographical Research,* Milton Keynes, Open University Press.

Rogers, C. (1975) 'Empathic: an unappreciated way of being', in C. Rogers (1980) *A Way of Being,* Boston, Houghton Mifflin.

Rogers, C. (1987) 'Comments on the issue of equality in psychotherapy' *Journal of Humanistic Psychology,* 27, 38–40.

Rogers, C.R. (1961/2002) *On becoming a Person: A Therapist's View of Psychotherapy,* London, Constable.

Rose, H., and Rose, S. (2000) *Alas, Poor Darwin: Arguments against Evolutionary Psychology,* London, Jonathan Cape.

Rosenthal, T. (1993) 'To soothe the savage breast', *Behaviour Research and Therapy*, 31, 439–62.

Ross, J.W. (2011) *Specialist Communication for Social Workers. Focusing on Service Users' Needs*, Basingstoke, Palgrave Macmillan.

Ruch, G. (2004) 'Reflective practice in contemporary child care social work', unpublished PhD thesis, University of Southampton.

Ruch, G. (2005) 'Relationship-based practice and reflective practice: holistic approaches to contemporary child care social work', *Child and Family Social Work*, 10(2), 111–23.

Rutter, M.(1972) *Maternal Deprivation Reassessed*. Harmondsworth, Penguin.

Rutter, D.R. and Maguire, G.P. (1976) 'History-taking for medical students: II Evaluation of a training programme', *Lancet*, September, 11, pp. 558–60.

Sadler-Smith, E. (2008) *Inside Intuition*, London, Routledge.

Salzberger-Wittenberger, I. (1976) *Psycho-Analytic Insight and Relationships: A Kleinian Approach*, London, Routledge & Kegan Paul.

Sapolsky, R. (2004) *Why Zebras Don't get Ulcers*, 3rd edn, New York, Henry Holt.

Sayers, J. (1982) *Biological Politics: Feminist and Anti-Feminist Perspectives*, London, Tavistock.

Schaffer, H.R. and Emerson, P.E. (1964) *The Development of Social Attachments in Infancy*, Monographs of the Society for Research in Child Development.

Scheflen, A.C. (1964) 'The signifance of posture in communication systems', *Psychiatry*, 27, 316–31.

Schein, E. (1985) *Organizational Culture and Leadership*, San Francisco, CA, Jossey-Bass.

Schilling, J. (2009) 'From ineffectiveness to destruction: a qualitative study on the meaning of negative leadership', *Leadership*, 5(1), 102–28.

Schofield, G. (1998) 'Inner and outer worlds: a psychosocial framework for child and family social work', *Child and Family Social Work*, 3, 57–67.

Scott, W.R. (1992) 'Health care organisations in the 1980s: the convergence of public and professional control systems', in J.W. Meyer and W.R. Scott (eds) *Organisational Environments: Ritual and Rationality*, London: Sage.

Schultz, P. W., Nolan, J. M., Cialdini, R. B., Goldstein, N. J., and Griskevicius, V. (2007) 'The constructive, destructive, and reconstructive power of social norms', *Psychological Science*, 18(5), 429–34.

Schutte, N. S., Malouff, J., Bobick, C., Coston, T. D., Greeson, C., Jedlicka, E. et al. (2001) 'Emotional intelligence and interpersonal relations'. *Journal of Social Psychology*, 141(4), 523–36.

Schwarz, N. (1990) 'Feelings as information: Informational and motivational functions of affective states' in R. Sorrentino and E. T. Higgins (eds) *Handbook of Motivation and Cognition* (Vol. 2, pp. 527–61), New York, Guilford Press.

Schwarzer, R. and Knoll, N. (2010) 'Social support', in D. French, K. Vedhara, A.A. Kaptein and J. Weinman (eds) *Health Psychology*, 2nd edn, Oxford, BPS/Blackwell.

Scott, C., and Myers, K. K. (2005) 'The socialization of emotion: learning emotion management at the fire station', *Journal of Applied Communication Research*, 33(1), 67–92.

Segal, J. (1993) *Melanie Klein*, London, Sage.

Seligman, M.E.P.(1995) *What You Can Change ... And What You Can't*, New York, Fawcett Columbine.

Seligman, M.E.P. and Fowler, R.D. (2011) 'Comprehensive soldier fitness and the future of psychology', *American Psychologist*, 66, 82–6.

Sheldon, B. (2001) 'The validity of evidence-based practice in social work: a reply to Stephen Webb', *British Journal of Social Work*, 31(5), 801–9.

Sheldon, K.M. and Kasser, T. (2001) 'Goals, congruence and positive well-being: New empirical validation for humanistic ideas', *Journal of Humanistic Psychology*, 41, 30–50.

Shemmings, D., and Shemmings, Y. (2011) *Understanding Disorganized Attachment: Theory and Practice for Working with Children and Adults*, London, Jessica Kingsley.

Sheppard, M., Newstead, S., Di Caccavo, A., and Ryan, K. (2000) 'Reflexivity and the development of process knowledge in social work: a classification and empirical study', *British Journal of Social Work*, 30(4), 465–88.

Simpson, P., and French, R. (2005) 'Thoughtful leadership lessons from Bion', *Organizational and Social Dynamics: An International Journal of Psychoanalytic, Systemic and Group Relations Perspectives*, 5(2), 280–97.

Skinner, B.F. (1953) *Science and Human Behavior*, New York, Free Press.

Skovholt, T. and M. Trotter-Mathison (2010) *The Resilient Practitioner. Burnout Prevention and Self-care Strategies for Counselors, Therapists, Teachers, and Health Professionals*, 2nd edn, London, Routledge.

Smith, A., Goodwin, D., Mort, M. and Pope, C. (2003) 'Expertise in practice: an ethnographic study exploring acquisition and use of knowledge in anaesthesia', *British Journal of Anaesthetics*, 91(3), 319–28.

Smith, C. R. (1982) *Social Work with the Dying and Bereaved*, London, Macmillan.

Smith, J.B. (1993) 'Teachers' grading styles: the languages of feeling and thinking', *Journal of Psychological Type*, 26, 37–41.

Smith, P. (1992) *The Emotional Labour of Nursing: Its Impact on Interpersonal Relations, Management and the Educational Environment in Nursing*, London, Macmillan.

Smith, V., Collard, P., Nicolson, P., and Bayne, R. (2012) *Key Concepts in Counselling and Psychotherapy: A Critical A–Z Guide to Theory*, Milton Keynes, McGraw-Hill/Open University Press.

Spera, S.P., Buhrfeind, E.D. and Pennebaker, J.W. (1994) 'Creative writing and coping with job loss', *Academy of Management Journal*, 37, 722–33.

Spillius, E. (2007) *Encounters with Melanie Klein*, London, Routledge.

Stein, M. (2005) 'The Othello Conundrum: the inner contagion of leadership', *Organization Studies*, 26(9), 1405–19.

Steiner, J. (1985) 'Turning a blind eye: the cover up for Oedipus', *International Review of Psycho-Analysis*, 12, 161–72.

Stevenson, O. (1986) Guest editorial on the Jasmine Beckford Inquiry, *British Journal of Social Work*, 16, 501–10.

Stokes, J. (1994)' Institutional chaos and personal stress', in A. Obholzer and V. Zagier Roberts (eds) *The Unconscious at Work: Individual and Organizational Stress in the Human Services*, London, Routledge.

Strier, R. (2007) 'Anti-oppressive research in social work: a preliminary definition', *British Journal of Social Work*, 37(5), 857–71.

Sugarman, L. (2001) *Lifespan Development: Frameworks, accounts and strategies*, London, Taylor & Francis.

Taylor, S., and Tyler, M. (2000) 'Emotional labour and sexual difference in the airline industry', *Work, Employment and Society*, 14(1), 77–95.

Tepper, B. J. (2000) 'Consequences of abusive supervision', *Academy of Management Journal*, 43(2), 178–90.

Thompson, K. (2010) *Therapeutic Journal Writing: An Introduction for Professionals*, London, Jessica Kingsley.

Tieger, P.D. and Barron-Tieger, B. (2000) *Just Your Type: the Relationship You've Always Wanted Using the Secrets of Personality Type*, London, Little, Brown.

Tieger, P.D. and Barron-Tieger, B. (2007) *Do What You Are*, 4th edn, London, Little, Brown.

Tizard, B. (1975) *Adoption: A Second Chance*, London, Open Books.

Tourish, D. (2008) 'Challenging the transformational agenda: leadership theory in transition?', *Management Communication Quarterly*, 21(4), 522–8.

Tuckman, B. W. (1965) 'Developmental sequence in small groups', *Psychological Bulletin*, 63, 6, 384–99.

Twelvetrees, A. (1982/2008) *Community Work*, London: Macmillan – now Palgrave Macmillan.

Tyler, M., and Abbott, P. (1998) 'Chocs away: weight watching in the contemporary airline industry', *Sociology – the Journal of the British Sociological Association*, 32(3), 433–50.

Uhl-Bien, M. (2006) 'Relational leadership theory: exploring the social processes of leadership and organizing', *Leadership Quarterly*, 17(6), 654–76.

Ussher, J.M. (2006) *Managing the Monstrous Feminine*, London, Taylor & Francis.

van Knippenberg, D., and Schippers, M. l. C. (2007) 'Work group diversity', *Annual Review of Psychology*, 58(1), 515–41.

Vangen, S., and Huxham, C. (2003) 'Enacting leadership for collaborative advantage: dilemmas of ideology and pragmatism in the activities of partnership managers', *British Journal of Management,* 14, S61–S76.

VanSant, S. (2003) *Wired for Conflict,* Gainesville, FL, CAPT.

Vazire, S. (2010) 'Who knows what about a person? The self–other knowledge asymmetry (SOKA) model', *Journal of Personality and Social Psychology,* 98, 281–300.

Vince, R., and Broussine, M. (1996) 'Paradox, defense and attachment: accessing and working with emotions and relations underlying organizational change', *Organization Studies,* 17(1), 1–21.

Von Bertalanffy, I. (1956) *General Systems Theory,* New York, George Braziller.

Walsh, D. and Bull, R. (2010) 'Interviewing suspects of fraud: an in-depth analysis of interviewing skills', *Journal of Psychiatry and Law,* 38, 99–135.

Walsh, R. (2011) 'Lifestyle and mental health', *American Psychologist,* 66, 579–92.

Ward, J., and Winstanley, D. (2006) 'Watching the watch: the UK fire service and its impact on sexual minorities in the workplace', *Gender Work and Organization,* 13(2), 193–219.

Webb, S. (2001) 'Some considerations on the validity of evidence-based practice in social work', *British Journal of Social Work,* 31(1), 57–79.

Wellington, C. A., and Bryson, J. R. (2001) 'At face value? Image consultancy, emotional labour and professional work', *Sociology – the Journal of the British Sociological Association,* 35(4), 933–46.

Westcott, H. L. (2003) 'Are children reliable witnesses to their experiences?', in P. Reder, S. Duncan and C. Lucey (eds) *Studies in the Assessment of Parenting,* London, Brunner-Routledge.

Westcott, H.L. and Kynan, S. (2004) 'The application of a "story-telling" framework to investigate interviews for suspected child sexual abuse', *Legal and Criminological Psychology,* 9, 37–56.

Weston, S. (2008) *Leadership: A Critical Text,* London, Sage.

Whiteley, J. S. (1997) 'Ethical issues in the therapeutic community', *Israel Journal of Psychiatry and Related Sciences,* 34(1), 18–25.

Willmott, H. C. (1986) 'Unconscious sources of motivation in the theory of the subject: an exploration and critique of Giddens' dualistic models of action and personality', *Journal for the Theory of Social Behaviour,* 16(1), 105–21.

Wilson, A., and Beresford, P. (2000) ' "Anti-oppressive practice": emancipation or appropriation?', *British Journal of Social Work,* 30(5), 553–73.

Windle, G. (2012) 'The contribution of resilience to healthy ageing', *Perspectives in Public Health,* 132(4), 159–60.

Winnicott, D. (1949) 'Hate in the countertransference', *International Journal of Psycho-analysis,* 30, 69–74.

Yalom, I.D. (1989) *Love's Executioner and Other Tales of Psychotherapy*, Harmondsworth, Penguin.

Yalom, I.D. (2001) *The Gift of Therapy: Reflections on Being a Therapist*, London, Piatkus.

Yarnal, C. M., Dowler, L., and Hutchinson, S. (2004) 'Don't let the bastards see you sweat: masculinity, public and private space, and the volunteer firehouse', *Environment and Planning A*, 36(4), 685–99.

Zagier Roberts, V. (1994) 'The organisation of work: contributions from open systems theory', in A. Obholzer and V. Z. Roberts (eds) *The Unconscious at Work*, London, Routledge.

Zeanah, C. H., Berlin, L., and Boris, N. W. (2011) 'Practitioner review: clinical applications of attachment theory and research for infants and young children', *Journal of Child Psychology and Psychiatry*, 52(8), 819–33.

Zeidner, M., Matthews, G., and Roberts, R. D. (2004) 'Emotional intelligence in the workplace: a critical review', *Applied Psychology*, 53(3), 371–99.

Zeisset, C. (2006) *The Art of Dialogue: Exploring Personality Differences for more Effective Communication*, Gainesville, FL, CAPT.

# Index